No. 976
$9.95

MOPED
Repair Handbook
By Paul Dempsey

TAB BOOKS
Blue Ridge Summit, Pa. 17214

FIRST EDITION

FIRST PRINTING—NOVEMBER 1977

Copyright © 1977 by TAB BOOKS

Printed in the United States
of America

Library of Congress Cataloging in Publication Data

Dempsey, Paul.
  Moped repair handbook.

  "Tab 1976."
  Includes index.
  1. Mopeds--Maintenance and repair. I. Title.
TL444.D45   629.28'8'72   77-15621
ISBN 0-8306-7976-6
ISBN 0-8306-6976-0 pbk.

Cover photo by Coleman Photographers.

If you want economical transporation, the maintenance that mopeds demand cannot be farmed out to a dealer. For example, one manfuacturer suggests that the rear hub, a collection of parts that would put a bicycle coaster brake to shame, be dismantled every 6000 miles. Another suggests that the ignition contact points be adjusted or replaced every six months or 3000 miles, whichever comes sooner. Another would have the cylinder and exhaust system decarbonized at 1500-mile intervals, and the spark plug serviced every 500 miles. Clearly, if you want the combination of economy and reliability, you must do some maintenance yourself. This book shows you how to handle all routine maintenance from adjusting the carburetor to truing the wheels.

Even the best maintained moped can fail suddenly and without warning. Most of these surprises are caused by the fuel and electrical systems. I have included detailed troubleshooting and repair procedures, as well as descriptions of the way each component functions, for you cannot repair what you don't understand.

Major engine and transmission overhaul is treated in depth, often going beyond factory manuals, and on the assumption that the reader is unfamiliar with the work. Even readers who are knowledgeable about motorcycles and small engines generally will find that mopeds require special repair techniques, techniques that are strange to American mechanics.

The emphasis is on practical repairs, on restoring the machine to its original specifications. Legal restrictions limit power in most states; for those who are interested, there is information on how to bring these engines up to European standards.

The first chapter is an overview of moped technology, and should be read by a potential buyer. For mopeds are not all alike; each has different capabilities and handicaps, virtues and vices.

I want to thank the manufacturers and importers who have contributed information and, in some cases, bikes and engines for this book. Special thanks to Columbia Manufacturing Company and to Mr. "Bud" Poole, a Steyr-Daimler-Puch dealer in Sabillasville, Maryland.

Paul Dempsey

Contents

Chapter 1
The Mopeds
are Coming

Most Americans have never seen a moped. But times are changing: in the 23 states where mopeds were legal last year, nearly 100,000 pedal-poppers were sold. Sales are expected to double this year and the next, peaking out in the 1980s when mopeds will be as common as 10-speed bicycles.

What are mopeds? The name means "motor-assisted pedals," and that just about sums it up. Mopeds are heavy-duty bicycles with tiny motors attached. The rider can pedal for exercise or relax and let the one to two-horsepower engine do the work. Mopeds should not be confused with the old-fashioned motorbike. Motorbikes were, for the most part, unsprung, brakeless wonders suitable only for the very young and brave. Mopeds have large, positive-acting brakes, sturdy frames, and, with one or two exceptions, spring suspensions. Anyone who can balance on a bicycle can ride a moped.

Nor should mopeds be confused with motorcycles, which require coordinated clutch and gear manipulation and have the power to get you in trouble before you can say Banzai. Mopeds are quiet, almost sedate vehicles which go solely upon command of the throttle grip. Hand levers, one for each wheel, stop the bike. Speeds are limited to 20 or, in some jurisdictions, 30 mph.

Mopeds are lightweight machines, able to dart nimbly through traffic and comfortable enough for trips of 20 miles and more. While no one recommends this, Dick Hartnett, a student at the University of North Florida, rode a Vespa moped from Jacksonville to San Diego. This epic, 2617-mile journey earned Mr. Harnett a place in the *Guinness Book of World Records*. He reports that he did not have to pedal-assist the motor and that the only maintenance was changing the spark plug and cleaning the carburetor at the approach to San Diego.

The cross-country trip required 16.5 gallons of gasoline, which works out to 157 miles per gallon. Around the city, the typical moped delivers 130 to 150 mpg. The French Velosolex, the all-time economy champ, can squeeze out more than 200 mpg.

Initial cost ranges from $300 for stripped-down models to $500 for the most sophisticated. Liability insurance is usually not required and in those states that license and register the machines, the fees are nominal. Maintenance costs are low, particularly if you are willing to do the work yourself. In all, the manufacturers are probably right when they say that moped travel costs 1¢ a mile.

While mopeds are new to the United States, they are well known in other quarters of the world. Best estimates put the moped population at more than 20 million, with the greatest concentration in Europe, Africa, and Southeast Asia. Six million mopeds are registered in France alone.

THE LAW

Mopeds have been brought into this country sporadically for decades. New Yorkers might remember the bright yellow Velosolex that stood in the window of Papert, Leonig, & Lois back in the 60s. The ad firm, now defunct but then one of the hottest on the Avenue, had purchased marketing rights for the bike. They couldn't give them away. Some years later Mitsubishi had the same dismal luck with Batavus.

What changed matters was the oil embargo of 1974-75 and the quadrupling of the price of Persian crude that followed. The Federal Government began looking for ways to save energy. Mopeds, which had been classified as motorcycles, were exempted from some safety requirements. For example, turn signals were no longer mandated; stoplight output requirements were cut in half, and brake-fade standards were relaxed. Without these concessions, mopeds would be as heavy and cumbersome as motorcycles, without the cycle's saving grace of rapid acceleration.

However, this does not mean that moped manufacturers can sell anything they wish here. Mopeds must be equipped with two engine shutdown switches, horn, two-wheel brakes operated from the handlebars, speedometer, and, under just-amended rulings, a 12-square-inch rearview mirror.

Meanwhile, the moped manufacturers had not been idle. Three French firms, Motobecane, Sinfac-Velosolex, and Cycles Peugeot formed the Motorized Bicycle Association in 1975. Since then Motobecane and Sinfac-Velosolex have merged, and the BIA has opened its doors to 11 other manufacturers. Its membership accounts for some 80% of the bikes sold in this market. The purpose of the BIA is to do public relations for the manufacturers, act as a clearinghouse for information, and to lobby for changes in state legislation.

Once the federal government recognized mopeds as a class of vehicle distinct from motorcycles, it was not difficult to persuade the states to follow suit (Table 1-1). So far, 23 states recognize mopeds as "motor-assisted bicycles," "motorized bicycles," or simply "bicycles." Indiana legislators, perhaps in recognition of the fun value of mopeds, call them "therapeutic bicycles." More than half of these states do not require an operator's license, none require liability insurance or crash helmets, and the minimum age for riding a moped ranges from none to 17 years. Most do not require registration and only Texas insists on annual inspection.

Where legal, mopeds have about as many legal restrictions as bicycles.

On the other hand, the states did not give this freedom without imposing some restrictions. Mopeds cannot be used on limited-access freeways and are subject to the same traffic regulations as automobiles. Performance is curtailed by limits on engine displacement, horsepower, maximum speed, or all three in concert. Multispeed transmissions are legal providing they are shifted automatically and not by separate control.

Manufacturers have accepted the 50-cubic-centimenter displacement limit imposed in most states and do not build larger engines for use in those jurisdictions that allow them. Some detune their products for this market and sell 20, 25, and 30-mph versions of the same bike.

Table 1-1. Current Moped Legislation. New York Statutes Are Too Complex To Be Tabulated Here and, At Any Rate, Require Administrative Clarification.

State	Defined	Displacement	Horsepower	Max. Speed	Min. Age	License	Registration	Insurance	Helmet	Comments
ARIZONA	pedal bicycle with helper motor	50 cc or less	1.5 bhp or less	25 mph or less	16	any valid	yes	no (financial responsibility)	no	law effective 9/22/76
CALIFORNIA *bicycle license	motorized bicycle: automatic trans required, except if electric powered	none	less than 2 gross bhp	30	15	any valid or learner's permit		no (financial responsibility)	no	
CONNECTICUT	bicycle: automatic trans required	less than 50 cc	no more than 2 bhp	no more than 30 mph	16	any valid	no	no	no	
FLORIDA * may not operate at more than 25 mph	moped, under bicycle definition	none	max. of 1.5 bhp	*	15	no	no	no	no	
HAWAII	bicycle	none	1.5 bhp or less	none	15	no	no	no	no	
INDIANA	therapeutic bicycle	none	less than 1 bhp	none	none	no	no	no	no	
IOWA * any valid or motorized bicycle license. At age 14 no road test.	motorized bicycle or motor bicycle	no more than 50 cc	none	no more than 25 mph	14	*	yes	no (financial responsibility)	no	
KANSAS * any valid or written only at 14	motorized bicycle: automatic trans required	no more than 50 cc	no more than 1.5 bhp	no more than 25 mph	14	*	yes	no (financial responsibility)	no	law effective 1/1/77

State	Definition	no more than 50 cc	no more than 1.5 bhp	no more than 25 mph	Age	License					Notes
LOUISIANA	bicycle: automatic trans required	no more than 50 cc	no more than 1.5 bhp	no more than 25 mph	16	any valid	no	no		no	law effective 10/2/76
MARYLAND	bicycle	less than or 50 cc	less than 1 bhp	none	16	any valid	no	no		no	
MASSACHUSETTS	bicycle: automatic trans required	no more than 50 cc	no more than 1.5 bhp	no more than 25 mph	16	any valid or learner's permit	yes	no		no	
MICHIGAN	bicycle: friction trans	none	less than 1 bhp	20 mph	15	no	no	no		no	
NEVADA	moped: pedals required	none	none	30 mph	16	any valid	no	no		no	
NEW HAMPSHIRE	moped: automatic trans required	no more than 50 cc	no more than 2 bhp	less than 30 mph	16	any valid	yes	no (financial responsibility)		no	
NEW JERSEY	bicycle	less than 50 cc	no more than 1.5 bhp	25 mph	15	no	no	no (financial responsibility)		no	
NORTH CAROLINA	bicycle	none	less than 1 bhp	20 mph	16	no	no	no		no	
OHIO	bicycle: friction trans	none	none	20 mph	none	no	no	no		no	
PENNSYLVANIA	motorized pedalcycle: automatic trans required	no more than 50 cc	no more than 1.5 bhp	no more than 25 mph	17	yes	yes	no (financial responsibility)		no	law effective 7/1/77
RHODE ISLAND	motorized bicycle	none	no more than 1.5 bhp	no more than 25 mph	16	any valid	yes	no		no	
SOUTH CAROLINA	bicycle	none	less than 1 bhp	20 mph	none	no	no	no		no	
TEXAS	motorized bicycle *	less than 60 cc	none	20 mph	15	yes (written only)	yes	no		no	* annual inspection required
VIRGINIA	bicycle	none	less than 1 bhp	20 mph	16	no	no	no		no	

DEFINITION

OPERATING INSTRUCTIONS

While some states are expected to liberalize moped regulation there has been backlash in the East. The New Jersey State Police would have them reclassified as motorcycles. The troopers argue that it is difficult to enforce the minimum age (15 in that state) because kids do not carry identification and some mopeds can exceed the 25-mph speed limit. The police are also irked by drunks who ride mopeds recklessly with immunity from DWI charges.

THE CUSTOMERS

Who buys mopeds? The data is sketchy, but it is obvious that the market is not the same as for motorcycles. Executives at Steyr-Daimler-Puch, one of the largest manufacturers, suggest that they are suburban, middle-class, "opinion leaders." According to Chalek & Dreyer, the ad agency that handles Motobecane, the market is 70% male and between 25 and 55 years old. Other ad execs see a much broader market with retirees at one end of the spectrum and high school students at the other.

THE RISKS

A recent study of vehicular fatalities in Europe indicates that mopeds are three times safer than motorcycles and six times more lethal than bicycles, but there is no reliable data on moped safety in this country. This is partly because police departments and hospital emergency forms do not yet have a category for mopeds. In so far as the equipment is concerned, the Americanized moped should be somewhat safer than its European counterpart; it is typically less powerful and has superior brakes and lights.

At any rate, mopeds share the road with automobiles that outweigh them by a factor of 15. When the moped driver disputes passage with one of these behemoths, he is always wrong. The best passive safety measure is a good crash helmet.

The baseline of helmet quality is the Z90. 1 sticker (or its equivalent) of the AAMVA (American Association of Motor Vehicle Administrators). Helmets so identified meet minimum federal impact standards. An SHCA sticker means that the manfuacturer has submitted to inspection and quality-control procedures devised by the Safety Helmet Council of America. Since helmet testing is destructive, the helmet you wear has not been tested, but SHCA certification improves the odds that is will work when you need it. And finally, there is the hallmark of quality—the Snell Foundation sticker. Only a few helmets can meet Snell Foundation standards, which are much more rigorous than the Z90.1.

As mentioned earlier, 12-square-inch mirrors are required for new bikes. The reason for the requirement is that mopeds cannot keep up with fast traffic and must hug the shoulder, where they are subject to being struck from behind by overtaking autos. Bikes sold before the new standard was in effect should be updated with one of these mirrors (Fig. 1-1).

But passive measures—improved brakes and lights, helmets, and rearview mirrors—cannot substitute for alertness, skill, and the sense of vulnerability that all two-wheel motorists should cultivate. Be aware of the vehicles

Fig. 1-1. A rearview mirror that meets the new regulations and folds for storage.

behind you and of obstacles ahead. One very great danger, well-documented in bicycle safety literature, is autos that turn right, crossing your part of the lane. Another is the door that opens as you pass a line of parked cars. Motorists frequently don't see or hear a moped approaching from the rear. Use caution on steel bridge surfaces, and cross railroad tracks at right angles to the rails. A diagonal approach can mean loss of steering control and a spill.

THE MANUFACTURERS

While there has been no census of moped makers, they number in the hundreds. Mopeds are built wherever there is a supporting bicycle technology, from Taiwan to Norway. Most manufacturers are small and purchase engines, wheels, and sometimes frames from outside sources. Their markets are accordingly restricted. A few, like Motobecane, Puch, Peugeot, and Batavus, and giants with global ambitions, build almost every component under their own roofs. Design philosophies vary from the stark simplicity of the Velosolex to the baroque complexity of the Tomos.

Batavus

Batavus bikes are famous for their finish and workmanship, and because of this reputation for quality were among the first to be imported into the U.S. Chrome parts—fenders, rims, handlebars, and controls—are triple-dipped for durability (Fig. 1-2). The frames are painted with epoxy enamel, a product that retails for $40 a gallon. The most durable, fade-resistant paint known, epoxy is also used on commercial airliners and zero-maintenance merchant ships.

Their design philosophy is conservative, as befits a firm that dominates its home market in the Netherlands and has been manufacturing since 1904. The engine has the direct simplicity associated with a classic, with none of the compromises or afterthoughts that seem characteristic of contemporary designs. The crankshaft is counterbalanced by honest bobweights and supported on massive bearings; the crankcase halves are simple castings, joined on the vertical axis; the head and barrel are held down with studs, a practice made famous by Norton and other pioneer engine builders. One touch uncharacteristic of European engines is the use of

Fig. 1-2. The Batavus VA Deluxe is an example of honest Dutch craftsmanship.

reed valve induction. Reed valves generally improve midrange torque and always make for a more civilized idle. This engine was copied bolt-for-bolt by a competitor—the ultimate accolade.

Primary drive is by belt and pulley. Belt drive is hardly on the cutting edge of technology, but it is smooth, quiet, and inexpensive to repair when the belt finally wears out.

Batavus frames are made of mild steel tubing and, in theory at least, are superior to the steel stampings used by most other manufacturers. The VA series has the conventional step-through frame; the HS-50 (Fig. 1-3) is styled like a small motorcycle, with a top tube between the seat and steering head and a fairing forward of the rear wheel. It has the strongest frame in the industry and has additional advantages of a real, honest-to-God saddle and a fuel supply that gives 150 miles between fill-ups.

Motobecane

Motobecane is the General Motors of moped-dom. It was founded in 1923 to manufacture motorcycles and branched out into bicycles and mopeds a few years later. Since 1949, Motobecane S.A. has produced nearly 20 million mopeds,

Fig. 1-3. Excepting the frame, the 50 VL shares components with the VA series.

making it the largest and most experienced manufacturer in the world. New production facilities outside Paris have a capacity of a million units a year.

Motobecane offers a wider variety of models and accessories (Fig. 1-4) and spends more on R & D than any other manufacturer. Judging from results, the research effort is conservative—a matter of making a good product better, rather than seeking out new directions. The basic machine has not changed in more than a generation.

The size and growth of the organization—over 200 new dealers signed up in 1976 when mopeds were legal in fewer than 20 states—means that customers can expect good service and parts availability. Motobecane has five major warehouses sited throughout the U.S. and operates dealer schools on the east and west coasts. In contrast, some other manufacturers operate on a shoestring, not even supplying service manuals, let alone factory training.

Figure 1-5 illustrates the 50VL model. It features a stainless-steel front fender—much more durable than chrome—and a variable-ratio belt transmission. This moped shifts automatically from low to high range, giving better acceleration than fixed-speed models. The frame is well thought out, with side luggage racks and a covered storage

Fig. 1-4. Accessories from Motobecane: (A) A clip-on basket and nylon panniers. (B) chrome or vinylized double baskets and cycle carrier. (C) the Godzilla of moped locks.

Fig. 1-5. The elegant Motobecane, perhaps the best-realized moped.

space for small items. Other models have single-speed transmissions and, at the bottom of the line, dispense with the rear shocks. All share the same engine, derated as necessary to meet various state requirements.

The engine is superbly finished with clean castings, high-quality bearings, and a chromed cylinder bore. Chrome makes a more durable cylinder than cast iron (used on most other bikes) and provides a better seal against the rings. Production tolerances are meticulous: there are eight stock piston-cylinder combinations for the same engine, allowing the piston to be perfectly matched with the bore. Not surprisingly for a machine of this refinement, dealer mechanics report almost no warranty claims. Though it may be lacking in flash, the Motobecane is as reliable as the Brooklyn Bridge.

Velosolex

Velosolex has a claim on anyone who loves mopeds. Until recently it was the moped of France, as much a part of Gallic scenery as pretty girls and sidewalk cafes.

Mention Velosolex to a competitor and he will mutter darkly about friction drive, springless suspension, and the tiny engine, some 15 cc smaller than the maximum under the law. Even in its heyday, when you could buy one at the factory door for $80, the Velosolex was an anachronism. Other machines were more powerful, rode better, and looked more modern.

The Velosolex is the Model T of mopeds, a resemblance that was even closer when it came only in black (Fig. 1-6). Like that earlier vehicle, the 'Solex put a generation on wheels by using radically simple solutions to problems. Friction drive may not be entirely positive, but as long as the tire and drive roller are free of oil, it works. And friction drive invites the simplest imaginable clutch—the drive roller, engine and all, is lowered against the tire. While the engine rides high over the front wheel, it looks more intrusive than it is. The engine weighs only a few pounds and the rider soon learns to compensate for its effect on steering. Nor is the ride as harsh as a solid suspension would suggest; compliance built into the wheels and frame muffles most road irregularities.

While its power is nothing to write home about, the bike weighs only 68 pounds. Pedal assistance is not that much of a

Fig. 1-6. The Velosolex, the Model T of mopeds: reliable, unbreakable, and aging.

chore, and the owner may get some satisfaction from the fact that the Velosolex is the most economical form of motorized transportation known to man. Under ideal conditions, a 'Solex will travel 218 miles on a gallon of fuel.

Motobecane purchased Velosolex a few years ago and markets the machine in this country as "The Horse." Velosolex owners benefit from the parent company's extensive training programs and parts distribution network.

Puch

There seem to be three ways to produce a quality moped: build it from long experience, with improvements made as the need arises; scale down a motorcycle, simplifying the controls and detuning the engine; or build it from a pool of engineering talent, borrowing techniques from several specialities. The Puch is an example of the last method.

Steyr-Daimler-Puch is a giant industrial complex, the result of the merging of three pioneer Austrian manufacturers of motorcycles, automobiles, and airplanes. Two of the greatest names in automotive history—Dr. Ferdinand Porsche and Hans Ledwinka—were in their employ. Today, in addition to mopeds, the conglomerate builds auto accessories, utility and military vehicles, motorcycles, bicycles, and the famous Mannlicher rifle.

Steyr-Daimler-Puch is making a serious effort to increase its share of the American market. Hundreds of dealerships have been established, many of them veterans of the snowmobile trade and thus familiar with two-cycle engines. The firm has set up training programs and has gone to great lengths to assure the availability of spare parts. Even some internal parts for the rear shocks are inventoried—something unheard of in the rest of the industry.

The Puch (pronounced "pook") Maxi has clearly had the attention of an industrial designer. Wheels, fenders, headlamp, fork, and frame are integrated so that the bike seems of a piece, and not a collection of miscellaneous parts (Fig. 1-7A). Wiring and control cables are unobtrusively tucked out of the way.

The finish is on a par with a high-class automobile and much superior to the average European motorcycle. Thoughtful touches abound. The luggage rack is spring-loaded to hold small parcels; two chromed handles assist in getting

Fig. 1-7A. The Puch Maxi—big-time technology in a small package.

the bike up on its center stand; front fender and engine covers are molded in soft, resilient plastic on the judo principle that it is better to give way than to stand and be broken.

The engine is obviously a moped engine, designed from the start for this purpose. The cylinder is horizontal to use space more efficiently and to keep the center of gravity low (Fig. 1-7B). Engine castings are clean and crisp, which indicates a heavy investment in foundry equipment. Fins and bearing

Fig. 17-B. The Puch engine and transmission reflect careful design.

25

Fig. 1-8. If Motobecane is the General Motors of French mopeds, Peugeot is Ford and Chrysler. The 103-U3, shown here, features Ceriani-type forks and an automatic transmission.

webbing appear to have been computer-designed for best effectiveness. The cylinder bore is plated with long-wearing chrome and the piston is hand-fitted. The internal finish and the cleanliness of new engines is evidence of careful assembly.

Primary drive is through a centrifugal clutch and gear train running in oil. Oil-cooled clutches are theoretically superior to dry or air-cooled clutches and can take more abuse before failure. Separate pedal and engine chains are used, a somewhat anachronistic feature, but one that simplifies the transmission. New models can be purchased with attractive cast-aluminum wheels that are stronger, lighter, and require less maintenance than spoked wheels.

Peugeot

Like other products from the house of the rampant lion, the Peugeot moped combines engineering elegance with visual appeal (Fig. 1-8). The engine is famous for its durability, and durable it should be. The castings are simple, heavily webbed for stress, and thicker than they have to be. Chrome plate protects the cylinder bore and the crankshaft rides on main bearings that would do justice to a truck transmission.

Primary drive is through a V-belt which, on the 103-U3, is combined with a speed-sensitive engine pulley. As the engine speeds up, the pulley flanges move together, progressively gearing the bike higher. The rims are 17 inches in diameter—an inch larger than most—for better stability and responsiveness. Another nice touch is the way the spoke holes are dimpled for strength. Peugeot supports its product with a six-month warranty, twice as long as the industry average.

No motor vehicle, however durable, is entirely free from service problems. Peugeot recognizes this and has set up a factory school in Gardena, California for dealer mechanics and interested owners. No other factory has been so thorough in the matter of special tools. There is a tool for almost every job on the bike. Not all of these tools are absolutely necessary—an owner can get by without most of them—but they make the job go better and faster.

Columbia

The Columbia Commuter is unique: the only moped to be assembled in the United States (Fig. 1-9). The Columbia

Fig. 1-9. The Columbia Commuter is the first to be designed specifically for this market and assembled by American labor. It may be the herald of a new industry.

Manufacturing Company of Westfield, Mass., is a major bicycle manufacturer, tracing its lineage back to the nineteenth century when it was founded by the legendary Colonel Pope. Two years ago the firm decided to enter the moped business, assembling components purchased in Europe. As sales warrant, Columbia intends to build more and more of the bike here.

For the customer this means a somewhat lower cost for a quality bike, while imported bikes are subject to duty, most duties do not apply to parts. Columbia contacted parts makers early while the better components were still available, and maintains a complete inventory of spares on this side of the Atlantic. Today the parts factories are working at full capacity and a newcomer would have to take what he could find.

The bike uses a series 505 Fichtel & Sachs engine, designed specifically for mopeds by the largest small-engine maker in Europe. Sachs occupies the same position in the European utility engine industry as Briggs & Stratton does here. In addition, the sprawling complex in Schweinfurt, West Germany builds motorcycle and snowmobile engines, antifriction bearings, and transmission components. In 1976 their sales totaled $413.9 million.

The 505 is the most modern moped engine on the market (Fig. 1-10). Others may be as good, but none benefit more from contemporary skills. Sachs' engineers probably know more about two-cycle engines than any other firm's: the 505 is prime evidence.

First of all, a moped engine must be compact and should house the primary drive components. The 505 crankcase halves enclose the primary gear train—with helical teeth for silence—and the pedal mechanism. The entire package is only 16 inches long, 85 inches wide, and 7.5 inches high. The all-up weight is just under 24 pounds with muffler attached.

Another requirement is that the engine be adaptable to different markets. Where appropriate, the 505 can be purchased with a two-speed, manually shifted transmission and 2.5 horsepower. The version used by Columbia is detuned to 2.0 hp at 4500 rpm, but has a torque curve as flat as West Texas.

The carefully shaped ports, the seemingly casual disposition of the cooling fins, and the brutal simplicity of the transmission attest to years of experience. Sachs engineers can distinguish between what is important—port profiles and and transmission-shaft rigidity—and what is not—fin symmetry.

A moped engine should be durable, and the Sachs promises that. The crankshaft is massive, fully counterweighted, and mounted on large-diameter antifriction bearings. The connecting rod has needle bearings on both ends, at the wrist pin as well as the crankpin.

When overhaul time does roll around, you'll appreciate the horizontally split crankcase. The engine opens as easily as a sandwich. All other moped engines are split vertically and require a safecracker's touch to get them apart without permanent damage to the castings.

The Commuter frame is a rugged piece of work, obviously tailored to this market. Slightly larger than the run of European bikes, it rides on 21-inch wheels for stability in the rough. Large, motorcycle-type hub brakes provide sure stops and the frame is reinforced. Chrome plating, always expensive and never as weather-resistant as paint, has been kept to a minimum. Fenders have rolled edges to resist cracking and the engine cowlings are made of shock-absorbing plastic.

Jawa

Jawa is a big name in off-road motorcycle competition, but what is not so well known is that the Czech firm makes a very advanced moped (Fig. 1-11). The Babetta is an honest moped, with few concessions to the mass market. While the frame is made of pressed steel, the angles are sharp and clean; front forks and centerstand appear almost spindly; the steering head, the most important single part of the frame, stands naked and unshrouded. Even if the angularity of the bike wasn't a sufficient clue, the black anodized engine and lightening holes in the headlamp bracket should tell you this is a serious moped, built by people who have dominated European motorcross racing for a generation.

The engine is typically Jawa—thick, clustered fins, antifriction bearings on all shafts, needle bearings on both ends of the con rod. A complex double-chain drive transmission is enclosed within the engine castings. Major repair work is not for the amateur. The Babetta is the only moped with a transistorized ignition system, guaranteed to extend spark plug life and make starting easier.

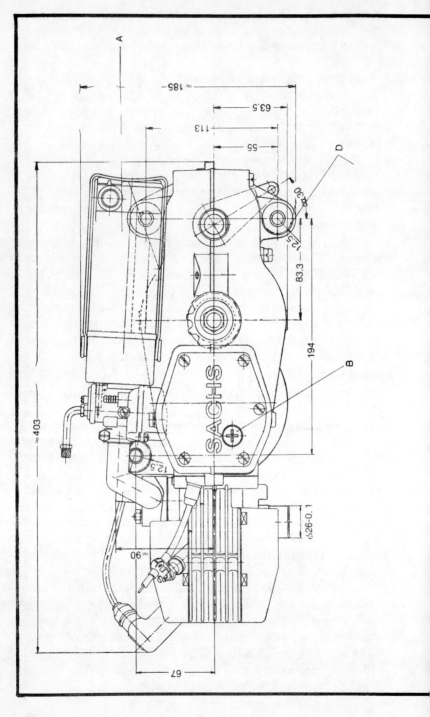

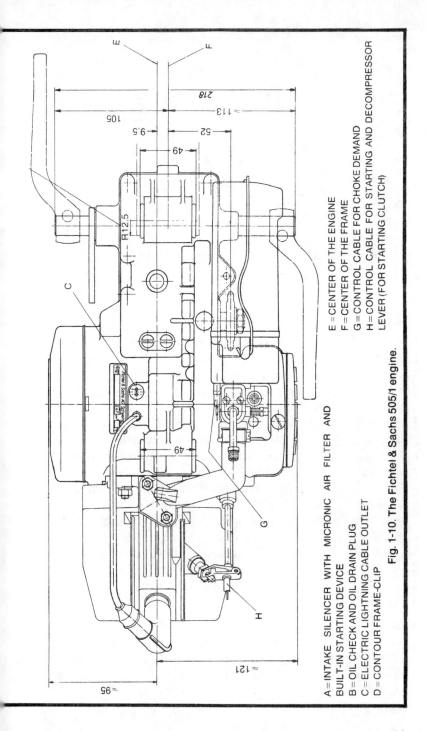

A = INTAKE SILENCER WITH MICRONIC AIR FILTER AND
BUILT-IN STARTING DEVICE
B = OIL CHECK AND OIL DRAIN PLUG
C = ELECTRIC LIGHTNING CABLE OUTLET
D = CONTOUR FRAME-CLIP

E = CENTER OF THE ENGINE
F = CENTER OF THE FRAME
G = CONTROL CABLE FOR CHOKE DEMAND
H = CONTROL CABLE FOR STARTING AND DECOMPRESSOR
LEVER (FOR STARTING CLUTCH)

Fig. 1-10. The Fichtel & Sachs 505/1 engine.

31

Fig. 1-11. The Jawa Babetta—a thoroughbred.

Cimatti

The Cimatti City Bike is the most inviting of all mopeds, styled with excitement and verve (Fig. 12 A). The frame is tubular and the fuel tank mounts, logically enough, over the rear wheel. The bike has been proved in the marathon of the moped world—rental service.

Its Minarelli V1 engine is used by several other manufacturers, a testament to its durability and a convenience for owners, who thus have several sources of parts and service (Fig. 1-12B). While the basic mechanism—a piston-ported cylinder, single-speed gearbox, and integral pedal mechanism—is fairly simple, the detail engineering is first rate. For example, the primary gears are helically cut to reduce noise and the final drive is by a single chain to the rear wheel. All engine-driven shafts are mounted on ball bearings pressed into the heavily webbed crankcases. A flywheel fan keeps air moving over the cylinder fins to prevent piston seizure after long periods at idle.

Tomos

Tomos Koper is known throughout eastern Europe as a builder of bicycles, motorcycles, outboard motors, and other leisure products. Current moped production is pegged at 200,000 a year. Two models are imported to this country: the 30-mph A 3S and the 20-mph A 3S Super Sport.

Fig. 1-12A. The Cimatti City Bike

Fig. 1-12B. A closeup of the Cimatti's Minarelli engine

Fig. 1-13. The Tomos A3S—mechanical sophistication in an unpretentious package.

Tomos bikes are state-of-the-art machines with features that would do justice to a luxury motorcycle (Fig. 1-13). All engine and transmission shafts ride on antifriction bearings; primary drive is through a fully automatic, two-speed gearbox; secondary drive is via a single chain to the rear wheel; both wheels have full-width hubs, and the front fork is hydraulically damped. No other moped has all these features.

On the debit side, Tomos does not, as yet, have much of a dealer organization. Parts and service are hard to find in some areas; the owner is on his own and will not get too much help from the shop manual, which is poorly translated and illustrated. However, replacement parts are reasonably priced and can be ordered through the central depot in Summerville, South Carolina.

Chapter 2
Engine ABCs

Moped engines have three moving parts: *piston, connecting rod,* and *crankshaft* (Fig. 2-1). The piston moves up and down in the cylinder bore. The small end of the connecting rod reciprocates with the piston, and the big end describes a circle, driving the crankshaft.

The cylinder, sometimes called the barrel or jug, is finned for cooling (Fig. 2-2). The part that closes off the top of the cylinder is called the cylinder head. It is secured by several bolts and may be fitted with a soft metal or composition gasket to make a gas-tight joint over the barrel. The spark plug threads into the head, also using a gasket for sealing.

The piston is a close fit in the bore and, for a more perfect seal, is grooved to accept a pair of piston rings. The rings expand under gas pressure and hug the bore, forming a barrier to leakage. The wrist pin passes through the piston and is held by a circlip on each side.

Both ends of the connecting rod usually ride on needle bearings, although some engines use bushings at the small end. Figure 2-3 shows the small-end bearings clearly; the big end bearings are hidden by the crankshaft webs. The crankshaft is supported in the crankcase by needle and ball bearings. A steel thrust washer locates the crankshaft fore and aft in the case. Seals on the outboard sides of the bearings prevent crankcase gases from escaping around the crankshaft

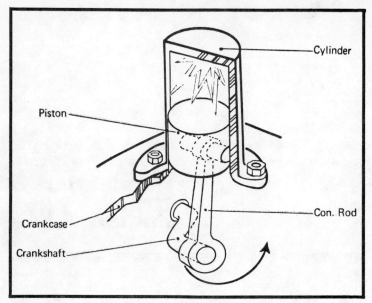

Fig. 2-1. Basic engine nomenclature. (Courtesy Pacific Basin Trading Co.)

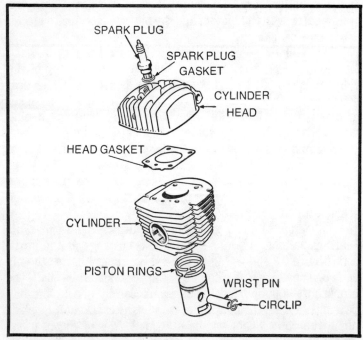

Fig. 2-2. The Motobecane upper engine assembly—typical of mopeds.

ends. The crankcase is split for easy access and is usually, though not always, gasketed.

OPERATION

Gasoline engines work on a cycle of five events: intake of the fuel charge, compression of the charge, ignition, expansion of the burning gases, and exhaust. Current imported moped engines accomplish this in a single revolution of the crankshaft or, phrasing it another way, in a single up-and-down stroke of the piston. Engines of this type are known as two-stroke or two-cycle engines.

Piston-Ported Engines

There are two varieties, distinguished by the way fuel and air is admitted into the crankcase. *Piston-ported* engines—the most popular—employ a cylinder pierced by three holes known as the inlet, transfer, and exhaust ports. The inlet port opens to admit the air-fuel mixture into the crankcase; the transfer port conducts this mixture into the cylinder; and the exhaust port channels the spent gases out of the cylinder and into the muffler. The ports are opened and closed by the movement of the piston.

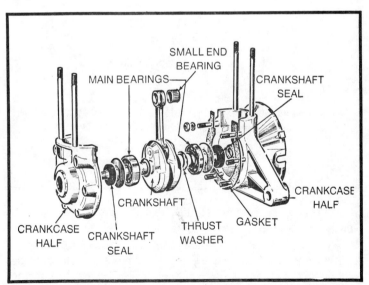

Fig. 2-3. The lower engine assembly converts the reciprocating motion of the piston into rotary motion. This Peugeot block illustrates typical moped practice.

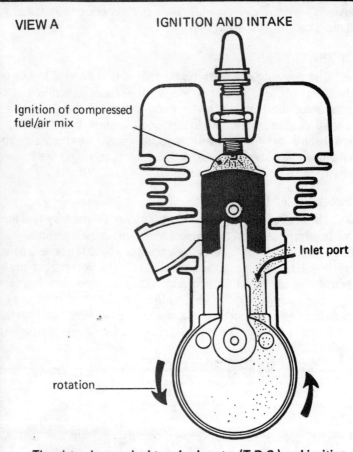

VIEW A   IGNITION AND INTAKE

Ignition of compressed
fuel/air mix

Inlet port

rotation

The piston has reached top dead center (T.D.C.) and ignition
is taking place. Note the inlet port below the piston; arrow
shows path of incoming fuel/air mix from carburetor.

Several events occur simultaneously, and you must look
closely at the drawings in Fig. 2-4. View A shows the piston at
the top of its stroke, a position called top dead center (TDC).
At this point, the exhaust and transfer ports are closed. The
inlet port is open and a fresh charge of air and fuel is entering
the crankcase, below the piston. At the same time, the top, or
crown, of the piston has compressed air and fuel in the

VIEW B

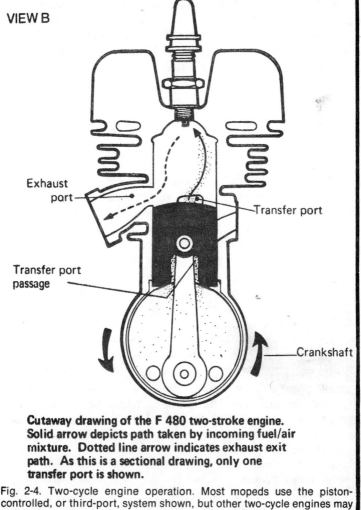

Exhaust port

Transfer port

Transfer port passage

Crankshaft

Cutaway drawing of the F 480 two-stroke engine. Solid arrow depicts path taken by incoming fuel/air mixture. Dotted line arrow indicates exhaust exit path. As this is a sectional drawing, only one transfer port is shown.

Fig. 2-4. Two-cycle engine operation. Most mopeds use the piston-controlled, or third-port, system shown, but other two-cycle engines may use a rotary or leaf inlet valve. (Courtesy Pacific Basin Trading Co.)

cylinder. This highly explosive mixture, more explosive than an equal weight of TNT, is ignited by a spark from the spark plug.

In Fig. 2-4B the piston, impelled by the force of burning gasoline and superheated air, has moved to bottom dead center (BCD). Early in its downward travel the piston closed off the inlet port, trapping the air-fuel charge in the crankcase.

The upper edge of the exhaust port is uncovered and then, a few degrees of crankshaft rotation later, the piston passes the transfer port.

As the piston falls it compresses the air-fuel charge below it. Once the inlet port closes, there is no escape for the charge until the transfer port is uncovered. When this happens the charge passes out of the crankcase and into the cylinder where it will be burnt during the next crankshaft revolution.

To return for a moment to events above the piston: the exhaust port is always cut higher in the bore than the inlet port and so opens earlier. This is to allow most of the spent (but still high-pressure) gases to "blow down" or exit through the exhaust port. Blow-down ceases when the pressure of the gases equals atmospheric pressure, so some exhaust residue remains in the cylinder and must be forcibly ejected— otherwise the fresh charge would be contaminated. The process of purging the cylinder is called *scavenging*, and has given two-cycle designers many a sleepless night.

There are several ways to scavenge a cylinder; all of them depend on using the incoming fuel charge as a kind of battering ram to force the spent gases out the exhaust port. The trick is to do this without losing too much of the fresh charge in the process.

Moped engines use what is called *cross-flow* scavenging. The incoming charge is divided between two transfer ports on opposite sides of the cylinder. The piston is slightly domed and the transfer-port exit ramps are angled to converge the charges at the center of the chamber. The charge streams meet and loop, forming a miniature hurricane that drives the exhaust gas out before it.

Reed-Valve Engines

Batavus, Peugeot, and Puch bikes use *reed-valve* engines. While piston-ported engines have three ports, reed-valve designs have only two—a transfer and an exhaust port. (Fig. 2-5). The reeds are made of spring steel and are mounted between the carburetor and the crankcase. They open when crankcase pressure drops below atmospheric pressure, and close, trapping the mixture, when the pressure relationship is reversed. Piston-ported engines have a tendency to spit back through the carburetor at low speeds, upsetting the mixture and covering the carburetor with a layer of oily grime. A reed

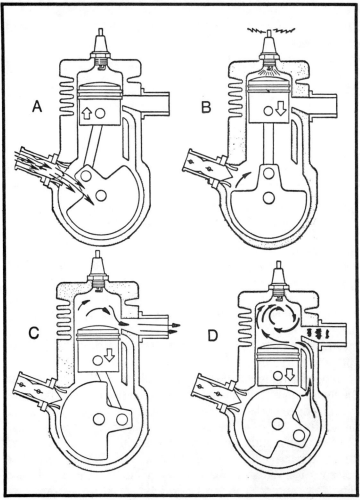

Fig. 2-5. A reed-valve, loop-scavenged engine. As the piston climbs in the cylinder, crankcase pressure drops in its wake. The reed valve opens (view A). The sparkplug fires (view B), igniting the mixture and sending the piston back down the bore (view C). Crankcase pressure closes the reed while, at the same time, the exhaust port is uncovered. Most exhaust gases blow down. Further downward piston movement (view D) opens the transfer port, and the cylinder fills with a fresh charge. The port is angled to loop the charge.

valve keeps the mixture in the crankcase where it belongs and, since the valve responds to vacuum, the engine is fed as much fuel as it can consume at all speeds. Torque is improved over piston-ported designs, especially at part throttle.

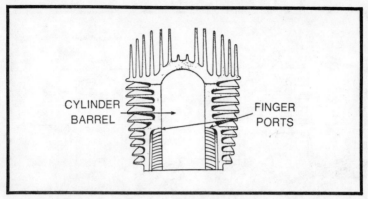

CYLINDER
BARREL

FINGER
PORTS

Fig. 2-6. "Finger ports", ports that open to the bore along their full length, are used on some moped engines. The illustration shows the dual, diametrically opposed finger ports on a Peugeot.

As a point of interest, Peugeot and Puch transfer ports are open to the bore along their full length (Fig. 2-6). While go-kart engines are sometimes modified this way to increase port area, the reason here seems to be manufacturing convenience.

The easiest way to tell whether an engine is reed-valve or piston-ported is carburetor placement. The carb on a piston-ported engine is always positioned with its intake tube (the single-cylinder equivalent of an intake manifold) leading to the base of the cylinder. A reed-valve engine's carb is mounted on the crankcase.

ENGINE DIMENSIONS

The basic dimensions of any engine are the bore and stroke (Fig. 2-7). The bore is the diameter of the cylinder; the stroke is the distance the piston travels between bottom and top dead centers. The stroke is determined by the throw, or offset, of the crankshaft.

Moped engines are built in countries that use the metric standard of measurement. Bore and stroke dimensions are expressed in millimeters (mm). For example, the Jawa Babetta has a bore of 39 mm and a 41 mm stroke. In American terms these dimensions are expressed as 1.55 × 1.61 inches.

Displacement

Displacement is a measure of how much air and fuel the engine "inhales" during each revolution of the crankshaft. It is the volume that the piston sweeps as it moves from top to bottom dead center, and is equal to the stroke times the area of the bore. Displacement does not include the clearance volume above the piston at top dead center.

Displacement is important in the legal definition of a moped. In most jurisdictions, "motor-assisted bicycles" are limited to 50 cubic centimeters of displacement. The reason for this restriction is to limit the power of the engine. In engines of equal refinement, power is directly related to displacement: the greater the displacement, the more horsepower and torque developed. A quick formula for calculating displacement is:

Bore × Bore × Stroke × Number of Cylinders × 0.7854.

Since all moped engines are single-cylinder devices, we can disregard the number of cylinders. It is important to use uniform units of measure. If we express bore and stroke in inches, the answer will be in cubic inches (cu. in. or, sometimes, CID for cubic inches of displacement). If we use millimeters the answer will be in cubic millimeters, a legitimate but rarely used unit of measure—it is traditional to express metric displacement into cubic centimeters (cc). To convert cubic millimeters in cubic centimeters, divide by 1000.

The displacement of the Babetta calculates as:

$$39mm \times 39 \times 41mm \times 0.7854 = 48978.33mm^3$$

$$\frac{48978.33mm^3}{1000} = 48.98 \text{ cubic centimeters}$$

We can convert to cubic inches by converting the millimeters into inches or by multiplying the cc displacement

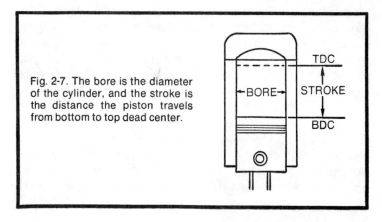

Fig. 2-7. The bore is the diameter of the cylinder, and the stroke is the distance the piston travels from bottom to top dead center.

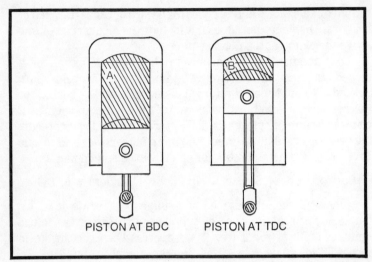

PISTON AT BDC   PISTON AT TDC

Fig. 2-8. Compression ratio is the ratio of the cylinder volume with the piston at bottom dead center to the volume at top dead center.

by 0.061. The Babetta displaces 2.99 cu. in. As a point of comparison the Chevrolet workhorse V-8, by no means the largest engine in the stable, displaces 350 cu. in.

Compression ratio is the cylinder volume at bottom dead center divided by the volume at top dead center (the clearance volume). Mopeds have compression ratios of about 8:1 (Fig. 2-8). Higher compression ratios give more power, but increase engine temperatures and require high-test fuel.

Engine power is expressed in units of horsepower and torque. These two terms are distinct, but interrelated. Torque is a measure of instantaneous twisting force. You exert torque when you open a jar lid, pedal a crank, or turn a wrench (Fig. 2-9). In our system, torque is expressed in pounds-feet, e.g., 10 pounds of force acting on a lever 1 foot long produces 10 pounds-feet of torque. The metric system uses kilograms and meters to measure torque. For an engine, torque translates as acceleration and the ability to keep slogging under load.

Unlike torque, which is a force sensed at a given moment, horsepower involves the concept of time. One horsepower is the ability to lift 550 pounds one foot in one second. One hp equals 550 ft-lb of work per second, or 33,000 ft-lb per minute. Horsepower and torque can be estimated from a vehicle's performance, but exact measurements of an engine's output requires a dynamometer.

44

A dynamometer is a machine that monitors rpm and torque while a brake applies a variable load to the engine. Some dynamometer brakes are mechanical, others are electrical; most are hydraulic and use water as the working fluid. Figure 2-10 illustrates a Go-Power engine dyno, intended for small two-cycle engines. The engine is bolted to

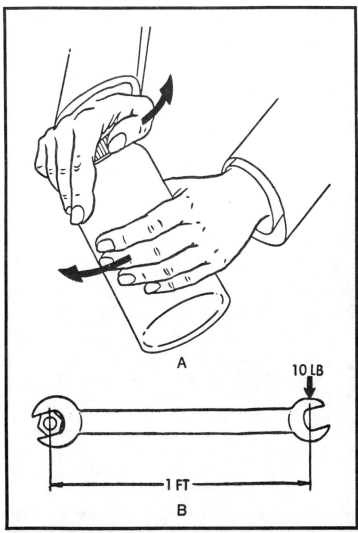

Fig. 2-9. Torque is a term for twisting force. You exert torque when you open a jar (view A) or turn a wrench (view B). A force of 10 lb exerted on a lever 1 ft long is 10 lb-ft of torque.

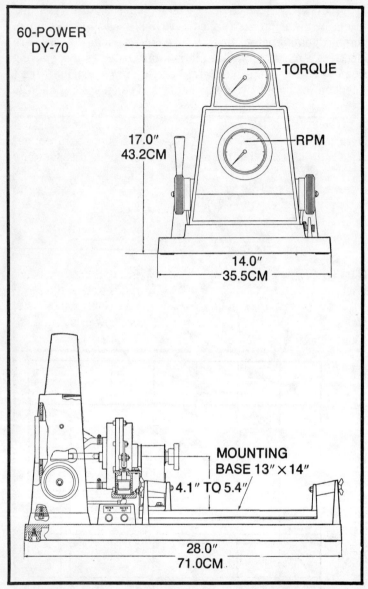

Fig. 2-10. Horsepower yields speed, but the relationship is not linear.

the mounting plate which is suspended on flexible rubber snubbers; the crankshaft is coupled by an adaptor to the driveshaft of the water brake. The amount of water going to the brake and the drag it generates is controlled by the valve on the right of the instrument stand. Two instruments are provided, a mechanical tachometer and a torque gauge.

This and most other engine dynos work on a very simple principle known as Newton's First Law of Motion: every action has an equal and opposite reaction. The force generated by the crankshaft to overcome the drag imposed by the water brake is the action. The reaction is the tendency of the engine to rotate around the crankshaft: this rotation has the same force as the crankshaft output, but is in the opposite direction. It acts through the flexible mounting base and is measured by the torque gauge.

Once rpm and torque are known, it is simple enough to convert to horsepower:

$$\text{brake horsepower} = \frac{\text{rpm} \times \text{torque (lb-ft)}}{5250}$$

The term brake horsepower (bhp) signifies that the figure has been measured on a dyno and is not estimated or guessed at.

Horsepower translates as speed, but the relationship is not linear. As speed increases, more and more power is needed to

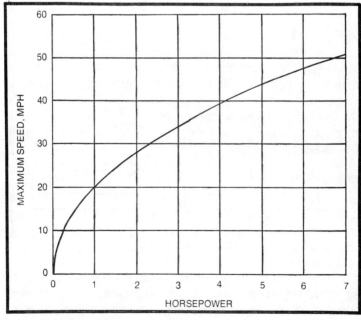

Fig. 2-1. Basic nomenclature. (Courtesy Pacific Basin Trading Co.)

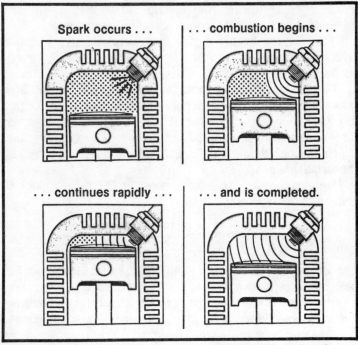

| Spark occurs . . . | . . . combustion begins . . . |
| . . . continues rapidly . . . | . . . and is completed. |

Fig. 2-12. Normal combustion. (Courtesy Champion Spark Plug Co.)

overcome air resistance, the friction losses in the transmission, and the rolling resistance of the tires. Figure 2-11,
prepared from data supplied by several moped
manufacturers, illustrates this. One horsepower will propel a
moped and a 160-lb rider at approximately 20 mph. Doubling
the horsepower increases the speed to slightly less than 30
mph; tripling the power only gives 35 mph. About 6 hp would
be required at 50 mph.

COMBUSTION

Normal combustion is an orderly process, a kind of
controlled explosion initiated by the spark plug. The spark
leaps between the plug's electrodes, ignites the mixture near
the spark plug, and the flame front moves progressively out
and into the far reaches of the chamber.

As you can see from the drawing at the left of Fig. 2-12, the
spark occurs early, before the piston reaches top dead center.
About 0.03 second is required for the flame front to move
across the chamber and generate peak pressure. Unless the

spark is advanced (occurs before TDC), the pressure will peak late, after the piston has descended in the bore. Most of the explosive energy would be wasted.

There are two forms of abnormal ignition. One is called preignition, or early ignition, and the other is detonation. Preignition occurs when the mixture is ignited by a local hot spot before the spark plug fires (Fig. 2-13). The piston rises against increasing pressure and the two flame fronts—one generated by the hot spot and the other by the spark plug—collide, generating more heat and pressure. The result can be a melted piston, as shown in Fig. 2-14.

Most hot spots are caused by partially detached carbon deposits that glow incandescent red when the engine is working under load. Other culprits are "hangnail" spark plug threads extending down into the chamber, the edges of the exhaust ports, or a head gasket that overlaps the chamber. Inadequate lubrication or dirty cooling fins can raise internal temperatures enough to contribute to the problem.

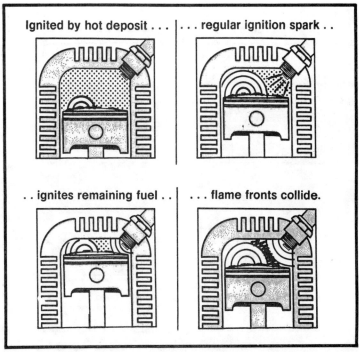

Ignited by hot deposit . . .   **. . . regular ignition spark . .**

. . ignites remaining fuel . .   **. . . flame fronts collide.**

Fig. 2-13. Preignition occurs early, before the spark plug fires. (Courtesy Champion Spark Plug Co.)

Fig. 2-14. Preignition does this to a piston. (Courtesy Champion Spark Plug Co.)

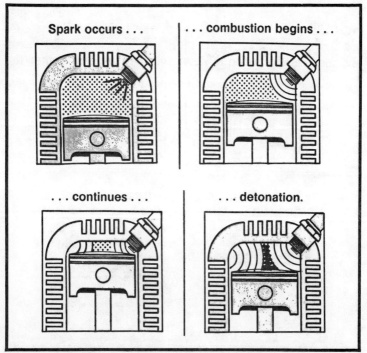

Spark occurs . . . **. . . combustion begins . . .**

. . . continues . . . **. . . detonation.**

Fig. 2-15. Detonation occurs late, after normal ignition. (Courtesy Champion Spark Plug Co.)

Detonation is a maverick explosion that occurs *after* normal combustion has begun. The spark plug fires and the flame front moves out into the chamber (Fig. 2-15). As it moves it compresses the unburnt charge ahead of it. Under certain conditions this unburnt charge can detonate, releasing a tremendous burst of energy, and you can actually hear the piston and cylinder head "ping" under its impact. The result is a dented or holed piston (Fig. 2-16).

Detonation is caused by too much ignition advance, poor-quality (low-octane) fuel, fuel-lean mixtures, or carbon deposits in the cylinder that raise the compression ratio beyond factory specs. Dirty cylinder fins and inadequate lubrication can also contribute.

Good combustion begins with the shape of the chamber. The one shown in Fig. 2-17 follows the best modern practice: spark plug threads are recessed and the outer edges of the chamber are undercut to form a squish band. The relief at the spark plug port protects the threads and reduces the possibility of one coming unglued and extending into the chamber where it would be a source of preignition. The swish band increases the turbulence of the fuel-air mixture: the greater the turbulence, the more quickly the mixture burns and the less likelihood of detonation. At top dead center the

Fig. 2-16. Detonation makes short work of pistons. (Courtesy Champion Spark Plug Co.)

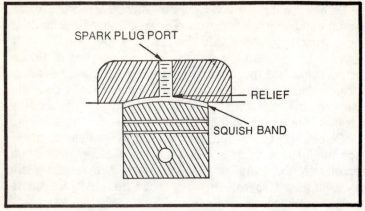

Fig. 2-17. A moped chamber in cross-section.

piston almost touches the squish band. Fuel trapped there squishes inward, toward the spark plug and the flame front.

LUBRICATION

Two-cycle engines are lubricated by oil mixed with the fuel. Since the crankcase is part of the intake tract, there is little choice in the matter. While a few European service stations sell premixed fuel, or petroil, in this country the owner must do his own mixing. The fuel-oil ratio varies with the manufacturer and the type of oil.

Check the owner's manual for instructions that apply to your machine. Too lean a mix can result in piston seizure and connecting rod failure; too rich a mixture will fog the neighborhood, foul the spark plug, and may cause overheating and detonation.

The proper way to mix the fuel is in a separate container. Pour the gasoline in first, add the oil, screw the cap down, and shake vigorously. In extreme cold, things go better if you warm the oil. Premix is fairly stable, but if the bike has been idle for several weeks, it is a good idea to shake it from side to side before starting.

The amount of oil going to the engine depends on the throttle setting. Under most conditions this works out fine, since the engine's need for lubrication and cooling is proportional to speed, but it can cause problems when on long downgrades. The throttle is almost closed while the engine is turning rapidly. Enough of this and the piston will run dry and seize in the bore, welding itself to the cylinder walls. Prevention is simple—merely open the throttle occasionally to introduce a fresh charge of oil.

COOLING

Moped engines are air-cooled, and depend on fins to dissipate the heat generated by combustion and internal friction. Most of the fins are clustered near the sources of heat, on the cylinder head and barrel. A few engines have one or two vestigial fins on the crankcase, more for looks than for function. The fins radiate some heat, but most cooling, more than 90% of it, is done by convection.

Convection depends on a current of air passing over the fins. The current does not have to be very strong, but it must keep moving. Velosolex and Minarelli V1 engines use a flywheel fan and shrouding to divert air to the fins. The engine is cooled whenever it runs. While such forced-air cooling is admirable, it may not be necessary for mopeds and does cost a little power, since the energy required to drive the fan is taken from the crankshaft.

Other manufacturers depend upon the forward movement of the vehicle to generate the air current. Engines built on this system are called free-air cooled, since no power is absorbed by the cooling system. Most motorcycle engines are cooled this way, as are high-performance snowmobile plants.

The designer must allow for fairly long periods of idle, when the vehicle is stationary. These periods are more frequent in a moped than in recreational vehicles. In addition, the designer must consider that moped engines are subject to occasional overheating when climbing long hills and sudden cool-down on the reverse slope.

Figure 2-18 is a cutaway of the Sachs 505/1 free-air cooled engine. The cylinder fins are shown clearly. Note their wide spacing, for good air flow at low velocities. Fan-cooled engines have narrower, more thickly clustered fins cast symmetrically and enclosed in a shroud (Fig. 2-19).

Free-air engines gain temperature stability from the mass of the finning, which is large in comparison to the size of the bore. The Sachs engine has fins stacked atop fins. The engine is slow to heat, which means that it can tolerate some abuse before the piston sticks, and it is slow to cool, giving some protection from overcooling on long hills. Stacked fins are

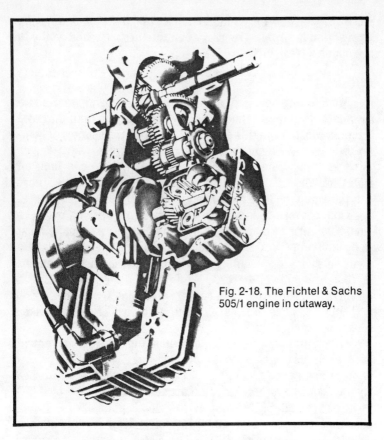

Fig. 2-18. The Fichtel & Sachs 505/1 engine in cutaway.

almost unknown outside of moped technology, but are a mark of the better engines.

The Puch Maxi engine is another example of careful fin design. Figure 2-20 illustrates the cylinder barrel. Note the displacement of fins to the left, two of which have a second fin grafted onto them. The reason is to balance the cylinder mass on the offset block in order to give the engine the appearance of symmetry. While this is not an engineering consideration, it does give some insight into the level of professionalism that can go into moped design.

While you would have to measure the fins to notice this, those on the lower side of the barrel are slightly longer than those on top. This is an engineering consideration; the additional fin length is needed to cool the exhaust port. The small hole on the face of the cylinder is the exit port for the compression release fitted to European models. Rather than release pressure to the outside of the cylinder, where the fuel and oil mix would dirty the fins, Puch engineers have diverted it to the exhaust.

The cylinder head is detachable (much to the mechanic's convenience) and deeply finned. The horizontal spark plug interferes with finning much less than the angled plug used by Sachs. A heat dam, formed by the absence of fins at the head/barrel joint, prevents heat from bleeding out of the head and into the barrel, where it could damage the piston.

DETUNING

You will recall from Chapter 1 that moped engines undergo one or more detuning stages to make them legal in various states. It is interesting to consider how this is done, since it is the reverse of most engineering practice. In other

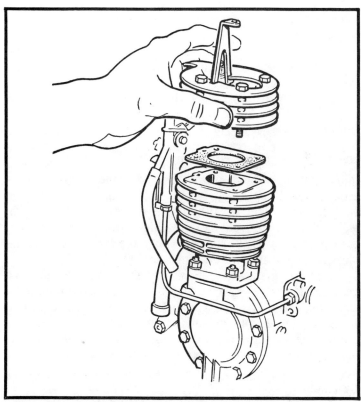

Fig. 2-19. The symmetry and narrow spacing of Velosolex fins are a dead giveaway that the engine is fan-cooled.

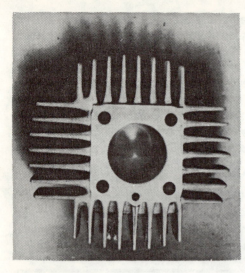

Fig. 2-20. A Puch cylinder barrel.

industries the emphasis is on more, rather than less, performance.

The most obvious way to cut power is to reduce the engine's displacement, but few manufacturers go to this expensive extreme. There are easier ways.

One method is to reduce the compression ratio, for the more tightly the air-fuel mixture is compressed, the more power it releases during combustion. Puch engines have as many as three paper-thin aluminum spacers between the cylinder head and the barrel. While these spacers do not seem thick enough to have much effect, together they drop the compression ratio by one point. Removing them gives the engine more power than the frame can comfortably absorb, and converts a pussycat into a real tiger. Other manufacturers use a relatively thick gasket between the cylinder barrel and block for this market and a paper gasket in Europe.

Another approach, often combined with a lowered compression ratio, is to restrict the size of the carburetor bore. Again using Puch as an example, 12-mm carburetors are fitted to the 17 and 20-mph machines; 25 and 30-mph bikes have 14-mm carburetors. Jawa bikes lose 0.6 hp in translation by virtue of a restrictor plate between the carburetor and cylinder. The plate blocks most of the intake port, throttling the engine.

Two-cycle engines are very sensitive to exhaust back pressure. Moped designers understand this and may include a deliberately restrictive muffler in their recipe for less power. Batavus has three sets of baffle plates, each more restrictive than the last, for the 30, 25, and 20 mph machines.

In addition to engine modifications, gearing may be changed to accomodate the law. For example, the Puch 20-mph bike has a 13-tooth engine sprocket; along with other changes, the 25-mph machine has a 14-tooth sprocket for slightly "taller" gearing. The rear wheel turns further with each revolution of the engine, enabling higher speed at a given engine rpm.

Chapter 3
Tools

The tools supplied with the bike are adequate for 90% of maintenance and repairs. The other 10% requires a small collection of standard mechanic's tools and a few special tools that are peculiar to mopeds.

WRENCHES

Mopeds are built on the IS, or metric, standard. No American tool will exactly match a metric bolt or nut. Half-inch and 9/16-inch wrenches will turn 12 and 14-mm bolts, but the fit is sloppy and invites butchering the bolt head and your knuckles. The first priority is to invest in a set of metric wrenches.

Open-end and Box-end Wrenches

There are three basic wrench varieties—open-end, box-end, and socket (Fig. 3-1). If you are on a budget, the open and box-end wrenches in the bike's tool kit will carry you a long way, but these wrenches tend to be crudely finished and wear quickly. Open-end wrenches are more essential than box-ends, since fuel fittings and the like cannot be worked on with a 360 degree jaw. And open-ends are faster to use. However—and this is a minor point—open-end wrenches tend to wear and distort in heavy use. A really tight fastener will spring one. Box-end wrenches are stronger and less liable to

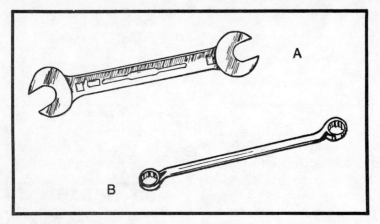

Fig. 3-1. Open-end wrenches are the most basic (view A), but need to be shortstopped by box-ends (view B).

round bolt faces, and are the second choice after a 4 to 19-mm set of open-ends.

The third choice, one that is a luxury for most Saturday-afternoon mechanics, is a set of combination wrenches in the same 4 to 19-mm span (Fig. 3-2). These wrenches have an open-end jaw on one side and a closed-end on the other. Both jaw sizes are the same. The idea is to use the open end to rapidly run the threads and the closed end for initial loosening or final tightening. Combination wrenches are expensive, since you must purchase one wrench for each bolt size and because these wrenches will not do anything that open and box-end wrenches will not do.

Socket Wrenches

Some nuts and bolts are positioned so that access is from above—the sides of the fastener are masked by other parts. The only wrench that will work under these circumstances is a socket.

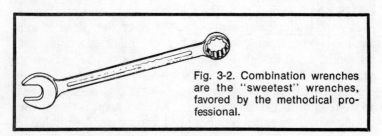

Fig. 3-2. Combination wrenches are the ''sweetest'' wrenches, favored by the methodical professional.

Fig. 3-3. Sockets are available in 6 and 12-point styles. For reasons explained in the text, the 6-point is preferable.

It is cheaper and less frustrating to purchase a complete set of sockets at one fell swoop. While there is a trend to standardize metric fasteners in even sizes on motor vehicles, not all moped manufacturers follow this convention. You will encounter some odd-numbered sizes, and will need sockets from 7mm to 19 mm in 1-mm increments. If possible, specify 6-point, as opposed to 12-point, jaws (Fig. 3-3). Six-point sockets exert a stronger grip, especially if the fastener is worn and rounded, and last much longer than the 12-point variety. The standard length, or reach, is adequate for everything except the spark plug which requires a 5/8-inch deep-well socket (Fig. 3-4). The popular 3/8-inch square-drive—this is the size of the hole in the back of the socket—is the best choice for small engine work. Quarter-inch drive tools are a little fragile and are not built to give the leverage; half-inch drive tools are heavy and get in their own way on moped castings.

Ratchet Handles

A simple T-handle driver is all that you need, at least in the beginning. Later you will want to invest in a ratchet handle, sometimes called a ratchet wrench. Ratchet handles come in a variety of shapes, sizes, and finishes. Each mechanic has his favorite brand, with some 70% choosing S-K.

The primary advantage of the S-K handle is its close-acting ratchet, made possible by the use of

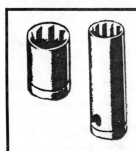

Fig. 3-4. Standard reach and deep-well sockets. (Courtesy Big Joe Industrial Tool Corp.)

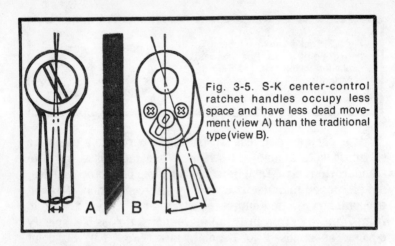

Fig. 3-5. S-K center-control ratchet handles occupy less space and have less dead movement (view A) than the traditional type (view B).

aircraft-quality steel in the ratchet wheels and pawls. Cheaper wrenches must have large gear teeth for strength; consequently, there is 10-20 degrees of dead movement at the handle before the ratchet engages (Fig. 3-5). The S-K tool requires no more than 9 degrees of dead movement and as little as 5.1 degrees.

Some mechanics prefer Snap-on tools, which are about the most expensive, and are surely the best finished, on the market. The Snap-on "Ferret" series handles require 18 degrees of handle movement between engagement points. Sears Craftsman ratchets have as little as 4 degrees of dead movement, but—with all apologies to Sears—are somewhat sloppy in action and finish. The real advantage of Craftsman tools and the reason why many amateurs and more than a few professionals are loyal to them is the warranty. Craftsman socket handles have an unlimited unconditional warranty which includes the ratchet mechanism. No other manufacturer gives such complete buyer protection.

TORQUE WRENCHES

The bane of beginning mechanics is stripped or pulled-out threads. Most of the fasteners you are dealing with on a moped are threaded into aluminum, and aluminum is not a forgiving metal. Run the fastener in crooked and the threads will cross and strip. Draw down the fastener too hard, and the threads will pull out.

Working mechanics do not have this problem. They avoid cross-threading by running the fastener in at least three turns by hand, before picking up a wrench. Spark plugs might get four or five turns, since the threads on the spark-plug port are subject to wear. And professionals have educated hands that sense how tight is enough. Without being conscious of it, the mechanic takes into account the diameter of the fastener, its threaded depth, the metal it threads into, and the length of the wrench handle. He stops tightening well short of that soft feeling that means the threads have begun to crumple. If this point is reached, the threads have been compromised, but will generally hold. Continued turning will strip the fastener.

A torque wrench indicates how much twisting force, or torque, is being applied to the fastener. It is a very good substitute for professional experience, and it must be used on critical fasteners. No mechanic, however competent, can consistently sense the difference between 8 ft-lb and 10 ft-lb. Some engine components can and the difference may be catastrophic.

There are many types of torque-indicating wrenches, each with advantages in particular applications. An amateur and most professionals are best served by a deflecting-beam wrench (Fig. 3-6). It is the simplest and least expensive, requiring no maintenance over its life span of several million cycles. The principle may not be entirely obvious from the drawing: force acting on the handle can turn the fastener or it can bend the beam. Initially the fastener threads easily, and the beam hardly bends. As the fastener is tightened it resists movement, and this resistance is read on the dial as torque. The dial is secured to the beam and deflects with it; the pointer is attached to the drive end of the wrench and remains straight.

There is some confusion about the units of torque. Torque is a measure of twisting force, expressed in units of weight, acting through a bar whose length is expressed as a unit of

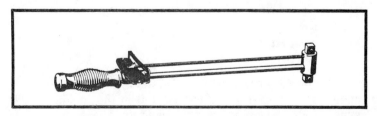

Fig. 3-6. This Fichtel & Sachs torque wrench is calibrated in mkg, and can be ordered from factory headquarters in Dorval, Quebec.

distance. In our system we use pounds as the unit of force and inches or feet as the unit of distance. Larger wrenches, intended for general automotive work, are calibrated in feet; smaller-capacity wrenches, of the kind that would be used on mopeds, are calibrated in inches. In Americanized shop manuals, specification sheets, and mechanic's conversation, torque is described as so many inch-pounds or foot-pounds. Engineers and the scientific community sometimes reverse the notation and say pound-inches or pound-feet. As far as this book is concerned, either term is okay. In the discussion of torque and horsepower in the previous chapter, the pound-foot was used since this is the way dyno gauges read.

Mopeds are built on the metric standard; inch-lb and ft-lb specifications are a courtesy extended to the American mechanic by some manufacturers. The traditional metric unit of torque is kilogram-meters, abbreviated kgm or, for scientific notation, mkg. However, by a recently passed law, West German torque specifications are published in Newton-meters, or Nm. Other European countries are expected to follow suit.

Torque specifications may be in four basic units: inch-lb, ft-lb, kgm, and Nm. The relationship between these units can be summarized:

TO CONVERT	MULTIPLY BY
in-lb to ft-lb	0.0833
in-lb to kgm	0.0115
in-lb to Nm	0.133
ft-lb to in-lb	12
ft-lb to kgm	0.138
ft-lb to Nm	1.36
kgm to in-lb	86.8
kgm to ft-lb	7.23
kgm to Nm	9.8
Nm to in-lb	8.85
Nm to ft-lb	0.738
Nm to kgm	0.102

Purchase a wrench with a 0-150 in-lb (0-2.0 kgm, 0-20 Nm) range. Most moped specifications fall in the middle of this range, where the wrench is most accurate. The wrench should be stored away from other tools, since the pointer and the plastic "floating" handle are fragile. If the pointer should be damaged, the wrench can be recalibrated by bending the pointer so zero torque is indicated under no load.

Factory torque specifications assume that the nuts, bolts, and other fasteners to be torqued are like-new and lubricated. Damaged threads or threads filled with rust and carbon will give wildly inaccurate torque readings since the wrench cannot distinguish between friction and tension on the fastener. Both are read as resistance to turning.

A common shop practice is to clean threads with a power-driven wheel. A light brushing probably doesn't hurt anything; heavy brushing, of the sort required to remove carbon, dulls the threads and makes a torque wrench useless. If the fastener is carbon-impacted or rusted, soak it in carburetor cleaner and brush it by hand.

In addition, the threads and the underside of bolt heads and nuts should be lubricated. Motor oil is most often used, and is generally adequate, but for best results, purchase a small tin of antiseize compound.

Aluminum castings can easily distort in assembly. Bolts should be drawn down together, if possible, to stress all areas of the casting equally. If there are only two bolts, as in the case of a carburetor flange, tighten one a few turns, then the other. Work in this criss-cross fashion until the bolts are snugged; then if you have the specs, finish the job with a torque wrench. Head bolts are tightened in the same manner, moving from one an other across the long axis (Fig. 3-7). Go through the sequence in three increments: 1/3 torque, 2/3 torque, full torque. All torque-limit specifications available at this writing are included in Chapter 6.

SCREWDRIVERS

American screwdrivers fit metric screws reasonably well, although you may want to file the screwdriver that you use for

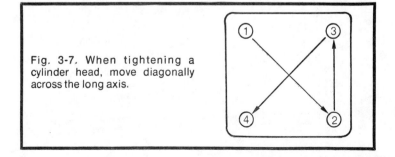

Fig. 3-7. When tightening a cylinder head, move diagonally across the long axis.

PHILLIPS   **SLOTTED**

Fig. 3-8. Phillips-recess and single-slotted screwheads. (Courtesy Star Stainless Screw Co.)

point adjustments to an accurate fit. A butchered point screw is a frustration.

Some manufacturers use Phillips, or cross-slot, screws to hold the major castings (Fig. 3-8). While this approach simplifies manufacturing—Phillips screws can be run in with automatic drivers—and gives the bike a clean look, it causes headaches for the mechanic. The screws get tighter as the machine is run and removal with an ordinary screwdriver is

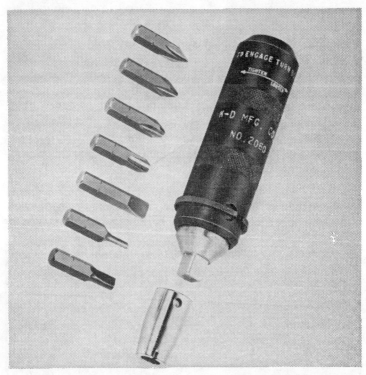

Fig. 3-9. A K-D impact driver.

Fig. 3-10. Needle-nosed pliers are more elongated versions of long-nosed pliers, useful for positioning parts. Neither of these tools tolerates much torque. (Courtesy Big Joe Industrial Tool Corp.)

almost impossible. Sometimes the screws can be shocked loose with a hammer blow on the end of the driver. One may be reduced to turning the screws crabwise with a small chisel which, of course, ruins them.

The solution to this and other vexing fastener problems is an impact driver (Fig. 3-9). The bit is positioned in the screw slot and the tool given a healthy wallop with a hammer. The bit is forced deeper into the slot and, thanks to an internal cam, rotates. No Phillips screw with any kind of slot left is proof against an impact driver.

PLIERS

Ordinary slip-joint pliers, the kind that most people keep in a kitchen drawer, are adequate for most jobs. Long-nosed pliers are convenient for holding small parts, and the needle-nosed variety is even more so (Fig. 3-10). The best source of either is an electronics supply house.

Vise-Grip Pliers

Vise-Grip is a trade name applied to a group of plier-like tools (Fig. 3-11). The bolt adjusts an internal toggle to the approximate jaw size needed; squeezing the handles generates a force of some two tons for the 8-inch size and correspondingly more for larger tools. Vise-Grips have no specific use on a moped—you should not be in a situation that requires two tons of force—but they have scores of miscellaneous uses. The tool can be mounted in the vise to hold

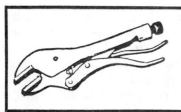

Fig. 3-11. Locking pliers. (Courtesy Big Joe Industrial Corp.)

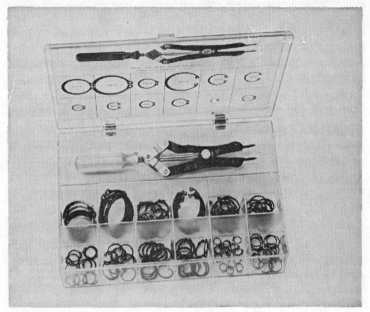

Fig. 3-12. A K-D combination snapring tool. The snapring assortment is inch standard and of no use on metric equipment.

irregularly shaped parts, used as a clamp to secure parts during assembly, and can generated leverage on other tools. The central use, and the reason these tools have displaced water pump pliers in most mechanic's tool boxes, is to remove rusted and battered fasteners.

Purchase the original Vise-Grip or a tool of comparable quality. Cheap locking pliers are worse than useless, since the force generated by the handles merely warps the jaws.

But a word of caution: pliers are not wrenches and should not be used on bolts with good heads. Using Vise-Grips or other pliers on a fastener is an admission that the fastener is already damaged and must be replaced.

Snapring Pliers

Snaprings are used to secure the piston pin to the piston and may be found on clutch and transmission components. There are two types of snaprings, normally requiring separate plier-like tools. The K-D tool shown in Fig. 3-12 handles both inside and outside snaprings, expanding one and squeezing the other. The combination tool is no more expensive than the others, although it does take up more space in the tool box.

Of course, more people disassemble mopeds than have snapring tools. A knife blade in concert with a small screwdriver usually does the trick, but there is danger of damage to the parts. Damage to the snapring is of no consequence, since a careful mechanic discards them—particularly those on the piston pin—each time they are disturbed, but damage to the mounting surfaces can cause a loose or difficult fit.

HAMMERS

Hammers are strong medicine, particularly on white-metal castings, but strong medicine has its place. A carpenter's claw hammer is better than nothing, but the balance and the distance of the face from the handle is wrong for mechanical work. It is much better to purchase a machinist's, or ball-peen, hammer. The 8-ounce weight is about right.

A few precautions can prevent most embarrassments and minimize the danger of inury:

- Wear safety glasses. I realize that a mechanic may be laughed at if he dons safety glasses when he uses a hammer. But many who didn't wish they had.
- Keep the hammer clean. A greasy handle or face can cause injury to yourself or to the machine.
- A hammer requires some minor maintenance. In dry weather you may have to soak the hickory handle in water to swell the grin. Replace the handle at the first sign of a crack. And replace the head if it begins to peel and chip. Hammer heads are surface-hardened by a dose of carbon at the foundry, but the inner metal is as soft as pig iron: once the surface is compromised, it will throw chips.
- Use a hammer with discretion. Do not strike soft metal castings with a steel hammer.
- If it doesn't move, find out why. Be slow to apply more force.

A mallet is needed to separate crankcase halves. The traditional favorite is made of rolled rawhide, but these are getting expensive, and you may have to settle for plastic or, at the worst, hard rubber. But do not attempt any serious, elbow-deep, engine work without a mallet.

Cutting Tools

We think of saws, files, and chisels as construction tools, rather than as repair tools. There are times, however, when nicks and gouges have to be smoothed out and allegedly inter-changeable parts must be custom-fitted.

Hacksaws

As long as the frame is rigid, the most important part of a hacksaw is the blade. For precision work, use a 12-inch "all-hard" blade, such as the tungsten high-speed steel blade made by Disston. This blade is brittle and will snap if you force the saw or allow the blade to work loose in the frame. Disston Super Safe blades are flexible—so flexible in fact that they can be tied in knots without breaking—but their cut tends to wander.

Files

File technology was old when the pyramids were built, and there is a lot to learn about the subject. Basically, files are classified in terms of their cut, pitch (number of teeth to the inch), shape, and length. Some of these factors are interrelated. For example, the pitch number drops as the length of the file blank increases. A 4-inch file has more teeth to the inch than the same style in the 12-inch length. In other words, smooth work requires a short file.

The cut refers to the way the teeth are milled. If formed by a single pass of the cutter, the teeth are in parallel rows and the file is classified as single-cut. A second pass, diagonal to the first, produces a double-cut file. The teeth have a diamond shape, falling off from a point in the center. Single-cut files are slow, but leave a smooth surface; double-cut files rip the metal.

Tooth size or pitch is described in general terms as fine (smooth) cut, medium (second) cut, and bastard. As explained in the previous paragraph, the pitch is related to the length. A 12-inch fine-cut has larger teeth—leaving a coarser work surface—than a 4-inch bastard.

For general cutting and sharpening, use a flat mill bastard in the 8-inch length (Fig. 3-13).* A rattail of about the same length is useful on curved surfaces and doubles as a poor

---

*This is the standard file in the metal-working trades. The adjective "mill" is a carry over from the past, when these files were used primarily to sharpen circular mill saws.

Fig. 3-13. If you buy only one file, make it a mill bastard. (Courtesy American Saw & Mfg. Co.)

man's reamer. Do not make the error of purchasing one of the round files meant for sharpening saw blades. A true rattail is tapered and has double-cut teeth for rapid material removal.

Purchase name-brand files, with the maker's logo stamped on the tang. Unmarked files are factory seconds and give disappointing results, since most rejects have faulty heat-treating.

A file will give years of service if you observe these rules:

- Always use a handle, for the control and protection it offers.
- Cut on the forward stroke, lifting the file off the work on the back stroke.
- Cut dry, without oil.
- Keep the teeth clean with a filecard. A filecard looks like a wire brush with a burr haircut. An ordinary wire brush or power-driven wheel will dull the teeth.
- If you keep you files in the toolbox, protect them with plastic sleeves.

GAUGES

When you begin to work on engines, it is satisfying enough to get the things running, but as a mechanic gets more experience, he takes a longer view. Not only is the engine supposed to run—that is expected—it's supposed to stay together for a long time. A real engine man goes beyond these considerations. The engine must not only run and stay together, but it must perform better than it did the day it left the factory. He begins where the factory finished.

At the heart of engine work is precision measurement. Inside and outside micrometers, dial indicators, vernier calipers, and gauge blocks to keep the instruments accurate are what distinguish the engine man from the ordinary, however-talented, mechanic. The mechanic can estimate piston-to-cylinder clearance accurately by wobbling the piston with his fingers; a thumbnail nail dragged across a bearing journal gives him some indication of its finish. But the engine

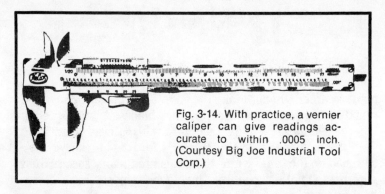

Fig. 3-14. With practice, a vernier caliper can give readings accurate to within .0005 inch. (Courtesy Big Joe Industrial Tool Corp.)

man starts where the mechanic finishes. His touch provides the clue that reveals an imperfectly-fitted part; his instruments enable him to fit it to a ten-thousandth.

The beginning mechanic has little experience to guide him and less in the way of precision gauges. In this book I will describe, as well as I can, the correct feel for bearing clearances, piston fits, and the like. But if you really want to build the engine right, invest in a vernier caliper (Fig. 3-14). You can purchase a fairly good one for about $30, and with practice will be able to take readings accurate to 0.0005 inch. The instrument may be used as inside and outside calipers, and doubles as a depth gauge.

Feeler Gauges

Feeler gauges are indispensible. The gauge shown in Fig. 3-15 combines two types of feeler gauge into a single tool. The round wire gauges are used to measure spark plug gap, since spark-plug electrodes wear rounded and the gauge must conform if it's to give honest readings. The flat leaves are used to set ignition point gap and measure clearances between machined parts.

Most moped manufacturers have been considerate enough to translate their metric specs into the inch system. Metric feeler gauges are available, but you can use inch gauges if you remember that 1 mm equals 0.04 inch. Say, for example, that the specification calls for a contact point gap of 0.3 mm. Multiplying 0.3 by 0.04 gives 0.012 inch.

Round gauges are less subject to error then flat ones, which is why some mechanics use them whenever they can. A flat gauge must be held dead parallel with the parts measured, while a round gauge can move in one plane without affecting the reading. There should be a slight drag as the gauge is moved between the parts. The feel of zero clearance cannot be described in a book, but you can learn to recognize it with practice. The ignition points are a good teaching aid, particularly if the points are new and the contact faces are square. Set the gap to specification. Now insert the next smallest leaf between them. It should move with an almost-imperceptible resistance, indicating that both sides of the leaf are in light contact. Then try the leaf on the wide side of the specification. It should be in solid contact with the points.

Compression Gauges

A compression gauge is used to diagnose piston ring and cylinder bore wear (Fig. 3-16). The gauge fitting screws into or is held over the spark plug port, and registers peak compression as the engine is cranked. One-shot readings are not as useful as a carefully recorded series of readings taken once or twice a year. In a new or rebuilt engine, compression will usually be low for the first few hundred miles and climb steadily as the rings seat. It will remain on a plateau for many miles, and then gradually fall off as wear takes its toll. The rings should be renewed at the falloff point. New rings should reach and hold the original compression plateau, once they are broken in. If the rings leak, soon after installation, the cylinder bore or piston is worn and should be replaced.

SUPPLIES

Engine and drive-train maintenance and repair requires a variety of solvents, sealers, and lubricants.

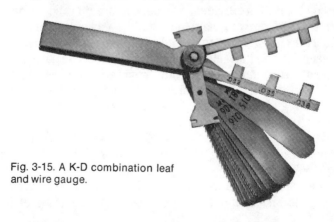

Fig. 3-15. A K-D combination leaf and wire gauge.

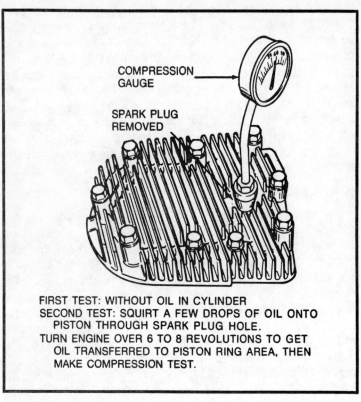

COMPRESSION GAUGE

SPARK PLUG REMOVED

FIRST TEST: WITHOUT OIL IN CYLINDER
SECOND TEST: SQUIRT A FEW DROPS OF OIL ONTO
    PISTON THROUGH SPARK PLUG HOLE.
TURN ENGINE OVER 6 TO 8 REVOLUTIONS TO GET
    OIL TRANSFERRED TO PISTON RING AREA, THEN
    MAKE COMPRESSION TEST.

Fig. 3-16. A compression gauge is a good diagnostic instrument.

Solvents

The first priority is a general-purpose solvent. One of the best solvents, available if you're lucky enough to work where it is used, is trichlorethylene. Stoddard's is the brand name of another good solvent, and one that is easier to find than trichlorethylene. The third, and most economical, choice is kerosene. But do not, under any circumstance, use gasoline as a solvent. Gasoline boils at room temperature and below. The vapor is heavier than air, and moves out in long, ground-hugging streamers. These streamers act as fuses. In one case on record, an open container of gasoline was ignited by a welding torch 162 feet away. When mixed with the proper proportion of air, gasoline is more explosive than an equal weight of TNT.

The pungent, burnt-candy odor you detect around motorcycle shops and airplane hangers is Gunk, one of the most efficient degreasers known. When mixed with kerosene, Gunk turns grease and oil into soap. The disadvantages of Gunk are that it must be flushed with water—a problem around electrical equipment—and that is discolors paint.

Gunk Hydroseal is a favorite of aircraft mechanics, who use it to dissolve carbon deposits inside engines and on cylinder fins. Cylinder fins can also be brightened with oven cleaner, but test the cleaner on an unobtrusive part of the head before you spray the whole surface.

There are special carburetor cleaners, but most are sold in five-gallon cans for professional use. Gunk Carburetor Cleaner is available from most automotive stores in pints; one pint should do about a hundred moped carburetors. Perhaps the best solution is to purchase a spray can of Berkebile 2 + 2 Gum Cutter. The spray product is more potent (and expensive) than the 2 + 2 in pints. If nothing else is handy, you can clean most carburetors with lacquer thinner.

Mufflers eventually clog up and must be dismantled for cleaning. The job is easier if you submerge the muffler in a warm solution of water and caustic soda. Be careful when you are handling caustic—it does to flesh what it does to carbon. Nor are the fumes particularly wholesome. And caustic cannot be used on aluminum, only steel and cast iron.

Engine work produces large amounts of waste, and you should have a good supply of rags on hand. Cotton shop towels are best, but any lint-free, natural-fiber cloth is adequate. Somehow, old T-shirts are traditional around a shop. Some mechanics use heavy paper towels available from parts stores. Ordinary paper towels are better than nothing, and much better than dirty rags.

Lubricants

You will need several lubricants. Chassis lube is a bit heavy for wheel bearings and suspension swing arms, but it is inexpensive. Most shops use it, but specially refined and formulated greases such as Lubriplate are better choices and can add to the life of the machine.

If you run synthetic oil, use it as an assembly lube. If not, preoil the parts with SE-grade motor oil from a major refiner. Some petroleum-based motor oil is fortified with additives; fortified oil is the choice for use as an asembly lube. Or you may purchase an additive from a Big Three auto dealer—Chrysler, Ford, and General Motors offer well-tested additives under their own parts numbers.

Torque specifications can be more accurately met if you dab antiseize lubricant on the threads. This extreme-pressure lubricant is available in small cans from the larger automotive supply houses. Penetrating oil is useful on machines that are heavily weathered. Various chain oils are available, some of them containing exotic metals such as molybdenum, and others that spray on as a bubbling froth. Industrial chain users, the experts in this field, say that motor oil is okay, so long as the chain stays wetted. Silicon lubricants protect rubber and plastic parts and, should the need arise, can be sprayed on the magneto and spark plug leads to draw water out of the insulation.

Sealants

Gasket sealants are insurance against leaks and, used with moderation, add security to a repair job. The old favorite was 3M Weatherstripping Adhesive, affectionately known as "Yellow Death." It works very well, but is sensitive to heat and cannot be used on head gaskets or exhaust systems.

The current favorite, at least on the eastern Pennsylvania sprint car circuits, is Permatex Silicon ("Blue Stuff"). To use, spread a thin coat of Blue Stuff on both sides of the gasket and bolt it up immediately before the silicon has a chance to cure. The engine can be started upon assembly. Blue Stuff tends to harden in the tube after opening, but its shelf life can be extended to a year or more if it's stored in the refrigerator.

SPECIAL TOOLS

Figure 3-17 illustrates the complete tool set for the Sachs 505/1-series engine. Some of these tools are specific to the Sachs and will work on no other bike; a number of them, including the piston pin extractor (1), the clutch holding wrench (9), and the tachometer (12), can be used on other makes. Other tools in this series can be fabricated with a little ingenuity and patience; a few are European equivalents of familiar American mechanic's tools and can be purchased locally. The flywheel puller as well as clutch pullers for other engines can often be purchased at bicycle shops—the same tools are used to remove cotterless bicycle cranks.

ODDS AND ENDS

Collect several half-foot lengths of two-by-four to use as supports for precision parts. Machined surfaces such as the head gasket surface or the parting line on the crankcase halves should be placed on the supports, not directly on the bench. A brass rod 5 or 6 inches long and 5/8 or 3/4 inch in diameter protects steel parts from direct hammer blows. If you have a vise, you should fashion jaw covers from brass or copper sheets. Cut the covers slightly larger than the jaws and crimp the ends.

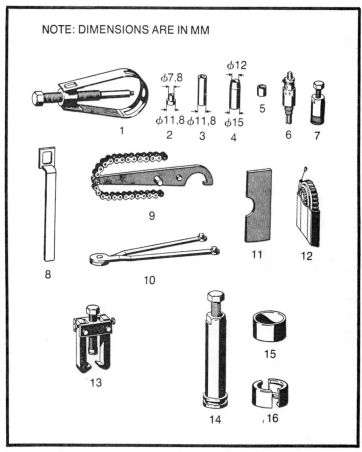

Fig. 3-17. Sachs factory tools include piston pin extractor 1, several sleeves 2, 3, 4, 5, a timing gauge 6, flywheel puller 7, offset wrench 8, clutch holder 9, flywheel holder 10, intermediate plate 11, tachometer 12, sprocket puller 13, bearing puller 14, and bearing puller adaptors 15 and 16.

Several repair operations take advantage of aluminum's rapid expansion when heated. You can use a propane torch for this, but a light touch is necessary. Too much heat or heat focused in one spot will distort the casting beyond repair. A safer method, and one that almost always can be substituted for a torch, is to heat with an electric hot plate. Where the shape of the parts prevents direct contact, you can use oil and rags as the medium. Heat the oil, keeping the temperature below 200 degrees F, pour it over rags wrapped around the casting.

Discarded ice trays and clean food tins make good cleaning containers. Kitchen brushes can be used to scrub parts, but a mechanic's brush is cheaper in the long run; specify the type with nylon bristles.

Chapter 4
Fuel System

The fuel system is—after the electrical system—the most complex and least understood system on a moped. In addition, there is an element of personal danger involved, a danger that is usually underestimated by anyone who has not been in the vicinity of a fuel tank explosion. Some repair operations involve dribbling gasoline from open fuel lines and carburetor float bowls. Do not spill fuel on a hot engine or, God forbid, on an engine that is running. Work in the open, well away from water heaters, cigarettes, and other sources of ignition. Do not crank an engine that is wetted with fuel; sparking at the contact points can easily start a fire.

The fuel system has these components:

- Filler cap
- Tank
- Fuel valve
- Fuel line(s)
- Carburetor
- Air filter
- Reed valve (Batavus and Peugeot)
- Fuel pump (Velosolex)

FILLER CAP

The filler cap should be fuel-tight, whether the tank is full or almost dry. Leaks mean that the cap gasket or entire cap

79

must be replaced. Particularly in dusty environments, it is possible for the vent to clog. The engine will run for a few minutes and quit when the fuel level drops and tank pressure becomes less than atmospheric pressure.

FUEL TANK

The tank may be integral with the frame or detachable. Columbia and Motorbecane integral tanks bear frame loads and, from an enginering viewpoint, are elegant: one part has the function of two. On the other hand, should the tank be damaged, one has the option of making a difficult repair or purchasing a new frame.

Contamination

The major problem with the fuel system, the ultimate cause of more than 90% of difficulties, is contamination. Fuel may contaminate spontaneously with age. Some of the hydrocarbons in gasoline oxidize and settle out as varnish and gum. Besides being difficult to ignite, stale gasoline attacks metal and plastics.

Some water is present in all gasoline because of condensation. As water content increases, the fuel turns gray and, in time, globules of greasy water settle out at the bottom of the tank. Water rusts the steel tank and corrodes the aluminum parts in the carburetor. Rust and aluminum oxide particles eventually detach and score the piston, leaving tiny vertical scratches. Large amounts of water may make the engine hard or impossible to start and can freeze off the fuel line in cold weather.

Dirt and sand can enter by way of a faulty air filter, air leaks between the filter and cylinder, and through careless fuel handling. The piston rings may take on a satiny finish, as if they were lapped (as indeed they were). The piston will show thousands of fine vertical scratches and, in severe cases, the chromium bore will be affected.

Rust is the number one contaminant. If you suspect rust in the fuel—the condition of the piston or an examination of the residue in the carburetor will provide confirmation—drain the tank and inspect its interior with a small flashlight. Turn the light on before you put it over the filler neck and off after you take it away, since the spark at the switch contacts may be enough to ignite the vapors. Another, and safer, way is to secure a piece of white rag to a wood dowel or brass rod and swab the floor of the tank. If rust is present, the rag will show it.

There are several things you can do about rust:

- Ignore it and attack the symptom by splicing a miniature filter into the fuel line. These filters are available from auto parts houses.
- Attempt to clean the tank.
- Purchase a new tank.

A severely rusted tank should be replaced, since the tank has been weakened and will almost certainly develop leaks. Minor rust can be contained with an inline filter and by keeping the fuel level above the rust line. The filter will catch most rust particles that float free and the oil in the fuel should prevent further rusting. Tanks that appear sound but are thick with rust can sometimes be salvaged by chemical cleaning. However, a word of caution: some detachable tanks are crimped together over a layer of plastic sealant. Bendix and other potent cleaners attack the sealant, leaving you with a more serious problem than before, one that is almost impossible to correct without replacing the tank. If the tank appears safe, and it would be wise to consult your dealer on this matter, remove the fuel valve, plug the hole, and carefully pour carburetor cleaner into the tank until the rusted area is covered. A half-hours soak should be enough, since carburetor cleaner is quite potent, dissolving paint and fingers about as readily as rust and carbon.

Leaks

Tank leaks may be caused by impact damage, faulty welds, and severe rust. If rust is the problem, the only practical cure is to replace the tank. Other leaks can usually be sealed with Produit D'Obturation, better known as Peugeot part No. 69158. To use it:

- With a piece of chalk, mark the leak site.
- Disconnect the fuel line and, if possible, remove the tank from the frame.
- Drain the tank completely, tilting it in the direction of the fuel valve.
- Blow out any fuel that remains with compressed air.

- Close the valve and pour one quart of trichlorethylene into the tank. Do not use kerosene or any other petroleum-based solvent.
- Shake the tank vigorously for several minutes.
- Drain and collect the solvent for reuse.
- Remove the fuel valve.
- Thoroughly dry the inside of the tank with compressed air.
- Position the tank so that the leak is at the lowest point.
- Pour a 30-cc bottle of Produit d'Obturation into the tank. This sealant has a shelf life of six months. If the bottle is not full, the sealant has undergone a chemical change and will not work.
- Allow 48 hours for the sealant to cure. Do not move the tank during this period.

Alternately, the tank can be sent out for welding. This is not a job for a beginner, for even the most vigorous cleaning does not eliminate the risk of explosion. At a minimum, the tank should be flushed with live steam for 30 minutes and flooded with carbon monoxide during the welding operation.

FUEL VALVE

Figure 4-1 illustrates a three-position fuel valve. The longer of the two inlet pipes opens in the *on* or *run* position; the shorter pipe comes the flow when the valve is turned to *reserve*. This particular assembly has its filter screen downstream of the valve; the more common moped practice is to mount the screen over the inlet pipes. Motobecane fuel valves are mounted on the side of the carburetor; other machines have their valves threaded on a nipple on the tank.

The valve should be removed once a year for cleaning. Drain the tank and undo the valve union nut. Some of these nuts are double-threaded; that is, the lower, or valve-side, threads are left-handed; the upper, tank-side, threads are right-handed and so are simultaneously disengaged by turning the union nut counterclockwise. Soak the valve assembly in solvent and work the lever through all three positions. Then blow the mechanism out with compressed air.

FUEL LINE(S)

After several years of service, the fuel line may grow brittle and develop cracks, particularly at the ends.

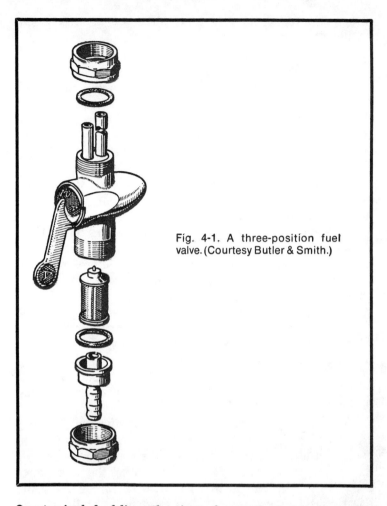

Fig. 4-1. A three-position fuel valve. (Courtesy Butler & Smith.)

Quarter-inch fuel line (the size refers to the inside diameter) can sometimes be purchased at auto parts stores. It should not be confused with vacuum or windshield-washer hose, neither of which are fuel-proof. Motorcycle dealers stock clear neoprene hose and clamps. Neoprene slowly deteriorates in sunlight, but is preferred by motorcyclists who want a positive indication that fuel is reaching the carburetor.

CARBURETORS

Moped carburetors are simple instruments, designed for ease of maintenance. There is nothing mysterious about them, but their principles of operation are less than obvious. Some theory is needed, if only to troubleshoot the instrument intelligently.

How They Work

The central principle of all carburetors, moped or automotive, is pressure diffential. The weight of the atmosphere presses down on the earth's surface with a force of 14.7 pounds per square inch. During the intake stroke the engine generates a partial vacuum, where pressure is less than atmospheric, in the cylinder. The carburetor provides the route between engine induced vacuum and atmospheric pressure, and the pressure imbalance forces air (and thereby, fuel) through the carburetor and into the engine.

A carburetor has three functions. It atomizes the fuel into a fine spray, regulates engine speed on demand from the rider, and adjusts the mixture strength for different operating conditions. I'll talk about each of these functions in subsequent paragraphs.

Liquid gasoline burns slowly and inefficiently. To drive the piston, the fuel must be converted into a vapor, so that each hydrocarbon molecule is surrounded by oxygen molecules. Atomization, the process of breaking the fuel into tiny droplets, is the first step toward vaporization. Once atomized droplets enter the engine, they absorb heat and boil off into vapor.

Moped carburetors use a piston slide throttle (Fig. 4-2, part No. 18), connected to the twistgrip by means of a Bowden cable. Withdrawing the piston from the bore allows more air and fuel to pass, and at idle the piston closes the bore almost completely. The coil spring, part No. 17, forces the piston down, closing the throttle, when the tension on the control cable is relaxed. Without the spring, the throttle could stick open, since cables are flexible and don't "push" well. In addition to regulating the amount of air and fuel, piston slide throttles have a second and sometimes third function, discussed later.

The most demanding job the carburetor has is adjusting the strength of the mixture according to the engine's needs. At cruise, an engine is happiest on a mixture of about 16 parts of air to 1 part of gasoline. At high speed the mixture should be slightly richer, in the range of 14 or 15 to 1: the additional fuel is needed to overcome mechanical friction and to cool the

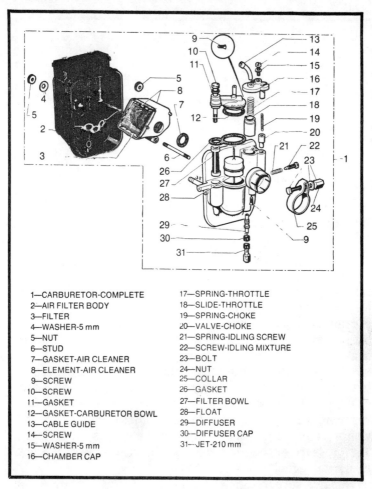

1—CARBURETOR-COMPLETE
2—AIR FILTER BODY
3—FILTER
4—WASHER-5 mm
5—NUT
6—STUD
7—GASKET-AIR CLEANER
8—ELEMENT-AIR CLEANER
9—SCREW
10—SCREW
11—GASKET
12—GASKET-CARBURETOR BOWL
13—CABLE GUIDE
14—SCREW
15—WASHER-5 mm
16—CHAMBER CAP

17—SPRING-THROTTLE
18—SLIDE-THROTTLE
19—SPRING-CHOKE
20—VALVE-CHOKE
21—SPRING-IDLING SCREW
22—SCREW-IDLING MIXTURE
23—BOLT
24—NUT
25—COLLAR
26—GASKET
27—FILTER BOWL
28—FLOAT
29—DIFFUSER
30—DIFFUSER CAP
31—JET-210 mm

Fig. 4-2. The Motobecane carburetor, developed specifically for moped service.

piston. At very low speeds the engine again needs a rich mixture to persuade it to run at all, since the cylinder is not very well scavenged, and the incoming charge is diluted by exhaust gases from the last cycle. Idle mixtures may be as rich as 8 or 9 to 1. Cold starting, when the fuel tends to condense back into a liquid, requires very rich mixtures on the order of 4 or even 3 to 1.

The carburetor makes these changes automatically, with no attention from the operator except for starting. This is what gives some complexity to even the simplest carburetor.

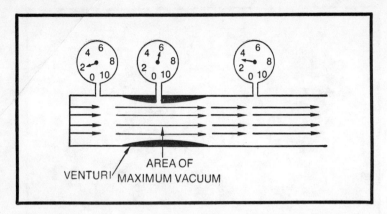

Fig. 4-3. Venturi action. The vacuum gauges read in inches of mercury.

Venturi

Although there is a pressure differential between the carburetor and the cylinder, it is not always sufficient to draw fuel into the engine. Help takes the form of a venturi, or vacuum generator. A venturi is a restriction in the carburetor bore; it may be streamlined as shown in Fig. 4-3 or it may be quite blunt.

Since just as much air enters the carburetor bore as leaves it, the velocity of the air at the venturi increases over its entry velocity. The boost in air speed helps atomize the fuel, whipping it into a fine mist, but the major benefit is that this velocity increase is "purchased" at the expense of pressure. The pressure of the air stream in the venturi section drops, encouraging fuel to flow into the bore.

Moped carburetors are a little different than those on typical automobiles and American small engines. Instead of forming the venturi as a *fixed* restriction or bulge in the sides of the casting, moped designers follow European practice and use a piston to form a *variable* venturi (Fig. 4-4).

At low speeds the piston masks off most of the carburetor bore, and the area of the venturi—the distance between the lower edge of the bore and the bottom of the piston—is small. Consequently, the air stream moves at high velocity, assuring a good vacuum draw. As the throttle piston retracts, the engine turns faster, and flow velocity is maintained by the increased air intake to the engine.

At full throttle the venturi effect no longer exists, since the piston is withdrawn completely from the carburetor bore, but some vacuum is generated by the bore itself. You can demonstrate the principle involved by cutting the ends off a cigar wrapper and blowing through it. The wrapper will collapse because the pressure of the moving air stream in the wrapper is less than atmospheric pressure.

Main Jet

In carburetor terminology, a jet is an orifice through which fuel flows. Jets are carefully calibrated so that only a preset amount of fuel flows through them at a given vacuum.

Most of the fuel consumed by the engine passes through the main jet circuit. The circuit is fed from the float bowl and discharges at the vacuum zone created by the venturi. The main jet is inserted at some point in the circuit; it may be just under the carburetor bore or it may be at some distance from the discharge point. In Fig. 4-2 the main jet is shown as No. 31; in Fig. 4-5 it's No. 17. Jets' numbering corresponds to their ability to pass fuel. Unfortunately there is no universal code; each manufacturer has a system of his own. In most cases, the higher the number the larger, more free-flowing, the jet.

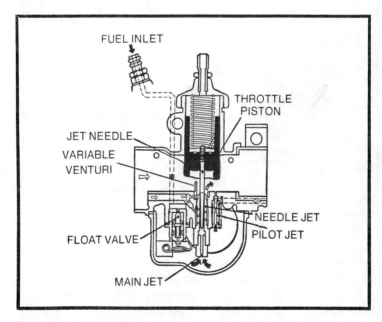

Fig. 4-4. At half throttle, the position and diameter of the needle determines fuel flow through the needle jet.

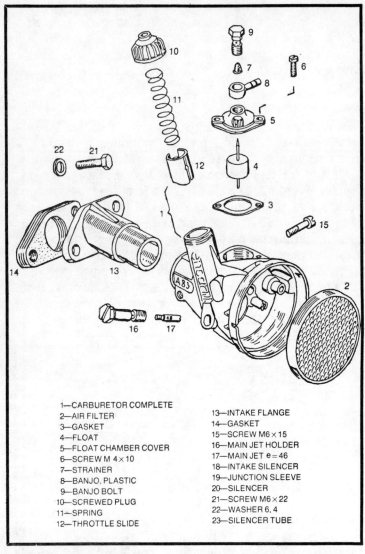

Fig. 4-5. The Encarvi carburetor and silencer as fitted to Tomos bikes.

1—CARBURETOR COMPLETE
2—AIR FILTER
3—GASKET
4—FLOAT
5—FLOAT CHAMBER COVER
6—SCREW M 4×10
7—STRAINER
8—BANJO, PLASTIC
9—BANJO BOLT
10—SCREWED PLUG
11—SPRING
12—THROTTLE SLIDE
13—INTAKE FLANGE
14—GASKET
15—SCREW M6×15
16—MAIN JET HOLDER
17—MAIN JET e=46
18—INTAKE SILENCER
19—JUNCTION SLEEVE
20—SILENCER
21—SCREW M6×22
22—WASHER 6, 4
23—SILENCER TUBE

Bing, Dell'Orto, Jikov, and other carburetors have a feature borrowed from motorcycles: flow through the high-speed circuit is, in part, controlled by throttle position. A tapered needle on the end of the piston moves up and down in the discharge nozzle which in this configuration becomes the needle jet. At low speeds, the piston is low in the bore and the thickest part of the needle almost fills the jet (Fig. 4-4). Very little fuel flows. As the piston retracts, the needle lifts out of the jet, progressively uncovering it. At full throttle the needle is almost completely withdrawn and maximum fuel flows. This arrangement provides a richer mixture at high speed and, because the position of the needle is adjustable, gives another opportunity for the carburetor tuner. Needle jet hardware is shown in Figs. 4-6 and 4-7.

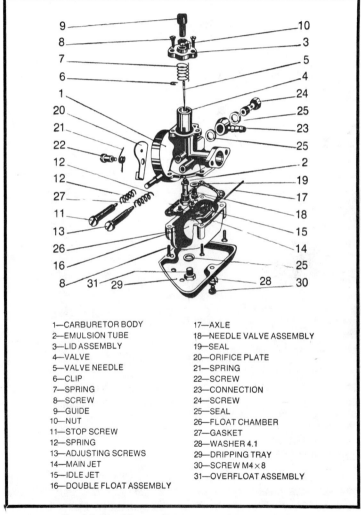

1—CARBURETOR BODY	17—AXLE
2—EMULSION TUBE	18—NEEDLE VALVE ASSEMBLY
3—LID ASSEMBLY	19—SEAL
4—VALVE	20—ORIFICE PLATE
5—VALVE NEEDLE	21—SPRING
6—CLIP	22—SCREW
7—SPRING	23—CONNECTION
8—SCREW	24—SCREW
9—GUIDE	25—SEAL
10—NUT	26—FLOAT CHAMBER
11—STOP SCREW	27—GASKET
12—SPRING	28—WASHER 4.1
13—ADJUSTING SCREWS	29—DRIPPING TRAY
14—MAIN JET	30—SCREW M4×8
15—IDLE JET	31—OVERFLOAT ASSEMBLY
16—DOUBLE FLOAT ASSEMBLY	

Fig. 4-6. The Jikov carburetor, used on Jawa bikes.

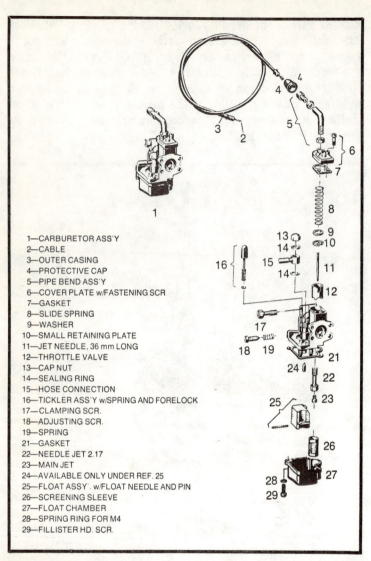

1—CARBURETOR ASS'Y
2—CABLE
3—OUTER CASING
4—PROTECTIVE CAP
5—PIPE BEND ASS'Y
6—COVER PLATE w/FASTENING SCR
7—GASKET
8—SLIDE SPRING
9—WASHER
10—SMALL RETAINING PLATE
11—JET NEEDLE, 36 mm LONG
12—THROTTLE VALVE
13—CAP NUT
14—SEALING RING
15—HOSE CONNECTION
16—TICKLER ASS'Y w/SPRING AND FORELOCK
17—CLAMPING SCR.
18—ADJUSTING SCR.
19—SPRING
21—GASKET
22—NEEDLE JET 2.17
23—MAIN JET
24—AVAILABLE ONLY UNDER REF. 25
25—FLOAT ASSY'. w/FLOAT NEEDLE AND PIN
26—SCREENING SLEEVE
27—FLOAT CHAMBER
28—SPRING RING FOR M4
29—FILLISTER HD. SCR.

Fig. 4-7. Bing is a famous name in German carburetors, found on such prestige products as the BMW motorcycle. This example is used on the Columbia bike.

Low-Speed Circuit

The low-speed circuit discharges just aft of the throttle piston. This auxiliary circuit is necessary because air flow becomes erratic over the main jet as the piston is lowered. Friction losses increase and, at some point while the engine is still running, air through the venturi reaches supersonic velocities. The main jet is caught in series of pressure waves and fuel delivery is unreliable.

Figure 4-8 shows a low-speed circuit typical of several moped carburetors. Note the way the throttle needle completely fills the needle jet, denying fuel from that source until the throttle is approximately one-third open. At low speeds the engine runs on fuel supplied by the low-speed, or pilot, jet.

The term "pilot jet" is a new one here and means that the low-speed mixture control is by way of an air screw. For reasons explained presently, some air is admitted to the jets before the fuel is discharged. This means that the low-speed mixture can be regulated by controlling the flow of fuel or the amount of air premixed in the fuel prior to discharge. Tightening the air screw (on the lower right of Fig. 4-8)

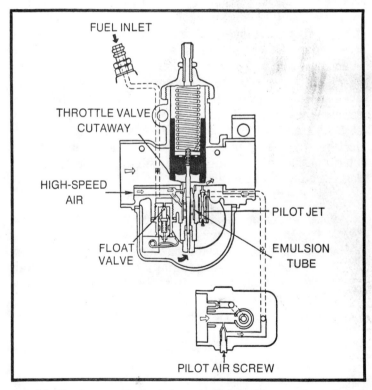

Fig. 4-8. The low-speed circuit is controlled, in this case, by a pilot air screw.

reduces the amount of air without affecting the amount of fuel flow. Consequently the mixture goes richer. Turning the needle out has the opposite effect.

Not all moped carburetors employ a pilot air screw; many adjust the low-speed mixture by means of a fuel-regulating screw. The term "pilot" is no longer applicable, and we speak of a low-speed jet and a fuel-regulating screw. The two screws look alike, although you will generally find a pilot air screw to be blunter and thicker than a fuel-regulating screw. The adjustment procedure is the reverse: tightening the fuel-regulating screw sends the mixture lean.

Air Bleeds

Fuel in both the high- and low-speed circuits is mixed with air before it enters the carburetor bore. The low-speed air bleed may be adjustable or not, as discussed under the previous head; the high-speed air bleed is, for practical purposes, fixed. Air enters the high-speed circuit from a port at the carburetor mouth, flows through a passage under the bore, and mixes with the fuel at some point between the main jet and the discharge nozzle.

Figure 4-8 illustrates the typical arrangement. Mixing takes place in a part generally called the emulsion tube, although the same part goes by several names, including main jet holder and diffuser. At any rate, the emulsion tube is identified by one or more cross-drilled holes in its side. Air enters the fuel column through these holes; should the holes clog, the high-speed mixture goes rich.

There are three reasons for air bleeds:

- An emulsion of gasoline and air atomizes better than fuel in the liquid state.
- Because each bubble has its own surface tension, emulsified fuel tends to stay put in the passages. Raw fuel would drop away from the jets when the throttle opened suddenly and vacuum momentarily disappeared. The engine would go lean under acceleration.
- Again because of surface tension, an emulsion is less likely to siphon into the crankcase.

Float

The Bing float is made of nitrogenated plastic, a foam-like substance that is lighter than gasoline. Gurtner carburetors use a hollow plastic cylinder as the float. The Jikov, a sophisticated design that was developed from the firm's motorcycle carburetors, employs a brass pontoon float.

Once fuel in the bowl reaches a predetermined level, the float closes the inlet valve (Fig. 4-9). This valve is generally known as the needle and seat assembly. The needle is usually made of chrome steel and may be acted on remotely as shown in Fig. 4-9, or may be attached to the float without any intermediary mechanism. The latter arrangement is illustrated back in Figs. 4-2 and 4-5. The seat is usually made of brass and, except on the most rudimentary carburetors, is replaceable.

The roof of the float chamber is vented to keep the fuel at atmospheric pressure. Where there is a float adjustment, this adjustment must be made with the greatest accuracy, for the distance the float moves before the needle closes determines the level of fuel inside the carburetor. All things equal, the higher the fuel level, the richer the mixture.

Cold Start Provisions

The engine needs a very rich mixture during cold starts. The traditional way to provide this is with a choke plate mounted on the mouth of the carburetor bore. The part described as an "orifice plate" (No. 20 in Fig. 4-6) is, in American terminology, a choke plate. When the choke is

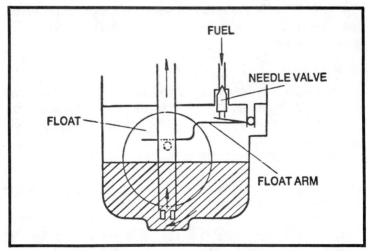

Fig. 4-9. A typical float and remote needle. (Courtesy U.S. Suzuki.)

athwart the bore, the engine pulls against it, creating a vacuum along the whole length of the intake passage. Both the main and low-speed jets flow.

French designers, in the best automotive and motorcycle tradition, use a starting jet, of which the Motobecane carburetor is typical (Fig. 4-2). Two fuel passages leave the floor of the float bowl; the upper passage supplies the main and low-speed jets, the lower passage runs under the carburetor and up to the choke valve, (No. 20). The valve is normally kept closed by the spring (No. 19). When raised, the valve allows fuel to flow to a discharge orifice in the aft part of the carburetor bore.

In addition to a choke or a starting jet, some carburetors feature what is quaintly called a "float tickler". The Bing, shown in Fig. 4-7, has this feature. Depressing the tickler sinks the float, flooding the jets for an extremely rich mixture. The tickler should be used with discretion and only on the coldest days.

TROUBLESHOOTING

Hard starting, "flat spots" during acceleration, misfiring, and loss of power are all symptoms of carburetor ailments—but are more likely to originate in the ignition system. Check the ignition system, giving particular attention to the spark plug and contact points, engine compression, and the exhaust ports and muffler before you turn to the carburetor. By the same token, resist the temptation to adjust the carburetor. Once in adjustment, it should remain there for many thousands of miles.

No Fuel

The prime symptom of no fuel is a dry spark plug nose after repeated cranking. If the engine is running when this condition occurs, it will miss, cough, pick up again, and finally stop.

First ascertain that fuel is getting to the carburetor. Momentarily disconnect the line at the carburetor end. If there is no fuel present, the diagnosis is an empty tank, a clogged fuel valve, line, or air vent in the filler cap.

If fuel is present, remove the float bowl to determine if fuel has passed the inlet needle and seat. If the bowl is dry, the inlet needle is hung in the seat or the inlet screen is clogged.

Fuel in the bowl and none—after persistent cranking—in the engine is a more serious affair. There are five possibilities; in order of frequency of occurrence they are:

- A clogged high-speed fuel circuit, usually stopped at the main jet.
- A massive air leak between the venturi and the engine cylinder.
- Less than 60 psi of cylinder compression.
- Broken or sprung reed valves (Peugeot).
- Leaking crankcase seals.

As a temporary repair, stoppages can be cleared by blowing through the high-speed circuit at the main jet. The jet is accessible with the float bowl removed. A broomstraw may be used if the stoppage is stubborn, but do not introduce wire into the jet or emulsion tube. A scratch on these parts is enough to upset calibration. At the first opportunity, disassemble and chemically clean the carburetor.

See that the intake pipe is secured to the carburetor and to the cylinder. An air leak serious enough to short-circuit engine vacuum implies loose hold-down bolts. Reed-valve and seal work is detailed in Chapter 6.

Flooding

A flooded engine is one whose mixture is too rich to ignite. A gasoline-soaked spark plug tip is the first visible symptom, but one that occurs relatively late in a hot engine: a fairly large amount of fuel must pass unignited through the engine before cooling the metal enough to condense the charge on the spark plug tip. Fuel evaporates upon contact with hot metal; if the vapor concentration in the chamber is greater than 6%, the mixture may be totally vaporized but still refuse to ignite. You may see a wisp of vapor curling out of the spark plug port as you remove the plug. Too much choke during cold starts and any choke during hot starts will flood the engine, making starting difficult or impossible. Once an engine's flooded, continued cranking adds to the problem.

Assuming for the moment that the carburetor is not at fault, there are several ways to clear a flooded engine. Minor flooding can sometimes be corrected by partially disengaging the spark-plug cable boot from the plug, leaving about a quarter-inch air gap between the cable terminal and the spark

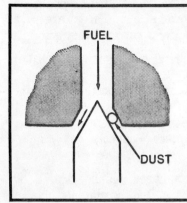

Fig. 4-10. The needle must make a fuel-tight joint with the seat; small particles of dirt or rust caught between these parts will flood the carburetor.

plug terminal. The spark will have to jump this gap before it gets to the spark plug. The ignition coil delivers only as much voltage as it has to; the air gap between the cable and spark-plug terminals increases the voltage output. With luck, the increase will be enough to ignite the over-rich mixture.

If this does not work, remove the spark plug and replace it with a known-good one. This procedure eliminates the spark plug as the cause of flooding and, unless the cylinder is sopping wet, may get the engine started. If you do not have an extra spark plug, dry the original with a cigarette lighter or match.

Severe flooding—when the chamber and crankcase are puddled with raw fuel—takes time to correct. One approach is to let the bike sit for an hour or so to give the fuel time to evaporate. Be sure to turn the fuel valve off. If you're in a hurry, you can drain the carburetor float bowl and try to dry the engine by cranking. Have a fresh spark plug ready when you open the fuel tap for the starting attempt. Compressed air introduced at the spark plug port speeds drying, particularly if the piston is brought down past the transfer ports.

Persistent flooding with the throttle wide open and the choke off means a problem with the carburetor's internal fuel-regulating mechanism. In severe cases, fuel dribbles from the carburetor mouth when the air cleaner is detached.

The needle and seat assembly is the usual culprit. The needle may be held off its seat by a particle of dirt (Fig. 4-10), or the needle may be worn so it no longer makes a fuel-tight seal with the seat. Dirt can sometimes be dislodged by giving the carburetor a sharp rap; a surer method is to drop the float bowl and turn on the fuel for a second or two. The rush of gasoline over the needle will clear it. A worn needle and seat should be replaced even if this means purchasing a new float bowl cover and float too. Fortunately, most carburetors have removable needles and seats. All that's required for the repair is a large screwdriver, ground to fit the slot in the seat, and the requisite parts. Use a new gasket and tighten the new seat firmly in the float bowl cover. You may wish to coat the threads with gas-proof sealant as further security.

Steel needles and brass seats can be temporarily repaired by lapping. Dip the tip of the needle in fine-grade valve grinding compound and rotate it in the seat with your fingers. Replenish the compound as needed, turning the needle so the full circumference is lapped. Wash off all traces of the compound with solvent—any that you miss will enter the engine and continue to lap there—and assemble the carburetor for test. Repeat the process until the valve stops leaking.

Some carburetors have an adjustable float. If the float rises too high in the chamber before it closes the needle against the seat, the engine will run rich and may flood. But the float will not spontaneously get out of whack; this condition can occur only if someone has changed the factory setting. See the "Overhaul" section in this chapter for further details.

Another possibility, one that is almost always confined to hollow floats, is leakage. Shake the float vigorously; if enough fuel is present to disable it, its weight will be felt and, in brass floats, heard. Since repairs are impractical and, at best, short-term affairs, the best bet is to replace the float.

Finally, there is a very remote chance that the float is binding, particularily if the float works off a pivot. Carefully examine the float and the sides of the chamber for wear marks; correct by making small bending adjustments to the pivot.

Rich Running

An over-rich mixture costs power, fuel, and spark plugs. The symptoms of this malady are:

- Black carbon deposits on the spark plug nose.
- Acrid exhaust odor which may be accompanied by black droppings from the exhaust pipe.
- Four-stroking. The exhaust note becomes irregular as the engine misses a beat and fires with almost a double charge on the next revolution.

If these symptoms persist across the rpm band, suspect a restriction in the air supply. Test the bike with the air filter element removed; if the problem disappears, the filter element is clogged and should be renewed. Puch and a few other bikes use a remote element, connected to the carburetor by a flexible hose; the hose may be pinched shut.

Dell'Orto carburetors have fixed jets. Others have an adjustment screw located on the outboard side of the carburetor, about midway along its length. Four-stroking at low speeds can be corrected by turning this screw counterclockwise if it is a pilot air screw and clockwise if it regulates the fuel flow. With the engine running, move the screw out one-eighth turn or less. Allow a few seconds for the adjustment to be felt; repeat until four-stroking stops. It may be necessary to increase the idle speed slightly, an operation that is described under "Adjustments."

Rich running at high throttle settings can be corrected by lowering the tapered needle in the throttle piston one notch. If a needle is not used, it may be necessary to insert the next-smaller main jet. However, you should remember that jet changing—particularly when it produces a leaner mixture—is not something one does casually. The jet that came in the carburetor should be approximately correct. The major exception to this rule is if the machine is operated at high altitude: in this circumstance, a smaller jet will correct the overly-rich mixture by matching the fuel delivery with the reduced oxygen content of the air, but it will not restore sea-level power.

Lean Running

A gasoline-starved mixture burns hotter than a normal mixture and produces less usable power. The first symptom is a dull white spark-plug tip. As the condition progresses, the tip turns china-white and the side electrode shows blue temper marks. Very little carbon will be left in the cylinder; that which remains will be scorched grayish-white. The end product is piston destruction, either from a hole in the crown or a melted skirt.

Determine whether the carburetor is receiving enough fuel. Two types of fuel line are used: transparent neoprene and black rubber. A rubber line can be loosened at the carburetor with the engine stopped. Fuel should gush out as the line is pulled toward the end of the barbed fitting. In a transparent line the fuel column can be seen. It should be solid, perhaps broken by an occasional small bubble. The usual site of fuel line obstructions is the screen at the fuel valve. Disassemble and clean it.

If adequate fuel seems to be getting to the carburetor, the next step is to remove the float bowl cover or float bowl, depending upon the construction of the carburetor. The bowl should be at least half full. If not, check the inlet screen and, if applicable, the float level adjustment. See that the inlet needle drops without binding or hesitation. Clean the needle and seat as required to restore its responsiveness.

Enough fuel to keep the float awash but a scarcity of fuel in the engine may mean a partial stoppage in the main jet or its feed circuit. Blow out the carburetor as described a few pages back under "No Fuel."

The fuel supply is only half the picture: there is also the possibility of air leakage between the carburetor venturi and the combustion chamber, particularly if the engine has many miles on it. Open the throttle piston cover; some covers are secured by small screws, others by a knurled ring. Carefully lift the throttle piston up and out. The piston is slotted and located by a pin or tab in the piston bore. Pull the piston straight up, clearing the needle jet without bending the needle in the process. Inspect the piston for scratches, wear marks, and carbon tracks that can mean air leakage between it and the bore. In some carburetors a severely worn piston will vibrate and rattle under load and at low speeds: the only cure is to purchase a new carburetor.

Install the piston dry, without lubricant. Align the slot and pin and center the needle over its jet. The piston should fall easily into the bore.

See that the carburetor is secure on the inlet pipe and that the pipe is fastened down hard on the cylinder head. Leakage at the head seems to be rather common on mopeds; it can be cured by coating the gasket with silicon sealant. A paper-thin coat is enough.

And, if worse comes to worst, there is always the possibility of crankcase seal failure. Fortunately this does not happen often; most seal failures occur early because of manufacturing error or very near the end of the engine's life, when the main bearing clearances have pounded out. See Chapter 6 for test and repair procedures.

99

Erratic Starting, Backfiring, Shutdowns in Extreme Cold.

Occurring separately, these symptoms mean ignition problems or water in the fuel. If they occur together, you can be sure that the fuel is water-logged. Drain the fuel system at the tank and the carburetor. It is a good idea to mix a few ounces of wood alcohol with the next load of fuel; the alcohol will absorb any moisture that remains.

OVERHAUL

Overhaul means cleaning, inspection, and replacement of worn parts. Berkebile 2 + 2 or lacquer thinner will dissolve soft gum and varnish; corrosion and calcified deposits can generally be removed with one of the commercial immersion-type metal cleaners.

Replace the needle and seat, if possible. As mentioned earlier, some moped carburetors have needles that are integral with the float and seats that are part of the float bowl cover. Others have a replaceable soft-tipped needle and pressed-in seat: when the seat wears the parent casting must be purchased.

If the throttle piston is excessively worn, the air will leak between it and the throttle bore. Most carburetors have high- and low-speed adjustments that can be used to compensate for this worn condition; however, extreme wear, signalled by 1/64 inch or so of clearance between the piston and bore, means that the carburetor should be replaced. The needle jet—the brass part that the throttle needle moves in—should not be in contact with the needle and, therefore, should not wear. Unfortunately this is not always the case. A small misalignment is enough to send the needle into the side of the jet. If this has happened, you will see wear marks on the needle, and both the needle and jet should be replaced. The low-speed adjustment screw should be replaced when it loses its profile (Fig. 4-11). Otherwise engine idle suffers.

Replace all soft gaskets and O-rings as a matter of course. Hard gaskets are washer-like affairs found on fuel-line fittings, and may be reused, if they are not grooved. Of course all nonmetallic gaskets should be removed before the carburetor is immersed in a chemical cleaner. Less potent cleaners, such as 2 + 2 Gum Cutter, do not have any immediate adverse effect on gaskets.

To dismantle the carburetor, first remove it from the engine. It is secured at three or four places:

- Air filter—on many bikes the filter is attached to the frame and connected to the carburetor by a flexible hose.
- Intake pipe—in some instances the pipe must be loosened at the engine end.
- Choke control—if a remote choke is fitted, remove the cable at the carburetor end.
- Throttle cable—disengage at the throttle piston.

The throttle cable mounts at the underside of the throttle piston. Remove the piston cover plate, the part that seals off the top of the piston bore (shown as No. 6 in Fig. 4-7). Most cover plates are secured by small screws; some of the older models used a knurled ring threaded over the top of the carburetor bore. Once the plate is free, carefully guide the piston up and out. Be particularly careful if the piston is fitted with a needle.

Turn the piston over and compress it against the return spring, so the cable end protrudes through the bottom of the piston. Move the free end of the cable through its disengagement slot and allow the piston to pull free of the cable. Bing carburetor needles are held in place by pressure

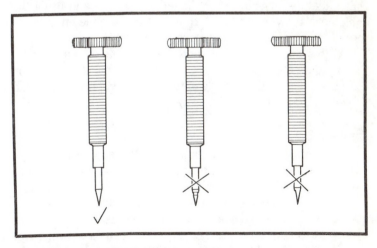

Fig. 4-11. Low-speed adjustment needles can wear out and produce an erratic idle.

from the return spring acting against a washer and retaining plate. There parts are shown as Nos. 9 and 10 in Fig. 4-7. Once the cable is released, the spring, needle, washer, and retaining plate are free (and easy to lose). Other needle-type carburetors secure the needle with a spring clip: the needle remains in place until the clip is removed. Regardless of the attachment method, note the position of the needle for assembly reference. Typically there are four grooves around the upper end of the needle, and the factory pins the needle at the third grove from the top.

Wipe off the piston with a paper towel or lintless rag soaked in solvent. Vertical scratches on the piston flanks mean that dirt is entering the system from a faulty air filter or a leaking cover gasket. Some discoloration on the bottom of the piston is more or less normal; heavy carbon deposits may indicate an out-of-adjustment carburetor, perhaps aggravated by long periods at idle.

Inspect as much of the control cable as you can see for frayed, broken, or splayed wires. Replacing the inner core of the cable is usually sufficient for repair; long-term wear, however, can damage the outer sheath. If the throttle binds after a new core has been lubricated and installed, replace both parts of the cable. In any event, the twist grip will have to be partly disassembled. Figure 4-12 shows a typical example.

Lubricate the twist grip threads and the inner cable core. Dab Vaseline on your index finger and thumb and draw the cable core between them. A thin coat of Vaseline on the grip threads and on the sleeve bearing is sufficient.

At this point we are ready to disassemble the carburetor. Clean the outside surfaces as a general sanitation measure—dirt on the outside of the casting will invariably find its way to the internal (critical) parts.

Disassembly

1. Remove the float bowl or float-bowl cover. The Motobecane carburetor in Fig. 4-2 and the Encarvi in Fig. 4-4 have float-bowl covers; other designs illustrated in this chapter have demountable float bowls.
2. Remove and discard the float bowl gasket.
3. Disengage the float. A typical pivot pin is shown as No. 17 in Fig. 4-6. Once it is withdrawn, the float and inlet needle can be lifted free. Other carburetors, such as

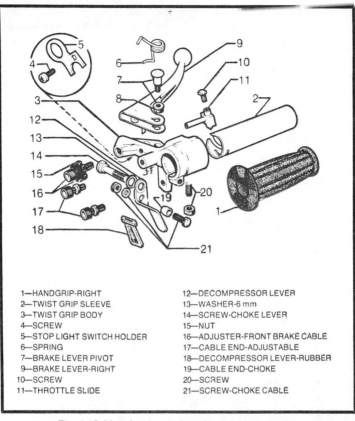

1—HANDGRIP-RIGHT
2—TWIST GRIP SLEEVE
3—TWIST GRIP BODY
4—SCREW
5—STOP LIGHT SWITCH HOLDER
6—SPRING
7—BRAKE LEVER PIVOT
9—BRAKE LEVER-RIGHT
10—SCREW
11—THROTTLE SLIDE

12—DECOMPRESSOR LEVER
13—WASHER-6 mm
14—SCREW-CHOKE LEVER
15—NUT
16—ADJUSTER-FRONT BRAKE CABLE
17—CABLE END-ADJUSTABLE
18—DECOMPRESSOR LEVER-RUBBER
19—CABLE END-CHOKE
20—SCREW
21—SCREW-CHOKE CABLE

Fig. 4-12. Motobecane twist grip and control cable.

those used by Peugeot, Motobecane, and Tomos have unsecured floats.

4. Take a close look at the inlet seat. If the seat is slotted for a screwdriver, remove it and the gasket on the underside. Bing and few other carburetors do not have replaceable seats. (More exactly, the seats are not replaceable unless you purchase the entire float bowl cover.)

5. Unscrew the main jet, using a screwdriver ground to mate precisely with the slots in the jet. Motobecane and Tomos carburetors have the main jet outside the float bowl for accessibility. The jet is turned with a box-end wrench.

6. Withdraw the emulsion tube, located in the passage above the main jet. On some carburetors the tube is

held in place by the main jet. A sharp rap on the casting is enough to dislodge it once the jet is removed. Other designs have the emulsion tube threaded into the casting; it is withdrawn with a screwdriver or a small wrench.

7. Count the turns required to seat the low-speed needle; this is the preliminary adjustment. Now back the needle out and inspect its tip for wear and distortion. Replace if necessary.

8. Some fuel-line fittings are integral with the carburetor body; others are secured by a gasketed banjo nut. If you are dealing with a banjo fitting, note the position of the inlet pipe before disassembly.

9. Remove the starting jet from Peugeot and Motobecane carburetors.

It is not necessary to dismantle the carburetor further. Some internal passages are sealed after manufacture with soft plugs or lead shot. In the unlikely event that these passages are clogged—and you can get an idea of their condition from the cleanliness of the parts that are visible—obtain replacement plugs before you disturb the originals. Moped dealers may not be much help and it's likely you will have to fabricate: large plugs from brass sheet and smaller ones from BB shot or brass rod. Seal the plugs with 24-hour epoxy.

Immerse the metallic parts in carburetor cleaner for 20-30 minutes. A very dirty carburetor will require a longer soak, but do not park the carburetor in the cleaner and forget it. Eventually the cleaner attacks the castings, leaching the soft metals and leaving you with a porous metal sponge. Once the carburetor appears clean, dip the parts in solvent to neutralize the cleaner.

The most critical aspect of assembly is float adjustment of Bing, Jikov, and other carburetors that use a hinged float. The distance the float moves before it shuts the inlet valve determines the internal fuel level in the instrument. This level affects the air/fuel ratio, and is therefore very critical. Specifications for all moped carburetors are not available at this writing, but examination of a number of mopeds and discussions with factory mechanics has produced a working rule: unless specifications say otherwise, the float should be parallel with the roof of the float casting (Fig. 4-13). Assemble the needle, seat, float, and pivot pin. Invert the assembly and sight between the float and casting. If the float is not parallel with the casting, make the correction by bending the tang, the torque-like projection between the float and the pin. Use needle-nosed pliers and do not use the inlet needle as a stop. That is, pull the float clear of the needle before you apply bending pressure. Steel needles can be damaged by forcing them into their seats; synthetic-tipped needles most certainly will be. Do not twist the float; it must be level and parallel.

Run in the low-speed adjustment screw finger-tight and back it out the number of turns you counted during disassembly. Mount the spring, retaining clips, and other hardware on the back of the throttle piston. Compress the spring and snap the cable into place, passing its end through the piston. Make sure the piston is clean and insert it into the carburetor bore. A slot on the piston flank engages a screw and cast rib on the barrel. Push the piston home, being careful not

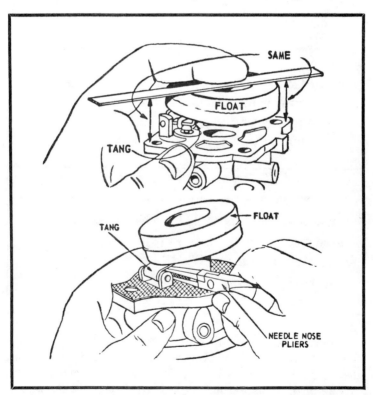

Fig. 4-13. Unless factory literature states otherwise, moped floats are set parallel with the casting.

to force it, since it is possible for the needle to hang on its jet. The piston is assembled dry, without lubricant.

Adjustment

The adjustment procedure is not as complex as it sounds. The first step is to identify the possibilities. All carburetors have some sort of idle rpm adjustment; most have a low-speed mixture adjustment; a few have a high-speed adjustment as well.

If the carburetor has	necessary adjustments are
no low-speed adjustment screw; no tapered throttle needle on the piston	idle rpm
knurled low-speed adjust - ment screw on the outside of the carburetor, just aft of the throttle piston.	idle rpm and low-speed mixture
knurled low-speed adjust- ment screw and tapered needle on the throttle pis- ton. May have main jet options	idle rpm, low-speed mixture, and high-speed mixture

Idle RPM. This adjustment controls the height of the throttle piston, regulating the quantity of air and fuel entering the engine with the twist-grip released. If you turn back to the picture of the Bing carburetor in Fig. 4-7, you will see what is called the pipe bend assembly, referenced as No. 5. This assembly is capped with a hollow bolt and locknut. The bolt or, more accurately, the barrel nut, is threaded. The control cable casing is moored at both ends, at the twist grip and at the barrel nut. Turning the barrel nut out puts a bend in the cable, making it effectively shorter: the piston rises and idle speed increases. Turning the nut clockwise lengthens the cable and lowers the piston. The locknut secures the adjustment.

A few motorcycle-bred carburetors, such as the Jikov shown in Fig. 4-6, have an idle rpm screw that bears against the lower edge of the piston. The barrel nut is still present, and is adjusted to give slack so that the distance the piston drops at idle is controlled solely by the screw. One or two designs have no idle-rpm adjustment at the carburetor; the cable is adjusted at the handlebar.

Low-Speed Mixture. When present, this adjustment takes the form of a knurled screw. Most moped carburetors follow European practice and have their low-speed mixture screws athwart the idle air bleed. This screw, called the pilot air screw, controls the amount of air mixed with the fuel. The Bing carburetor is one exception to this; their adjustment screws control the amount of fuel going into the low-speed circuit. The distinction between the two approaches is important: tightening a pilot air screw reduces the air flow and produces a richer mixture; tightening a fuel-control screw reduces the amount of fuel discharged and leans the mixture.

High-Speed Mixture. The position of the tapered needle controls the mixture between one-third and two-thirds throttle. Raising it in the piston puts a thinner section of the needle in the jet, which allows more fuel to pass, richening the mixture. Lowering the needle fills more of the jet, causing the mixture to go leaner. The factory setting—usually one notch rich—is correct for most bikes. The needle should be dropped a notch at high (over 2000 ft) altitudes and, if only as an experiment, raised a notch for extended full-throttle operation. Raising the compression ratio, removing intake and exhaust restrictions, polishing the head, and other modifications pretty well mandate a one-notch-richer mixture.

The main jet is removable in all carburetors, whether fitted with a needle or not. Under very unusual circumstances is may be necessary to replace the original jet with a different size. This is not a standard tuning procedure and is done only for high altitude operation or when the engine has been modified to give more power. Unfortunately, some moped importers can't seem to stock even standard parts, let alone alternates, and you may have to write the manufacturer to get alternate jets.

On Motobecane and other designs that don't use a needle, the main jet determines mixture strength from approximately one-quarter to wide-open throttle.

Making the Adjustments

The symptoms of carburetor maladjustment are difficult to overlook. An excessively lean mixture bleaches the carbon deposits on the spark plug tip and may cause a flat spot on acceleration. An overly rich mixture soots over the spark plug tip and can induce four-stroking at low rpm. The exhaust beat skips and misses—da da BAM da da BAM. Also, once you've been around engines awhile, you'll be able to smell a rich mixture

I'll assume that your carburetor has the full panoply of adjustments and that you have lost track of the original settings. Install a new, correctly gapped spark plug and see that the air filter element is clean. Top up the tank with fresh premix, blended according to the manufacturer's instructions.

Lightly seat the low-speed mixture screw and back it out one and one-half turns. This should get the engine started. Allow the bike to idle for a few minutes, but not so long that you smell hot metal. Moped engines, even those with forced air circulation over the barrel, overheat when stationary.

Thread in the mixture screw about an eighth of a turn, and wait a few seconds for the mixture change to be felt. If the engine picks up speed, you're moving in the right direction; tighten the screw another small increment. If rpm drops, back the screw out an eighth of a turn past the original setting. Continue to chase rpm until you are satisfied that the engine is running at its peak for that rpm setting. The adjustment is usually broad: tiny changes will not have an obvious effect.

Snap the throttle open about a quarter-turn. The transisiton from idle should be smooth and effortless. If the engine hesitates, richen the mixture a smidgen. The idle may be less then perfect, but that is less important than the ability to pull strongly.

Now that the low-speed mixture is correct, it may be necessary to reduce idle rpm. Make this adjustment as described previously. The engine should be turning over smartly, a few hundred rpm under clutch-in speed. An idle so slow you can almost count the revolutions may sound impressive, but it's harmful to the engine.

If the needle adjustment spec has been lost, begin one notch rich. Secure the typical four-groove needle at the second groove from the top. Take the bike out on the road and run it for a few minutes with the throttle between one-third and two-thirds open. Shut off the engine and brake to a stop. The spark plug tip should be brown—the color of coffee with a dash of cream—or tan. Lighter colors mean that the mixture is too lean; the needle should be raised a notch. Darker colors point to a surplus of fuel, and the needle should be lowered. Repeat the test after each change in needle position. With a two-cycle engine, err, if you must, on the dark side. About the worst a rich mixture can do is dirty the spark plug; a lean mixture may cook the piston.

The main jet controls fuel delivery from approximately one-third to full throttle in carburetors without the tapered needle and from two-thirds to full throttle in those with a metering needle. An oily and carbon-stained spark plug tip after a few minutes at full throttle may mean that the main jet is too large, or that the ignition system is missing at high speed, a condition often associated with the contact points.

By the same token, a lean mixture, one that bleaches the spark plug tip white, can mean that the main jet is too small, that the ignition is advanced beyond specification, or that there is an air leak in the induction tract. An air leak normally shows up at low speeds, but can be compensated for by adjustments. The main jet then becomes a kind of litmus test. That is, if you've unknowingly compensated for an air leak by richening the low-speed mixture, the air leak will be evident when the high-speed jet is in operation.

AIR FILTERS

Most carburetors are fitted with sponge-like polyurethane filters. Wire mesh or composition board filter elements are still encountered, but their use is a mark of obsolescence. Polyurethane filters' only required maintenance is cleaning in kerosene or hot water and detergent. Allow the filter to dry and reoil with no more than a teaspoon of engine oil. Knead the oil into the filter until it is completely wetted.

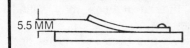

Fig. 4-14. Do not change the backing plate clearance on Peugeot reed valves.

5.5 MM

REED VALVES

Batavus and Peugeot engines use reed valves to contain the air/fuel mixture in the crankcase. The Peugeot valve has tow reeds; Batavus has four arranged in a triangular housing for maximum efficiency. In the normal order of things, these valves should outlast the engine. When it does occur, failure is dramatic: the engine stops as if someone had turned off a switch. It will refuse to start and the spark plug will remain stubbornly dry after repeated cranking. If you are sensitive to the engine you may detect a change in the cranking sound.

The valve assembly is located on the side of the crankcase, usually under the inlet pipe. It is held by two capscrews and gasketed on both sides. Once these gaskets are disturbed, they should be replaced.

The reeds should be in full contact with the mounting plate or lie a hair's breadth above it. Peugeot reeds have a backing plate which should not be disturbed for any reason. The correct distance between the backing plate and the mounting plate (Fig. 4-14) is 5.5 mm—more will allow the reeds to open wider and quickly fatique them. Treat the reeds gingerly, not touching them at all with your fingers. Look for cracks radiating out from the rivets and for deep pitting along the sealing faces. Using a small screwdriver, open the reeds only wide enough to see what their tips look like. If a reed is missing, it has been injected, and the engine must be torn down to determine the extent of damage.

FUEL PUMP (VELOSOLEX)

A fuel pump might seem out of place on a moped, but the Solex engine rides proud over the front wheel, where gravity-feed would be impractical. The pump contains a neoprene diaphragm and a plastic check ball. One side of the diaphragm is open to the crankcase and fluctuates with piston movement. Three lines connect to the pump body: the suction line provides fuel from the tank; the return line recycles fuel that is not used by the engine; and the output line connects the pump with the carburetor.

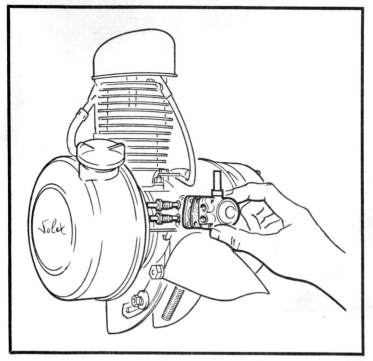

Fig. 4-15. Removing a Velosolex fuel pump.

Disassembly

Disconnect the fuel lines and remove the four pump holddown bolts. Lift the pump off (Fig. 4-15). If the plastic seating piece remains on the crankcase, gently pry it free. Replace the diaphragm each time the pump is disturbed. Clean the parts in solvent.

Assembly

Place the plastic seating piece over the crankcase port with the concave, or dished, side out. Tap it over the port lug. Without dropping the ball out of its recess, install the pump body. Tighten the screws in a criss-cross pattern to bring the body down square against the crankcase. Connect the fuel lines, running the metal fittings in at least three full turns by hand before you put a wrench on them. Crank the engine a few times; fuel should appear at the discharge port. If everything is copacetic, connect the pump-to-carburetor hose.

Chapter 5
Ignition and
Lighting Systems

Moped electrical systems are fairly simple, at least in terms of contemporary technology. But the nature of these systems is such that you cannot troubleshoot them or even do much purposeful work on them without some knowledge of the theory. Electrical parts do not make visual sense in the way that mechanical parts do. Almost anyone who looks at a piston comes away with some notion of its function; no one who is blankly ignorant of electricity can understand a capacitor or coil by merely looking.

I have taken some time to explain the theory of these systems in this chapter. Theory may be a bit tedious for someone who has a broken moped, but there are no shortcuts: what is not understood, cannot be repaired.

Here are some ground rules:

- Wiring diagrams are not pictorial. They show what's connected to what as simply as possible, and give you little idea how the actual wires are routed on the chassis.
- Current flows from negative to positive, that is, it moves from the negative terminal of the generator back to the positive terminal. This path is called a circuit.
- For current to flow the circuit must be complete and uninterrupted. A seemingly insignificant break, a few

thousandths of an inch between switch contacts, a film of rust, or a smudge of oil can open the circuit.

- The circuit may consist of insulated wire, or it may combine wire and the engine or frame. The junction between the insulated side of the circuit (called the "hot" or "live" side) and the metal parts of the bike is a ground. In wiring diagrams, ground connections are symbolized $\doteq$ or $\rightarrowtail$.

- Current will always take the easiest path back to the generator. Each circuit load—coil, horn, lamp, etc.—has resistance to electron flow. If possible, current will find a way to bypass, or short, the load. The problem is particularly severe when part of the circuit is grounded: any uninsulated part of the hot side will short to ground on contact with metal.

I IGNITION SYSTEMS

The ignition system generates a spark with enough voltage to ignite the air-fuel mixture in the cylinder, and times that spark to occur at some preset distance before the piston reaches top dead center.

SPARK PLUG

The spark plug is the final component in the ignition system and is, by far, the most stressed. Combustion temperatures heat the firing tip to 1700 degrees during normal operation; engine vibration can generate forces of as much as 50G; and while it is being heated and shaken about, the spark plug must contain combustion pressure and still do its primary job of releasing a spark across a high-pressure atmosphere of oil, gasoline, and air. A faulty plug can make starting more difficult or prevent it entirely. It may cause the engine to miss, particularly when cold or under heavy load. And a less-than-perfect spark plug can take the edge off performance without causing a noticeable miss: the engine will start easily, accelerate smoothly, yet go flat under full throttle.

It's not surprising that many experienced mechanics change the spark plug before they do anything else to the engine.

Construction

Figure 5-1 illustrates basic spark plug construction and nomenclature. The plug shown is a Japanese NGK which shares its plated finish with Champion and is otherwise quite similar to most American and German types.

1. Terminal nut—detachable on mopeds and European small engine applications generally.
2. Corrugation—protects against high voltage flashover, the same principle used on insualtors for high-voltage transmission cables.
3. Metal shell—offers purchase for the wrench and support for the spark plug components; 5/8-inch hex is standard.

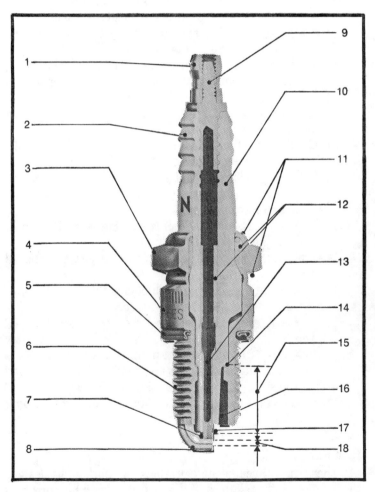

Fig. 5-1. Spark plug nomenclature. (Courtesy NGK Spark Plug Co., Ltd.)

4. Plated finish—for rust protection, generally preferable to a blued finish.
5. Gasket—seals the combustion gas.
6. Thread—the diameter is expressed in millimeters and the reach (the distance from the gasket flange to the end of the threads) is expressed in fractions of an inch. These dimensions are fixed by the engine maker.
7. Center electrode—usually thought of as the "hot" electrode, although in actual fact the direction of the spark is from the ground to the center electrode.
8. Ground electrode—sometimes called the side electrode, this electrode is grounded to the engine.
9. Stud—fixed to the insulator. If the stud is loose, the spark plug must be replaced.
10. Insulator—the part old-line mechanics call the porcelain because that was the material originally used. Today the insulator is made from fused aluminum oxide, a very hard ceramic, akin to rubies and sapphires.
11. Caulked portion—part of the defense against leaks between the insulator and shell.
12. Sealing powder—a kind of self-sealing gasket which compensates for the unequal rate of expansion of the shell and the insulator.
13. Copper core—NGK claims cooling benefits; most manufacturers use a steel core.
14. Inner gasket—the first line of defense against internal leakage.
15. Insulator nose—the part which has the most effect on the plug's operating temperature.
16. Gas volume—the space between the insulator and shell.
17. Insulator (firing end)—the nature and color of deposits on the firing end of the insulator reveal engine and combustion-chamber operating conditions.
18. Spark gap—the only adjustment normally made on a spark plug.

Heat Range

There are three basic variables in spark plug design: thread diameter, reach, and heat range. Thread diameter is hardly worthy of comment, except to say that it is impractical to salvage a stripped moped head by cutting threads for a larger spark plug. Even if you can obtain a larger plug with the same reach and heat range, the sheer volume of the plug will upset combustion-chamber geometry.

The reach is calculated to bring the firing tip even with the roof of the combustion chamber. A plug with insufficient reach will have its tip buried in the spark plug port, where it is remote from the action. Starting may be difficult and power will be down because of the additional clearance volume in the cylinder. A spark plug with excessive reach is almost sure to be hit by the piston.

Heat range refers to the cooling capacity of the spark plug. As you can see from Fig. 5-2, the ideal temperature for any spark plug is between 750 and 1800 degrees F. Below this temperature the firing tip carbons over and fouls; above it the tip glows and can ignite the mixture early, before the spark occurs.

Figure 5-3 shows four spark plugs in cutaway view. The plugs have identical thread diameters and reaches, but different heat ranges. The spark plug on the far left is the coldest of the lot; the heat range gets progressively hotter to its right. The primary difference is the distance heat travels

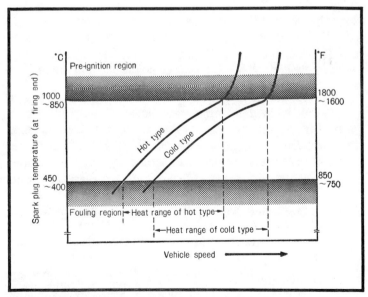

Fig. 5-2. Heat range walks the line between cold fouling and preignition. (Courtesy NGK Spark Plug Co., Ltd.)

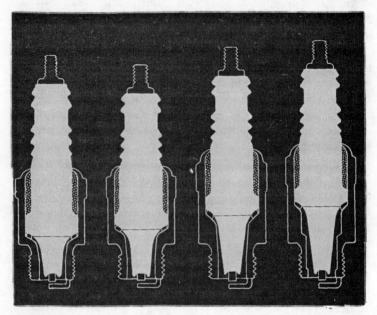

Fig. 5-3. Champion spark plugs in a heat range progression from (L) cold to hot (R).

along the nose of the insulator to the metal shell. Cold plugs have a short thermal path and cool down quickly; hot plugs have a longer thermal path and generally have a greater gas volume between the insulator nose and the inside of the shell.

Spark plugs are available in a wide variety of heat ranges. In general, what determines the choice of heat range for a particular engine is the temperature of the combustion chamber. Hot-running engines need cold plugs, and vice versa.

Heat range selection depends upon:

- The amount of carbon buildup in the cylinder. Carbon deposits can insulate the chamber, trapping heat.
- The air/fuel ratio. The ideal air/fuel ratio, the ratio that delivers the most power, also generates the most heat (Fig. 5-4).
- Ignition advance. Within limits, additional ignition advance means more power. Unfortunately, each degree of advance takes its toll as heat (Fig. 5-5).

118

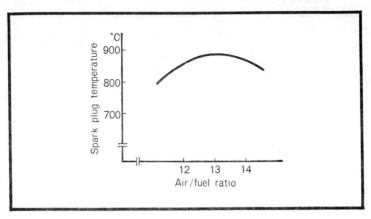

Fig. 5-4. The most power-efficient air/fuel ratio (around 13:1) releases the most heat in the chamber.

- Compression ratio. The higher the compression ratio, the more efficient the engine, and the hotter the chamber (Fig. 5-6).
- Spark plug tightening torque. Undertorqued spark plugs run hot because heat transfer depends upon the seal between the plug shell and the cylinder head (Fig. 5-7).

The spark plug furnished with the machine is a good choice for average use, but may not be if you've modified the engine for more power. Polishing the cylinder head and piston, smoothing the port profiles, boosting the compression ratio,

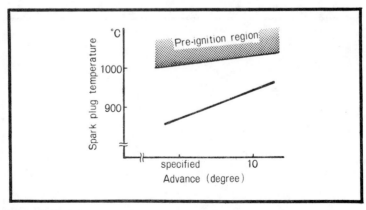

Fig. 5-5. Each degree of ignition advance entails higher chamber temperatures.

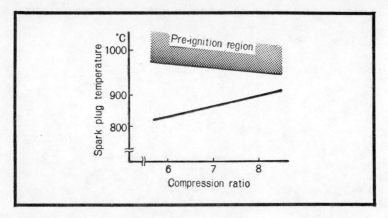

Fig. 5-6. A high compression ratio means power and high temperature.

increasing spark advance, and precision-tuning the carburetor mean higher combustion-chamber temperatures. Depending on the effect of modifications, the original spark plug can become a time bomb, waiting to go into preignition with the result shown in Fig. 5-8.

Service

Disconnect the spark plug cable by grasping the insulating boot and giving it a half-twist (Fig. 5-9). Moped spark plugs accept a 5/8-inch deep-well socket, sized to clear the insulator (Fig. 5-10).

Spark plugs wear out in 3000 miles or so of moped service. The electrodes round off and erode, and eventually become so

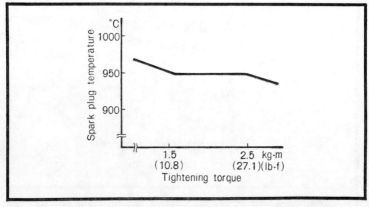

Fig. 5-7. A spark plug that is undertightened overheats.

Fig. 5-8. The woeful result of pre-ignition.

Fig. 5-9. To remove the spark plug cable, give the boot a twist and pull.

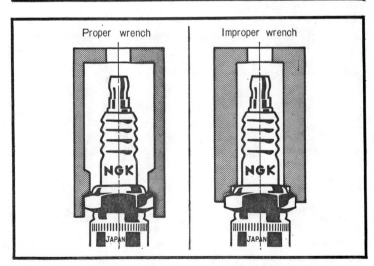

Proper wrench   Improper wrench

Fig. 5-10. The socket wrench must be in full contact with the hex shell and clear of the fragile insulator. (Courtesy NGK Spark Plug Co., Ltd.)

Fig. 5-11. A worn-out spark plug. (Courtesy Champion Spark Plug Co.)

fine they can overheat and send the engine into preignition (Fig. 5-11). But a slightly worn plug can be cleaned, filed, gapped, and used again.

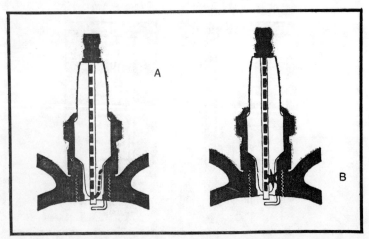

Fig. 5-12. Two maladies that can be corrected by cleaning: fouling (view A) and tracking (view B). (Courtesy Champion Spark Plug Co.)

Cleaning. The purpose of cleaning is to remove carbon deposits. These deposits can short out the spark, shunting it to ground before the plug fires, or build up in the gas volume area, forming a second spark gap deep inside the plug (Fig. 5-12). In either case, engine performance suffers.

Spark plugs may be cleaned by hand with a wire brush and a small screwdriver. Results with this method are reasonably good, but nothing to write home about. The professional approach is to use a sandblaster adapted to spark plug work. The plug is placed in the machine and wobbled under the blast so that the abrasives scrub deposits from the inside of the shell and insulator nose.

In theory, a sandblasted spark plug is as good as new; in practice this may not be the case. Abrasives do not have much effect on lead fouling, a kind of translucent patina that forms on the insulator and causes misfire during acceleation. Nor are plugs cleaned this way compatible with high-strung two-cycle engines. The newly cleaned plug will behave normally for a few miles and then misfire, costing 500 rpm or so at wide-open throttle. In addition, one must be very careful to remove all of the abrasive before the spark plug is put back into the engine. Even a few particles can do serious damage to the piston, rings, and cylinder bore. It's good practice to blow the plug clean and then let it soak for a few minutes in lacquer thinner.

Filing. After cleaning, reform the center electrode by filing it flat. In Fig. 5-13 the side electrode is straightened so

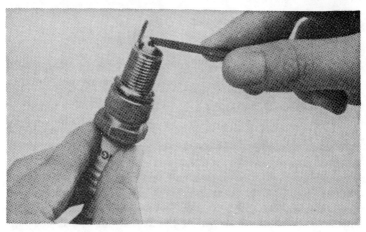

Fig. 5-13. File the center contact flat. (Courtesy NGK Spark Plug Co., Ltd.)

that the sandblast can reach all areas of the insulator nose. This practice is favored by Japanese mechanics, but is frowned on here; bending weakens the side electrode.

Gapping. Using a round feeler gauge, gap the plug to specification (Fig. 5-14). The gauge wire should pass between the center and side electrode with a light drag. If it binds, use the bending tool on the gauge to open the side electrode; if the gauge passes through without touching both electrodes, tap the center electrode on something hard. With a little practice you will be able to correctly gap a spark plug in a few seconds.

Installing. Clean the spark plug threads with a hand-held wire brush, not a power-driven wheel that could deform the thread edges. Wipe any carbon or oil deposits from the spark plug port in the cylinder head. Remember that the temperature of the firing tip depends upon the ability of the shell to pass heat to the head: a layer of carbon or a film of oil interferes with heat transfer.

Run the plug in by hand until the gasket bottoms. If you cannot turn it this far with your fingers, turn the plug at least two full revolutions before you apply the wrench. Otherwise, the spark plug may cross-thread and ruin the cylinder head.

Once the gasket is in contact with the head casting, one-half or three-quarters of a turn with a wrench is enough to secure it. Ideally, you should use a torque wrench to tighten the plug to the following specifications. The specs are for a cold engine, and should be used only if you don't have the specs for your engine.

Spark Plug Thread Diameter	Torque
10 mm	86-104 inch-pounds (1.0-1.2 kilogram-meters)
12 mm	125-175 inch-pounds (1.5-2.0 kilogram-meters)

Reading

Reading the spark plugs is the time-honored way of determining combustion chamber temperature and, by extension, of tuning the engine. The basic principle is that the hotter the chamber, the whiter the spark plug tip. If the plug has the correct heat range, the color of the insulator nose

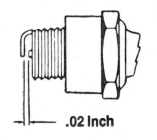

Fig. 5-14. Bend the side, or ground, terminal to adjust the gap. The specification is for Sachs-powered Columbia mopeds.

.02 Inch

should be neutral—either a rich tan or light brown. If temperatures are too high, the nose will turn white and may blister. In extreme cases, the side electrode can show blue temper marks. On the other hand, low chamber temperatures leave a fluffy black carbon residue on the nose.

The difficulty is getting consistent readings. A perfectly well-behaved spark plug will bleach white on a steep, full-throttle hill. The same plug will carbon during an extended period of idle.

Ignition system operation is usually checked by running the bike wide open for a short period, thereby subjecting the plug to maximum thermal stress, but carburetor tuning is best checked by operating the engine at a number of throttle positions and rpm ranges. In any event, the engine must be brought up to operating temperature and run for a quarter-mile or so at the desired speed. Shutdown must be abrupt in order not to leave false deposits. Chop the throttle, hit the kill button, and brake to a stop. Remove the spark plug and, holding it in the socket wrench to protect yourself from

Fig. 5-15. Normal: light tan or brown, electrode wear limited to the spark zone.

Fig. 5-16. Gap-bridged: a common malady of two-cycle engines, believed to be caused by dust. Wipe the whisker off and restart.

burns, compare the tip with the photographs in Figs. 5-15 through 5-20.

MAGNETO IGNITION

Figure 5-21 illustrates a typical moped magneto. The basic parts are:

- Stator plate that secures the stationary magneto parts to the engine block (3).
- Contact points which trigger the spark (7).
- Exciter coil which generates primary voltage (12).
- Cam that rotates against the movable point arm and separates the contacts (16).
- Rotor which acts as the flywheel and bears permanent magnets (17).
- Spark plug cable (20).
- Ignition coil (21).

Fig. 5-17. Wet fouling: damp black carbon coating over the entire firing end. May form sludge if the condition is chronic. Check spark plug heat range (the plug may be too cold), air/fuel ratio (too rich), fuel/oil ratio (too much oil), ignition system (misfiring). (Courtesy Champion Spark Plug Co.)

Fig. 5-18. Overheating: electrodes badly eroded, premature gap wear, gray or white insulator. Check spark plug heat range (too hot), ignition timing (too much advance), air/fuel ratio (too lean). (Courtesy Champion Spark Plug Co.)

Fig. 5-19. Preignition: melted electrodes and, in most cases, a white insulator. The insulator may be discolored due to a fog of debris in the overworked cylinder. Check for correct heat range, adequate lubrication, and for overadvanced ignition timing. Correct the problem before the engine is put back into service. (Courtesy Champion Spark Plug Co.)

Fig. 5-20. Scanvenger deposits: brown, yellow, or reddish deposits on the firing tip. These deposits are left by additives in the fuel and are not in themselves dangerous. Clean and return the plug to service. (Courtesy Champion Spark Plug Co.)

Figure 5-22 shows the Robert Bosch magneto, widely used on German and Italian machines. It combines the exciter and ignition coil in a single assembly. The next drawing shows one version of the CEV magneto, which can be interchanged as a unit with the Bosch (Fig. 5-23).

A diagram of the ignition side of the circuit is shown in Fig. 5-24. The exciter, or primary ignition, coil consists of several hundred turns of enameled copper wire, mounted on an iron form. One end of the exciter coil is connected to the ignition coil, which is mounted on the frame, outside of the magneto proper. The other end of the coil is grounded through a circuit that I will discuss under "Lighting Systems."

Operation

The flywheel has permanent magnets bonded to its rim. As the flywheel turns, the magnets sweep part the exciter coil, permeating its windings with magnetic lines of force. When a conductor—and the coil windings are a conductor—is subjected to a moving magnetic field, a voltage is generated in the conductor. The magnetic field must be moving: when the flywheel is stopped, no voltage is produced. At high speed, the exciter coil delivers as much as 300 volts to the ignition coil. But voltage is not constant. It depends upon the proximity of one of the magnets to the coil and upon the position of the contact points.

The points amount to a switch, connected in parallel with the exciter coil. The stationary contact is grounded to the stator plate; the movable contact is insulated and "hot." When the movable contact rests against the stationary contact,

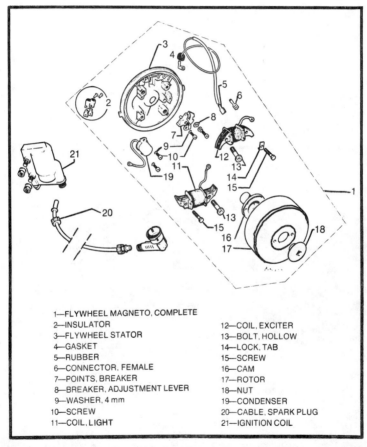

1—FLYWHEEL MAGNETO, COMPLETE
2—INSULATOR
3—FLYWHEEL STATOR
4—GASKET
5—RUBBER
6—CONNECTOR, FEMALE
7—POINTS, BREAKER
8—BREAKER, ADJUSTMENT LEVER
9—WASHER, 4 mm
10—SCREW
11—COIL, LIGHT

12—COIL, EXCITER
13—BOLT, HOLLOW
14—LOCK, TAB
15—SCREW
16—CAM
17—ROTOR
18—NUT
19—CONDENSER
20—CABLE, SPARK PLUG
21—IGNITION COIL

Fig. 5-21. The Motobecane magneto follows the general moped practice with a single lighting coil and two ignition coils. The exciter coil is housed under the flywheel and provides current for the frame-mounted ignition coil.

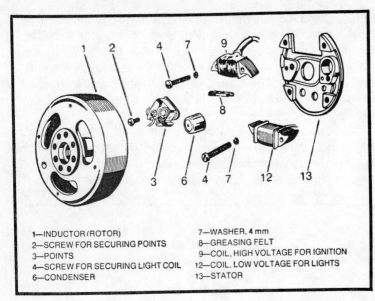

1—INDUCTOR (ROTOR)
2—SCREW FOR SECURING POINTS
3—POINTS
4—SCREW FOR SECURING LIGHT COIL
6—CONDENSER

7—WASHER, 4 mm
8—GREASING FELT
9—COIL, HIGH VOLTAGE FOR IGNITION
12—COIL, LOW VOLTAGE FOR LIGHTS
13—STATOR

Fig. 5-22. The Bosch Model KB6-B212 magneto is unique among mopeds in that the two ignition coils are wound together. (Courtesy Cimatti Ltd.)

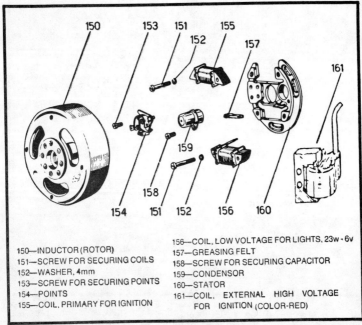

150—INDUCTOR (ROTOR)
151—SCREW FOR SECURING COILS
152—WASHER, 4mm
153—SCREW FOR SECURING POINTS
154—POINTS
155—COIL, PRIMARY FOR IGNITION

156—COIL, LOW VOLTAGE FOR LIGHTS, 23w - 6v
157—GREASING FELT
158—SCREW FOR SECURING CAPACITOR
159—CONDENSOR
160—STATOR
161—COIL, EXTERNAL HIGH VOLTAGE FOR IGNITION (COLOR-RED)

Fig. 5-23. The CEV Model 6932 can be substituted for the Bosch as a complete assembly. (Courtesy Cimatti Ltd.)

exciter coil output passes to ground: no voltage goes to the ignition coil. As the flywheel turns, it cams the movable contact open, denying ground to the voltage impressed on the exciter coil. The voltage goes out "seeking" a ground, and it finds it in the ignition coil. The moment of point opening coincides with (and causes) the ignition pulse and is the reference point for timing the engine.

The cam, contact points, exciter coil, and flywheel magnet work together as a team. The points open when a flywheel magnet is centered above the exciter coil, at the moment of greatest magnetic flux.

The condenser (or capacitor) is an electrical buffer. Electricity has a kind of inertia—once flowing it is reluctant to stop. As the points crack open, this "inertia" would continue current flow, arcing across the open points and burning them in the process. The condenser momentarily absorbs these electrons and releases them back into the circuit when the points close again.

The ignition coil is also known as the pulse generator. It consists of two windings: fairly heavy enameled copper wire is wound around the form some 400 times (the primary winding) and is covered by 20,000 turns or so of extremely thin wire (the secondary winding). The secondary winding terminates at the spark plug cable and delivers a wallop of 15,000-23,000 volts.

The operation depends upon magnetic lines of force. The exciter coil sends in one magneto, 300 volts into the primary winding. As the winding becomes saturated, it sends out

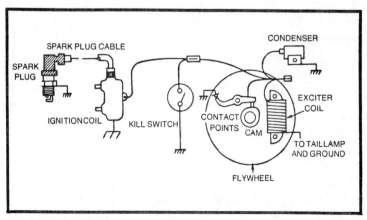

Fig. 5-24. The complete magneto circuit with kill switch and ignition coil.

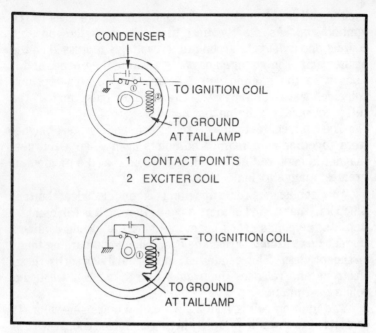

CONDENSER

TO IGNITION COIL

TO GROUND
AT TAILLAMP

1   CONTACT POINTS
2   EXCITER COIL

TO IGNITION COIL

TO GROUND
AT TAILLAMP

Fig. 5-25. The basic ignition circuit. When the points close, current flows through the exciter coil, its circuit completed through the grounded points at one end and the grounded taillamp at the other (view A). When the points open, current diverts to the ignition coil and the spark plug fires (view B).

magnetic lines of force, that move like the ripples on a pond. These moving lines of force cut through the second winding and generate a voltage in it which is proportional to the ratio of turns in the windings. This ratio—20,000 to 400 or 50:1—transforms the primary's 300 volts to 15,000 volts, plenty to jump the spark gap.

Spark Testing

Disconnect the spark plug cable at the spark plug by giving the boot a quarter twist and pulling. Do not pull on the wire. Insert a screwdriver into the boot so it makes contact with the cable terminal. Holding the screwdriver by its insulated handle, maneuver it to bring the blade within three-eighths of an inch of one of the cylinder fins. Turn the switch on and have a helper turn the pedals. If all is right, the spark will appear between the blade and the fin.

Observe the spark. It should be heavy, thick, and bright blue. A "nervous" spark, one that seems to go in all directions, means ignition problems, particularly if the spark is red or white. A really healthy system will deliver a spark that you can hear like a miniature thunderclap.

Service

The first step is to remove the flywheel nut. It's a standard thread and backs off when turned counterclockwise, but the flywheel must be held against wrench rotation. In Chapter 6 a universal flywheel-holding tool is described; most flywheels have access ports that accept a pin wrench (Fig. 5-26). In those few cases where the flywheel is closed and shrouded so there is no wrench purchase on its external surfaces, you can hold it with the starting clutch. Since the clutch will slip under wrench torque, shock the nut loose by giving the wrench handle a sharp rap with a hammer. A more sanitary method is to fix the piston with a tool that threads into the spark plug port. Break off the insulator on a discarded spark plug and have an extension brazed on its tip. With the tool in place, the piston contacts the extension at the top of its stroke.

Flywheel. Once the nut and (usually) lockwasher are loose, the flywheel must be withdrawn from the crankshaft stub. There are four ways to do this. In order of preference:

- Purchase the appropriate flywheel puller from your dealer, the moped importer, or from a bicycle shop. Some of these pullers are identical to European bicycle crank tools.

- Run the nut down flush with the end of the crankshaft and shock the flywheel off with the help of a brass bar and a hammer. Position the bar square against the

Fig. 5-26. Many flywheels have "windows" that accept a pin wrench. (Courtesy Steyr Daimler Puch.)

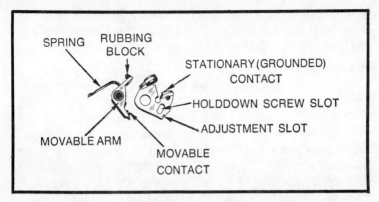

Fig. 5-27. A Bosch two-piece point set. Some sets have the movable arm secured permanently to the pivot post. (Courtesy American Parts Co., Inc.)

end of the shaft and hit it hard. This method is more dangerous than using a threaded knocker, since misalignment of the bar can snap the crankshaft stub.

● Run the nut down flush and strike the crankshaft end with a hammer. This technique is emphatically not recommended, since it does violence to both the shaft and the nut. But people have used it.

Any technique that shocks the flywheel loose involves the possibility of bending or breaking the crankshaft and scrambling the flywheel magnets. If the flywheel is stubborn, stop work until you can obtain a proper puller.

The most critical area of the flywheel is the fit of the crankshaft key. The key must be reasonably tight in both flywheel and crankshaft keyways; play between the key and its mating surfaces allows the flywheel to turn relative to the crankshaft and destroys one aspect of magneto timing. If the wear is relatively minor, the flywheel can be centered over the key and tightened down hard; if keyway wallow is severe, the flywheel and the crankshaft must be replaced.

Not all manufacturers supply crankshaft nut torque limits, but 25 ft-lb is an appropriate figure.

Contact Points. The points are the most vulnerable part of the magneto and should be considered as sacrificial items, with a life of less than 100 hours. Point failure can make starting difficult, cause misfire at high speed, or disable the engine altogether.

Figure 5-27 illustrates a Bosch two-piece point set. The movable arm bears against the cam at the rubbing block and pivots to contact the stationary arm. The stationary arm is grounded to the stator plate; the movable arm is electrically "hot," and connected to the exciter coil by means of the spring.

Examine the point set for physical damage, looking for breakage, wear on the rubbing block, excessive clearance between the movable arm bushing and its pivot, and for spring misalignment. On some installations, the spring can come into contact with the stator plate, grounding the ignition.

With a screwdriver, pry the movable arm away from the fixed contact. Inspect the contacts very carefully. The tungsten should be dull gray, with the contact faces slightly irregular and puddled. Replace the point set if the contacts look as if they have been torn apart, or if they are any color other than gray. Dark slashes under the points mean that too much grease has been used on the cam or that the crankshaft seal is passing oil into the magneto. Correct these problems before installing new points.

To install a new point set, follow these steps:

1. Remove the screws that hold the contact assembly to the stator plate and magneto side. Do not lose the lockwashers.
2. Lift the point set off the stator and disconnect the wire at the movable arm spring.
3. Wipe the point-mounting area of the stator plate with a rag dipped in laquer thinner. Oil between the point set and the stator can deny the ground connection.
4. Connect the coil wire to the replacement point set.
5. Mount the replacement point set on the stator plate, indexing any pins on the plate with holes in the stationary point assembly.
6. Run in the holdown screw(s) a few turns by hand and snug with a screwdriver. Tighten enough to overcome spring tension, but no so much as to make adjustment impossible.

Adjusting the point gap is a critical operation and must be done with precision (Fig. 5-28). The adjustment is by way of an eccentric screw or, more commonly, a screwdriver slot on the stationary contact assembly. The ignition cam may be secured to the crankshaft stub as shown in Fig. 5-29, or it may be integral with the flywheel (on the Bosch pattern). In the latter

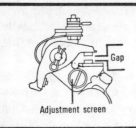

Fig. 5-28. The point gap is the distance contacts open at full extension. The gap on this point set is adjusted by means of an eccentric screw, a slightly more sophisticated arrangement than the slot shown in the previous figure.

Gap

Adjustment screen

case, when the cam is part of the flywheel, the adjustment is made after the flywheel is installed (Fig. 5-30). Place the wheel on the crankshaft stub, aligning the key. Working

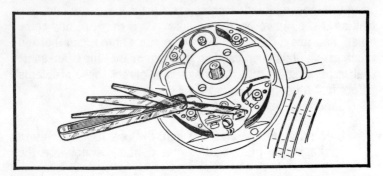

Fig. 5-29. The cam on the Motobecane magneto is located on the hub, allowing easy access to the points.

through one of the flywheel windows with a screwdriver, raise the movable contact so that it can ride on the cam: otherwise the contact may be jammed as you push the flywheel home.

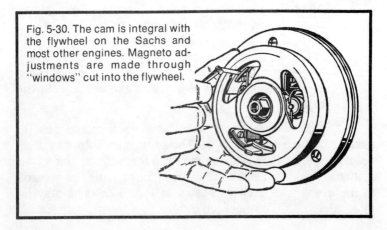

Fig. 5-30. The cam is integral with the flywheel on the Sachs and most other engines. Magneto adjustments are made through "windows" cut into the flywheel.

Watch the point contacts as you turn the flywheel: near the end of piston travel the points will part, reach their full extension, and begin to close. The interval at full extension is the point gap.

Point gap specifications are listed in Table 5-1. Select the appropriate feeler gauge blade and wipe it with a shop towel. Do not run the blade between your fingers. The oil on your skin, transferred to the blade and then to the contacts, is enough to disable the ignition. Insert the gauge between the points—the correct gap will produce a slight drag on the feeler. Adjust with the slot or screw provided, holding the feeler gauge in place as you move the stationary point towards or away from the movable point.

Table 5-1. Ignition System Specifications

MAKE	POINT GAP	IGNITION ADVANCE BEFORE TDC	SPARKING GAP
Batavus M-48	0.35-0.45 mm (0.014-0.018 in.)	2.0-2.2 mm (0.079-0.087 in.)	0.016 in.
Velosolex	N.A.	N.A.	0.015-0.020 in.
Garelli Eureka, Katia Kick, Katia M, Eureka Matic	0.30-0.50 mm (0.014-0-0.020 in.)	1.5 mm (0.059 in.)	0.020-0.024 in.
Fichtel & Sachs (engine) 505/1A 505/1ANL 505/1B 505/1C	0.35-0.45 mm (0.014-0.018 in.)	2.5-3.0 mm (0.098-0.118 in). see text for clarification	0.020 in.
Jawa Babetta	N.A.	1.5 mm (0.059 in.)	
Minarelli (engine) V1	0.35-0.40mm (0.014-0.018 in.)	1.67 mm (0.066 in.)	0.024 in.
Motobecane all models	0.35-0.40 mm (0.014-0.018 in.)	N.A.	0.015 in.
Peugeot 103 LS-U1, 103 LVS-U2, 103 LVS-U3	0.30-0.50 mm (0.012-0.020 in.)	1.5 mm (0.059 in.)	0.016 in.
Puch Maxi	0.40-0.50 mm (0.016-0.020 in.)	0.8-1.2 mm (0.031-0.047 in.)	0.020 in.
Tomas Automatic 3, A3	0.35-0.45 mm (0.014-0.018 in.)	1.8-2.0 mm (0.071-0.079 in.)	0.019 in.

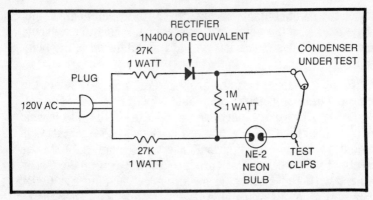

Fig. 5-31. Condenser checker. House the assembly in a clear plastic box.

Once you are satisfied that the gap is set, tighten the holddown screw. Recheck the gap, since it will have moved a few thousandths of an inch, the direction of movement depending upon the location of the holddown screw. Loosen the screw slightly and set the gap to compensate.

Condenser. Complete failure will keep the engine from operating, its ignition current grounded through a shorted condenser or the point set burned to a nub by an open condenser. But most failures are partial: the engine may be hard to start, may misfire, or may develop a large appetite for point sets. Occasionally a condenser will fail when hot, after a quarter hour or so of operation and, once cool, behave normally.

Condensers open, short, or change capacitance. Change in capacitance is a gradual process, caused by metal migration from one plate to the other or a deteriorating dielectric.

Opens and shorts can be detected by the device shown schematically in Fig. 5-31. Power is supplied by the line cord; about 150 volts DC appears at the test clips. One clip is connected to the condenser case, the other to its lead. Reducing the value of the two 27 kilohm resistors makes the device more sensitive, but increases the hazard of electrical shock. At their present value the output is less than lethal, although you should connect the clips *before* you plug the device in and leave the clips in place until you disconnect power. The 1 megohm resistor in parallel with the condenser is a discharge path for the condenser. If you take the condenser out of the circuit with power on, the condenser will "bite." Nothing lethal, but discombooberating.

The condenser is serviceable if the neon blub flickers once when power is connected. If the bulb does not react or if it continues to glow or blink, replace the condenser. Check the replacement before you install it; new condensers can also be faulty.

If you do not want to build or purchase a tester, the best course of action is to replace the condenser each time the points are serviced. The condenser is secured to the stator plate by a screw and strap arrangement. Remove the holddown screw (two on the Motobecane) and disconnect the lead between the condenser and the point set. On a few elderly mopeds the condenser lead is soldered. Heat the connection and pull the wire free.

Remove any oil accumulation under the mounting strap and install the replacement condenser. Snug the screw down tight, but not so tight that it pulls out the threads: remember, you are dealing with aluminum. Connect the lead to the point set. If the lead must be soldered, use a pencil-type gun and low-melting-point, rosin-core solder. Heat the connection until the solder melts and flows into the wires: too little heat leaves a lumpy, unreliable joint; too much can damage the condenser. And, however the wire is connected, check that it is routed away from the flywheel and the movable point arm.

Coils. Exciter and ignition coils, whether combined or in two separate units, are best tested by substitution. Generally, the exciter section fails first, for it is subject to engine heat and vibration.

External Circuit. Failure of the external circuit can also disable the ignition. Check the taillamp for continuity by disconnecting its lead and grounding it to the engine. If this solves the problem (the engine will run), the taillamp is burnt out or the taillamp ground is open. Take the kill switch out of the circuit by removing it physically from the handlebar. If the engine runs with the switch ungrounded, the difficulty is in the switch.

In rare instances the spark plug cable or the radio suppressor fitted between the cable end and the spark plug may fail. Again, the best test is by means of substitution.

SOLID STATE IGNITION

At present, Jawa's Tranzimo is the only solid-state ignition available on mopeds. The manufacturer is reticent about the

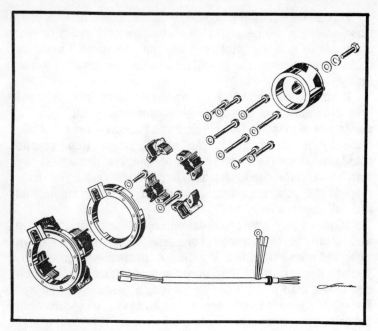

Fig. 5-32. The generating section of the Jawa Tranzimo, One large coil provides energy for the spark; the small coil atop the stator plate signals the transistor to conduct.

technology involved, but it appears to be quite unsophisticated. A transistor replaces the contact points; without points the engine should remain in time longer and tune-ups should be simpler. On the other hand, failure is absolute and unrepairable by the side of the road, unless you have a spare transistor.

Figure 5-32 illustrates the alternator, less the rotor. One coil, the uppermost in the drawing, generates power for ignition; the other three feed lights and accessories. The small coil on the stator plate is a trigger, generating a small command voltage for the transistor.

Figure 5-33 is a schematic of the circuit. The Tranzimo unit (2) houses the transistor and the secondary ignition coil. The transistor is connected to the primary ignition coil, the trigger coil, and the kill switch (8) on the handlebar. Internal connections are not shown, but a resistor is in series with the signal lead, and the output side of the transistor connects to the secondary coil. The rotor is keyed to the crankshaft and has permanent magnets in its rim. As the crank turns, one magnet generates voltage across the primary ignition coil. This voltage is blocked by the transistor until a second rotor magnet excites the trigger coil. The coil signals the transistor to conduct, and ignition voltage goes to the secondary ignition coil. There it is boosted to fire the spark plug.

In other words, the transistor is no more than a solid-state switch, under the command of the trigger coil.

Service

The following comments pertain to the Tranzimo, but, with some interpretation, can be applied to other makes.

Test the output as described under "Ignition System Troubleshooting." If the spark is weak, nonexistent, or erratic, begin with the obvious—the mechanical integrity of the generating section and its wiring. Remove the rotor cover and measure the clearance between the rotor and field coils. In the case of the Tranzimo, the specification is 0.012 inch. You can use a steel feeler gauge as long as you turn the rotor magnets away from the check points. Nonferrous gauges, used for

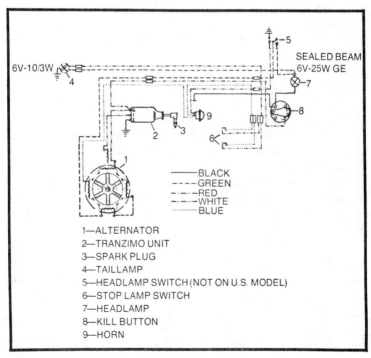

Fig. 5-33. The Tranzimo in schematic.

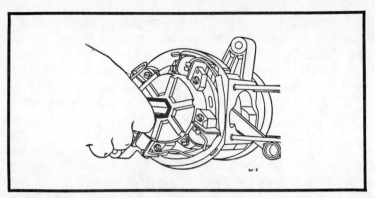

Fig. 5-34. Using a socket wrench for purchase, move the rotor up and down to detect main bearing wear.

air-conditioning clutch work, are available from auto supply houses, and give more consistent readings. If adjustment is necessary, loosen the coil holddown screws a few turns. The screws must be tight enough to hold the coils against the magnetic attraction of the rotor but no so tight that the coils cannot be gently tapped into place. Use a light hammer and a wooden dowel, positioning the dowel against the laminated iron coil shoes. Tighten the screws fully when clearance is correct.

Wear marks on the rotor edges, showing that the rotor has touched the coil shoes, mean that rotor-coil clearance is insufficient. This may be a simple matter of adjustment, or it may mean that the main bearings—the two bearings that support the crankshaft and the rotor—are worn. To determine if this is so, check the adjustment and then, using a socket wrench for purchase, bear bown hard on the rotor (Fig. 5-34). If the rotor moves down into contact with the coil shoes, the main bearings are no longer up to the job of locating the crankshaft and should be replaced, together with the crankshaft seals.

Hard starting and misfiring at high speed can sometimes be corrected by withdrawing the rotor from the crankshaft and polishing the rotor magnets and coil shoes (Fig. 3-35). Use fine sandpaper to brighten these parts; a thin patina of rust is enough to scatter the magnetic fields.

The wiring should be tucked clear of the rotor, well out of harm's way, and soldered to the field coils. Trace the circuit out of the alternator and to the Tranzimo switching unit on the frame. Make and break the bayonet connectors several times to reestablish solid contact. Heavy corrosion can be removed with television tuner cleaner, available in aerosol cans from electronic parts houses and large hardware stores.

The Tranzimo switching unit has several unique features, features that are not found on other solid-state systems. The back of the unit is sealed with a Bakelite cap, reminiscent of the distributor cap on an automobile. Remove the cap and scrutinize its inner and outer surfaces under a strong light. Not all defects are obvious to the eye; some appear as if someone had penciled marks on the cap. These carbon tracks glisten as the cap is turned under the light, and mean that there is a current path between the high voltage terminal and ground. But the path may be internal and hidden. When in doubt, replace the cap with a known-good one.

Another special feature of the Tranzimo is the external transistor, secured to the switching unit by its three soldered leads. Should the transistor fail, it will fail completely, like a light bulb. There will be no ignition output. Test by substitution: unsolder the leads and, using a small, pencil-type iron, solder in a new transistor. Carefully note the lead connections, since a wiring error may destroy the new part. Use rosin-core solder and protect the transistor with a heat sink. Commercial heat sinks are available, or you can fabricate a substitute by wrapping a rubber band tightly around the jaws of a pair of needle-nosed pliers. The rubber band clamps the jaws together and the steel pliers absorb and dissipate heat. Position the heat sink between the transistor and the joint to be soldered.

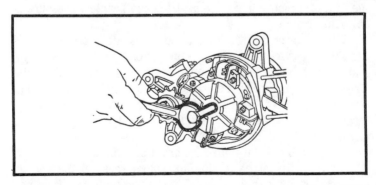

Fig. 5-35. Tranzimo rotor is extracted with Jawa special tool No. 16 65672 4. 3.

If these gambles fail—and replacing the transistor and an apparently good cap are gambles—then it is time to break out the voltmeter and do some serious troubleshooting. One must determine whether the fault is in the generating section or in one of the buried components of the switching circuit. The presence or absence of voltage is the diagnostic indicator.

The red wire is connected to one of the main generating coils and supplies current for the ignition pulse; the white wire is connected to the trigger coil and signals the transistor to conduct. Disconnect the red wire at the Tranzimo unit, and connect one probe of the voltmeter to it and the other to ground. Crank the engine to starting speed (some 600 rpm)—the meter should show at least 40 volts AC. If it does not, replace the generating coil and recheck. Make the same test with the white wire, expecting to find no less than 3 volts between it and ground. In the unlikely event that the trigger coil is defective, replace it, together with the stator plate. These parts are not available separately.

Suppose that both voltages are within specification. What then? By elimination, the fault is somewhere inside the Tranzimo switching unit. Since the circuits are buried in epoxy, the whole unit must be replaced.

IGNITION TIMING

As mentioned at the beginning of this chapter, the ignition system determines when the spark occurs. On all gasoline engines, the moment of sparking occurs early, before the piston has reached top dead center. This is to allow time for the air/fuel mixture to ignite, burn, and generate pressure. By the time the piston has gone past top dead center, pressure is at its maximum.

While some ignition advance is needed, too much is deadly—pressure peaks before the piston "goes over the top" and the piston is stressed by opposing forces. The inertia of the flywheel and the forward motion of the machine send it up, toward the top of the bore. At the same time, the explosive forces above it attempt to send the piston down, reversing the engine. The piston does not suffer long—it simply melts.

If the spark occurs late, the brunt of combustion energy is lost against the already sinking piston: most of the energy escapes out the exhaust port. The engine may be difficult to start and, once started, will produce little power.

144

Moped timing is fixed; once set it remains at a specific advance regardless of engine speed or load. Some readers who are familiar with the centrifugal and vacuum advance mechanisms on automobiles may wonder about the advisability of fixed timing. Some performance is lost, since the time required for combustion is almost independent of piston speed. At high speed a moped spark occurs late relative to peak combustion pressure. On the other hand, two-cycle engines are more tolerant of fixed timing than are automotive, four-cycle engines, and will run slightly retarded without much fuss.

Ignition occurs at the precise moment the contact points separate on conventional systems. Breakerless systems fire when the trigger coil and sensing magnet are in opposition. The purpose of timing is to match the moment of firing with a specified position of the piston, expressed as millimeters of travel before top dead center.

There are several ways to determine when the points break. The most accurate method is to use a continuity lamp, a buzzer, or an ohmmeter (Fig. 5-36). Connect one test lead to the movable arm of the point set, the other to a good, paint-and-oil-free engine ground. Turn the flywheel in the direction of normal rotation and watch the lamp or meter. The lamp should dim and the meter needle should drop as the points part. A more precise reading will result if you disconnect the lead between the point set and the exciter coil; the coil is grounded and fuzzes the results a bit.

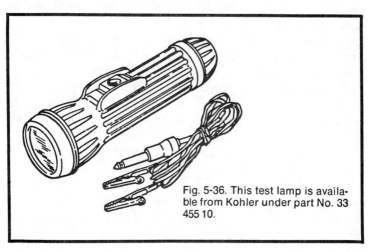

Fig. 5-36. This test lamp is available from Kohler under part No. 33 455 10.

Fig. 5-37. Minarelli engines have timing marks.

Another, less accurate way to determine when the points open, is to place a piece of cellophane between the contacts and turn the wheel until the cellophane is released. This is an emergency procedure only, since the timing will be off by the thickness of the cellophane.

Tranzimo rotors and stator plates carry timing marks. When these marks are in line with each other, the unit fires.

With magneto or solid state systems, the moment of firing can be adjusted by turning the stator plate in its elongated mounting holes. Turning the plate against the direction of crankshaft rotation advances the timing; turning it with crankshaft rotation retards the timing. Magneto systems have a second variable—the point gap. The wider the gap, the earlier the contacts open, and the more advanced is the ignition. Narrowing the gap has the reverse effect, which is why gapping the points to specification can do wonders for engine power.

The moment of firing must be coordinated with piston movement. Minarelli engineers have simplified matters by providing timing marks on the flywheel (Fig. 5-37). The mark identified by the letter "A" is the timing mark; it is 23 degrees in advance of "0," or top dead center. Timing these engines is simple:

- Set the point gap to specification—0.35-0.40 mm (0.014-0.018 inch).
- Loosen the stator plate holddown screws so that the plate can be turned.
- Mount the flywheel, but do not thread on the nut.
- Hook up a lamp or some other point-break indicator, with one lead on the movable point arm and the other lead grounded.
- Turn the flywheel in the direction of engine rotation—clockwise when facing the wheel—until the indicator shows point separation.
- If the "A" mark is not aligned with the pointer at the instant the points open, move the stator plate. Chances are the engine will not be far out of time and a few taps on the stator will be enough.
- Once you are satisfied that the "A" mark and point opening are synchronized, disconnect the timing indicator, tighten the stator plate holddown screws, and assemble the flywheel and nut. There are no torque specs for this nut; the manufacturer assumes that you will use the stubby 15-mm wrench supplied with the bike which, because of its length, has a built-in torque limit.

Flywheel marks are convenient, but not entirely accurate. Most manufacturers prefer to specify timing directly from piston position. timing becomes a matter of measurement, although there is a compromise available, represented by factory tools indexed for specific mopeds. The Motobecane is bottomed in the spark plug port and the flywheel turned against normal rotation. When the advance is correct the tool registers it.

The classic timing drill is more demanding; it begins with the search for true top dead center. You can use a plunger like the one shown in Fig. 5-38 or a dial indicator. The latter is the

Fig. 5-38. A timing plunger is an alternative to a dial indicator, although an inferior one.

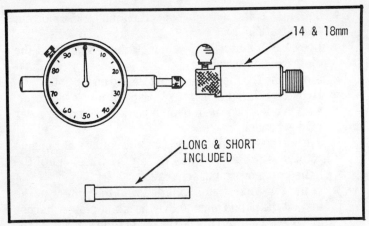

14 & 18mm

LONG & SHORT
INCLUDED

Fig. 5-39. This dial indicator and adapter kit is available from Kohler.

more precise instrument, with scale divisions of 0.01 mm. Several engine manufacturers offer mounting fixtures—bosses that thread into the spark plug port, with or without the dial indicator. Kohler, Suzuki, and Yamaha offer the complete kit (Fig. 5-39) under parts numbers 33 755 03, 09931 00111, and 908 90030 02 00, respectively. The spark plug port adapter is available from Puch as part number 905 6 32 101 0.

To time the engine with a dial indicator, gap the points to specification and follow this procedure:

1. Mount the indicator on the cylinder head, threading it solidly into the spark plug port.
2. Find top dead center by bracketing, i.e., move the crankshaft back and forth in progressively smaller increments.
3. Once you are satisified that the piston is at its high point, set the dial indicator at zero.
4. Connect an ohmmeter or test lamp to the points.
5. Determine the engine advance from Table 5-1 or by consultation with the dealer.
6. Turn the crankshaft against normal rotation to a point well beyond advance specification.
7. Turn the shaft in the direction of engine rotation to bring the piston to the advance specification. The points should just crack open.

If they don't, move the stator plate so they do, and tighten the holddown screws.

Most Fichtel & Sachs engines have timing marks on the flywheel and crankcase. "0" represents top dead center and "M" is the firing mark. However, some engines have come off the line withot these marks,and it is necessary to make them.

1. Find top dead center as before.
2. Mark the flywheel and crankcase at some visible spot to indicate TDC.
3. Turn the crankshaft against the direction of ratiotion. The spark advance on this engine is 2.5—3.0 mm. *Translated by the angle of the spark plug port this dimension is 3.5—4.0 mm (0.138-0.165 inch).*
4. Indicate this advance on the flywheel, adjacent to the previously made crankcase mark.
5. Gap the points at 0.35—0.45 mm (0.014—0.018 inch)
6. As described earlier, move the stator plate so that the points break with the flywheel firing and crankcase reference marks aligned.

Peugeot magnetos employ a rotor which is free to move relative to the crankshaft. This changes the timing drill somewhat; on other magnetos we can disregard the position of the flywheel magnetos, since they are part of the wheel, and keyed to the crankshaft. Follow this procedure with Peugeot engines:

1. Find true top dead center as before.
2. Turn the crankshaft (by means of the clutch drum) to bring the piston well in advance of top dead center.
3. Turn the drum to bring the piston 1.5 mm before top dead center.
4. Without moving the crankshaft, turn the rotor to align its timing mark "2" with the "1" mark on the stator.
5. Secure the rotor with Peugeot special tool No. 69646 or a pin wrench adapted to fit the holes.
6. The rotor is secured by a 16 mm capscrew. Torque it to 18 ft-lb.
7. Recheck the timing marks to be sure they have not slipped out of alignment.
9. Loosen the point holddown screw a bit. Insert a screwdriver blade in the adjusting slot on the stationary point assembly.

10. Adjust the gap until the points crack open. Tighten the holddown screw and recheck.

The nominal point gap is 0.40 mm (0.016 in.) but this consideration is secondary to the need for accurate timing. So long as the gap falls between 0.30 and 0.50 mm (0.012−0.020 inch), the magneto will function.

II LIGHTING CIRCUITS

Mopeds use 6-volt lighting systems. Three coils in the Tranzimo unit provide energy for the lights and horn; conventional magneto systems employ a single lighting coil for the headlamp and use the exciter to operate tail and brake lamps. The coils and magnets that generate energy for the system are known collectively as the alternator. Since the Tranzimo alternator is distinct from the ignition section (sharing only the rotor magnets), it has few problems for the serviceman. Magneto systems are another matter.

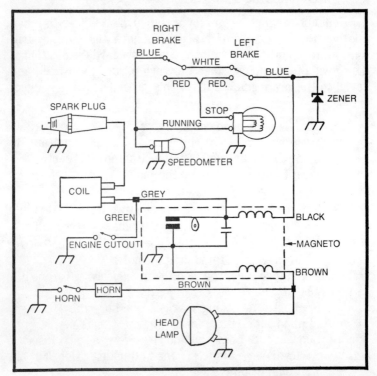

Fig. 5-40. A typical (magneto-fired) lighting and ignition system.

MAGNETO CIRCUITS

Figure 5-40 is a typical schematic. One side of the exciter is grounded when the contact points close; the other side is connected to the black wire, which joins the blue wire at a point near the handlebars. Both left and right brake levers incorporate stop-lamp switches; tripping either one operates the stop filament in the taillamp by way of the red wires. The blue wire continues through the tandem switches and provides power for the running filament.

Ignition Ground

Both the stop and running filaments are grounded at the lamp and provide a ground return for the ignition circuit. Current generated in the exciter flows through the closed points to ground and completes its circuit (or "circle," which is what the word means) at the taillamp. As long as this circuit is completed, there is ignition voltage. But if either of the tail lamp filaments open, there will be trouble. A broken or burned out stop filament will disable the ignition *when* the brakes are engaged; a broken running filament will disable the ignition *unless* the brakes are engaged.

Circuit Refinements

The *zener diode* in the upper right-hand corner of Fig. 5-40 limits voltage to the taillamp. The lamp is rated at 6 volts, a much lower voltage than the exciter coil delivers at high rpm. The zener "spills" the additional voltage to ground, protecting the lamp filaments. Should the zener short, all exciter current goes to ground, and there is no voltage available for the lamp or for the ignition coil. Should the zener open—the usual mode of failure—the taillamp burns out as soon as the throttle is opened.

In order to meet U.S. Department of Transportation standards, mopeds must be electrically clean; that is, the ignition system cannot transmit signals that interfere with radio and television reception. Most manufacturers meet this requirement by incorporating a resistor in the spark plug cable, usually at the terminal.

Peugeot has a fairly unique system: high-frequency oscillations, the oscillations that produce pips on TV screens and static in radio sets, are dampened by means of a *choke*, or *reactance coil* (Fig. 5-41). This coil has little effect on

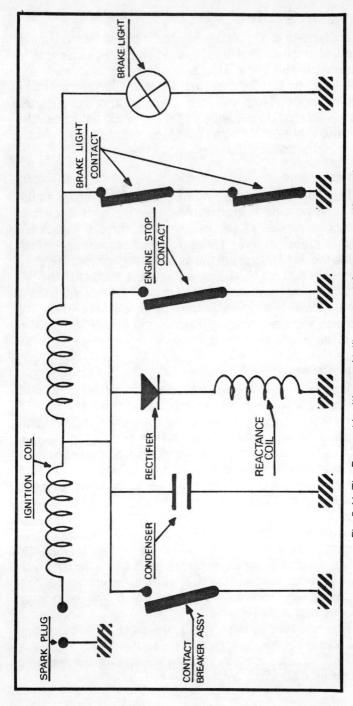

Fig. 5-41. The Peugeot ignition and taillamp circuit features a rectifier and reactance coil.

low-frequency oscillations. The current produced by the exciter coil alternates;this is,it moves to-and-fro in the circuit, peaking in one direction, falling to zero, and peaking in the other. The rectifier is a kind of traffic cop; it blocks half of the alternations to keep electrical traffic moving in one direction. Without it, exciter output would short to ground through the reactance coil, and there would be no ignition. Should the rectifier open, the circuit will continue to function, although it will radiate interference. Your TV-watching neighbors will know when you ride by.

Another interesting feature of the Peugeot circuit is that the stop lamp switches are connected in series and normally grounded. Because the resistance of the switch contacts is lower than the resistance of the stop lamp filament, no current passes through the filament unless one or both switches are opened. Any condition that denies ground will affect operation. For example, if the switch contacts are dirty, the stop lamp will burn continuously; if the stop lamp burns out, the engine will stop when the brakes are applied; if there is a break in the wire ahead of the switches, the engine will not run at all.

The usual European practice is to stop the engine with a compression release. To meet American standards, manufacturers have added and, in some cases, substituted a kill switch on the right handlebar. The kill switch is shown in Figs. 5-40 and 5-41. It is a simple grounding switch, wired to the ignition-coil side of the exciter. A mechanic should remember that a faulty kill switch can disable the ignition.

TROUBLESHOOTING

The bike's wiring diagram should be the basic tool for troubleshooting, and would be if we could trust them.Figure 5-42 is the wiring diagram for the U.S. version of the Cimatti City Bike. While the main outlines of the circuits are clear, things get a little fogged at the switch (2). But this is characteristic of all automotive diagrams, for these drawings combine schematic with pictorial elements, and do justice to neither. The wiring layout is quite functional, in straight lines from connection to connection, with no attempt to reproduce the tangle of wires on the actual machine. The lamps, ignition coil, and stop switches are pictorial, intended to call to mind the actual appearance of the object. The circuitry inside these pictures is incomplete or ignored.

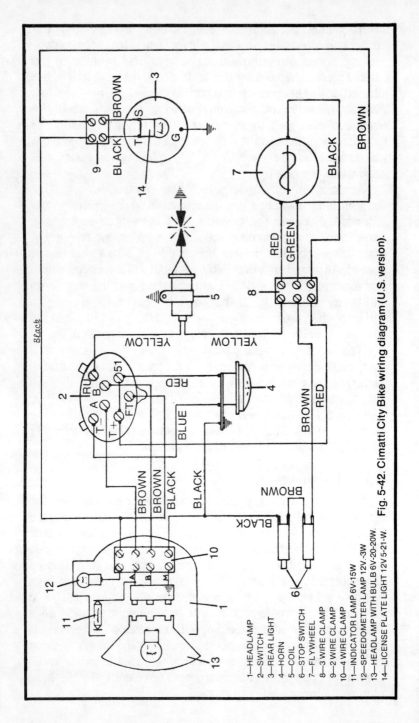

Fig. 5-42. Cimatti City Bike wiring diagram (U.S. version).

1—HEADLAMP
2—SWITCH
3—REAR LIGHT
4—HORN
5—COIL
6—STOP SWITCH
7—FLYWHEEL
8—3 WIRE CLAMP
9—2 WIRE CLAMP
10—4 WIRE CLAMP
11—INDICATOR LAMP 6V-15W
12—SPEEDOMETER LAMP 12V-.3W
13—HEADLAMP WITH BULB 6V-20-20W.
14—LICENSE PLATE LIGHT 12V 5-21-W.

154

Other moped manufacturers do worse. Some publish the European version of the diagram which includes a headlight switch. No moped sold in this country has such a switch, since DOT insists that the headlamp burn continuously. Certain circuit elements are forgotten, particularly circuit grounds. And the diagram may be deliberately incomplete, without the caption mentioning the fact.

The moral of all this is that wiring diagrams may add to the confusion. The diagram *will* tell you the color code and should give you an idea of the basic circuit components, but that's about it. In no way can a diagram substitute for a careful examination of the wiring on the machine.

After all is said and done, troubleshooting comes down to three basic techniques: *jumping, continuity testing*, and *substitution*.

Jumping

Jumping is a way of isolating a suspect component or circuit branch by shunting it out of the main circuit. An example—keyed to the diagram in Fig. 5-42—will make this clearer. Suppose that the engine has no spark and that you suspect the trouble is outside the magneto. Connect one end of a short length of wire to the brown/green terminal at the magneto clamp (8) and ground, and the other end to a clean, paint-free surface on the engine or frame. (Any fairly heavy-gauge wire with its ends bared will do, but if you expect to use such as jumper cable often, make one using gauge stranded wire and fit the ends with alligator clips or test probes.) If the tail light or its associated circuit is defective, the engine will start since the jumper has ground to the exciter coil.

The same technique can be used to test a switch; a jumper connected between switch terminals bypasses the switch. If the switch is faulty, the circuit will work with the jumper in place.

Continuity Testing

Continuity testing requires a test lamp (like the one shown in Fig. 5-26) or an ohmmeter (Fig. 5-43). The circuit inside the component must be complete; otherwise there can be no current through it. Some components are isolated from ground; others are grounded to their cases. If a kill circuit is always grounded, the engine will not run; on the other hand,

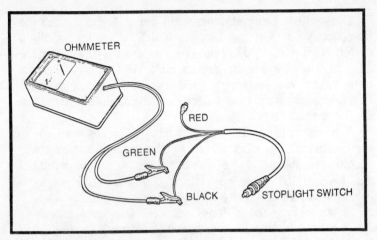

Fig. 5-43. Checking a Motobecane stoplight switch with an ohmmeter.

coils and many horns use the case as part of the current path. There should be continuity between a hot terminal and ground

Continuity checks also involve the ground side of the circuit. There should be an unbroken path from all ground connections to the engine block. An open ground circuit is just as disabling as a break in the insulated side of the circuit.

Subtitution

Substitution can be used as a crutch; when a mechanic doesn't know what else to do, he buys parts. But even the most knowledgeable mechanics must rely upon substitution at some point. For example, there are no coil testers that are calibrated to moped specifications; substitution is often the only way out. Horns can sometimes be disassembled and repaired, but horns are safety-related items and it is better to purchase a new one than take a chance fixing it. Even lamps are better substituted than checked. Filament breaks are not always obvious, and an ohmmeter does not say much about a defective lamp base.

REPAIRS

Once the trouble is spotted, electrical repairs are simple. Most involve defective grounds caused by rust, oil, or paint at the connections. Scrape the connections down to bare metal and make certain that they are secured by holddown screws or, in the case of lamp sockets, by spring pressure. The insulated side of the circuit usually fails because of dirty connections or broken wires. The most vulnerable wiring runs under the rear fender to feed the taillights.

Broken wires or wires that have lost their insulation and short can be replaced on one-to-one basis. This is, you can open the wiring harness, cut out the faulty wiring, and splice in new lengths. Use stranded wire, known in the automotive trades as primary wire, of at least the same gauge (thickness) as the original.

Gauge refers to the cross-sectional area of the conductive part of the wire, not to the thickness of the insulation. Mopeds generally use No. 16 or slightly heavier No. 14 wire. Hair-thin 20-gauge wire is sometimes used at the instrument nacelle. What is important to remember is that you can always go to heavier wire, but you're asking for trouble if you use thinner. Also remember that gauge number and thickness are inversely related: the higher the number, the thinner the wire (and the less current it will safely carry).

These connectors are fairly expensive and you have to purchase the crimping tool, but the speed and convenience is worth the investment. If you wish to use solder, purchase a roll of 60-40 rosin-core solder and some vinyl tape. Vinyl seems to hold up better than cloth friction tape and, since it can be stretched over the joint, makes a neater job. If the ends of the wires are to be joined, strip the insulation from both for about half an inch. Unwind the exposed strands so they are straight, and butt one wire against the other, interleaving the strands. Twist the strands together and heat the joint until solder melts and flows through it. Bend the resulting stub parallel with and against the wire and finish the job with several layers of vinyl tape.

If the wiring harness was opened, you can gather the wires with a good grade of vinyl tape. The tape ends should be protected from road splash and oil, or the whole thing will unravel. A better solution is to use spiral cable wrap, a precoiled plastic insulation that can be installed with the wires connected. Once in place, the plastic coils grip the wires in a tight, abrasion-proof bundle. Cable wrap can be purchased from electronics supply hose

The nice thing about the electrical system is that many components—wire, connections, switches, lamp sockets—can be purchased from nondealer sources. Six-volt sealed-beam headlamps are a standard item, used on small tractors and riding mowers. The quality of these parts is at least as good as those the factory supplies and the cost is less.

On the other hand, some electrical components are specific to mopeds. Taillamp bulbs are a good example—automotive bulbs draw too much current and, at any rate, do not have the reinforced filaments necessary to withstand motorbike vibration. And be careful about making modifications. A motorcycle horn—one that motorists can actually hear—may seem like a good idea. But moped alternators do not have power to spare , and the horn could burn out a coil.

Chapter 6
The Engine

Moped engines are rather complex (Fig. 6-1 through 6-4); major disassembly should not be entered into lightly. If you do decide to open the engine, go about the work in an orderly, patient manner with clean tools and hands. If the parts can be assembled wrong—some cylinder heads, for example, can go on three wrong ways and one right way—mark them while they are still together. The piston is very critical; it can be installed 180 degrees off unless you take notice of the factory mark or, if that mark is missing, make your own.

Another difficulty is that some manufacturers have not developed torque limit specifications, expecting that dealer mechanics develop a feel for these things. Torque limits that are available are included in Table 6-1; standard torque limits by bolt and screw size are in Table 6-2. The first table was compiled from factory manuals and has precedence over the second table. Both tables assume that the fastener threads are in good condition and are lubricated with clean motor oil.

DURABILITY

How long do moped engines last? The manufacturers are not saying, and few dealers have the experience to make more than a guess. Small motorcycles are superifially similar to mopeds; some of them are made by the same factories. These machines are not durable—the Department of Transportation is satisfied if they hold together for 20,000 miles—nor are they repairable in any true sense of the word. As mechanics say,

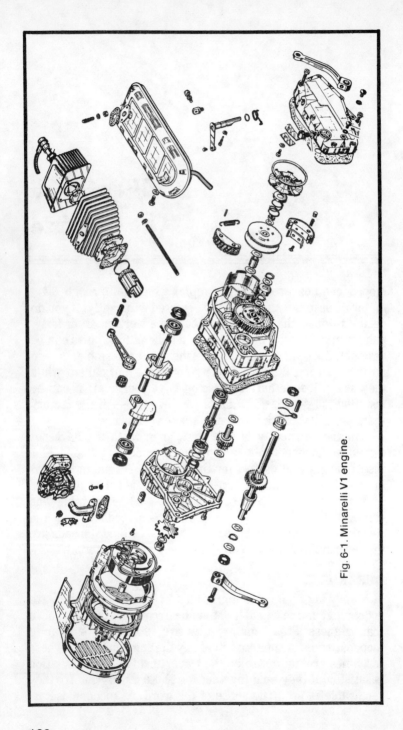

Fig. 6-1. Minarelli V1 engine.

" it's one ring job between the showroom floor and the junkyard."

But mopeds are different from motorcycles, different in concept, in market potential, and in purpose. Motorcycles, even the smallest of them, are leisure products sold on the promise of performance. Performance—and some 50 cc motorcycle engines can deliver upwards of 12 hp—is almost always gained at the expense of longevity. In contrast, mopeds are designed under legal restrictions that limit power and, in some cases, top speed. Moped engines are detuned for the European market and further detuned to meet American regulations. Few of them turn more than 5000 rpm and some develop no more than a hair over 1 hp.

Mopeds were originally intended as transportation for the working people of Europe, who insisted upon durability and, when something finally broke, repairability. While any small engine is a precision product, moped engines carry precision to a degree unknown elsewhere. No machine tool turns out

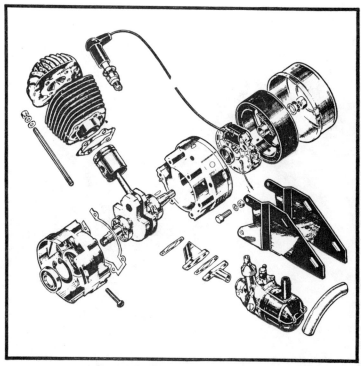

Fig. 6-2. Batavus (Laura) M48.01 engine.

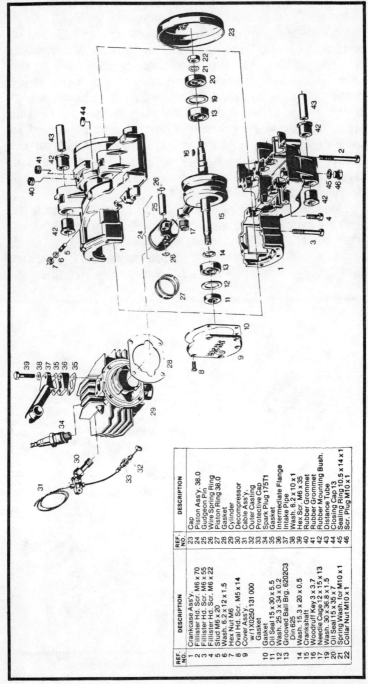

REF. NO.	DESCRIPTION
1	Crankcase Ass'y.
2	Fillister Hd. Scr. M6 x 70
3	Fillister Hd. Scr. M6 x 55
4	Fillister Hd. Scr. M6 x 22
5	Stud M6 x 20
6	Wash. 6.2 x 12 x 1.5
7	Hex Nut M6
8	Oval Hd. Scr. M5 x 14
9	Cover Ass'y. w/1X0250 131 000
10	Gasket
11	Oil Seal 15 x 30 x 5.5
12	Wash. 25.3 x 34 x 0.2
13	Grooved Ball Brg. 620203 Din 625
14	Wash. 15.3 x 20 x 0.5
15	Crankshaft
16	Woodruff Key 3 x 3.7
17	Needle Cage 12 x 15 x 13
19	Wash. 30 x 36.8 x 1.5
20	Oil Seal 15 x 35 x 7
21	Spring Wash. for M10 x 1
22	Collar Nut M10 x 1

REF. NO.	DESCRIPTION
23	Cap
24	Piston Ass'y. 38.0
25	Gudgeon Pin
26	Wire Spring Ring
27	Piston Ring 38.0
28	Gasket
29	Cylinder
30	Decompressor
31	Cable Ass'y.
32	Outer Casting
33	Protective Cap
34	Spark Plug 175T1
35	Gasket
36	Intermediate Flange
37	Intake Pipe
38	Wash. 6.2 x 10 x 1
39	Hex Scr. M6 x 35
40	Rubber Grommet
41	Rubber Grommet
42	Rubber Mounting Bush.
43	Distance Tube
44	Closing Cap 13
45	Sealing Ring 10.5 x 14 x 1
46	Scr. Plug M10 x 1

Fig. 6-3. Fichtel & Sachs 505/1A engine. (Courtesy Columbia Mfg. Co.)

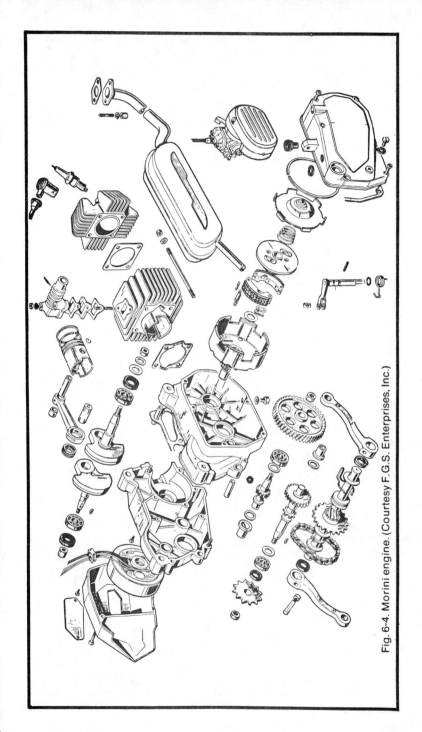

Fig. 6-4. Morini engine. (Courtesy F.G.S. Enterprises, Inc.)

Table 6-1. Torque Limits by Manufacturer

MAKE	Cylinder Head	Cylinder Barrel	Crankcase Fasteners	Flywheel Nut	Clutch Nut (Engine)	Motor Mount
Batavuus M-48						
Garelli	1.8kgm (17.9Nm) (13.0 ft-lb)	NA	0.9kgm (8.8Nm) (6.5 ft-lb)	3.3kgm (32.4Nm) (24.0 ft-lb)	3.5kgm (34.3Nm) (25.3 ft-lb)	NA
Eureka, Katia Kick Katio M, Eureka Matic		NA NA				NA NA
Fitchtel & Sachs (engine)	NA	(0.8-1.0 kgm) (7.8-9.8Nm) 5.7-7.2 ft-lb	(1-1.2 kgm) (9.8-11.8 Nm) 7.2-8.7 ft-lb	(3.7-4 kgm) 36.3-39.2Nm 26.7-28.9 ft-lb	(3.5-4.0 kgm) 3.6-3.9Nm 25.3-28.9 ft-lb	NA
Jawa						
Babetta	NA	NA	NA	NA	NA	NA
Minarelli (engine)						
all models	NA	NA	NA	NA	NA	NA
Motobecane						
all models	NA	NA	NA	NA	NA	NA
Peugeot						

Model						
Puch 103 LS-U1, 103 VLS-U2, 103 LVS-U3	1.1kmg (10.8Nm) (7.9 ft-lb)	NA NA NA	see note 1 see note 1 see note 1	4.0kgm (39.2Nm) (29.0 ft-lb)	4.0kgm (39.2Nm) (29.0 ft-lb)	2.5kgm (24.5Nm) (18.0 ft-lb)
Maxi	1.0kgm (10.0Nm) (7.3 ft-lb)	1.0kgm 10Nm 7.3 ft-lb	2.7kgm (27Nm) (19.5 ft-lb)	3.5 KGM (35Nm) (25.4 ft-lb)		0.8kgm (8Nm) (5.8 ft-lb)
Tomos Automatic 3	1.2kgm (11.8Nm) (8.7 ft-lb)	NA NA NA	1.0kgm (11.7Nm) (7.2 ft-lb)	3.0 kgm (29.4Nm) (21.7 ft-lb)	NA NA NA	NA NA NA
Velosolex	1.2kgm 11.5Nm 8.5 ft-lb	0.8kgm 8.2Nm 6.1 ft-lb	0.8 kgm 7.4Nm 5.4 ft lb	3.3 kgm 32.1Hm 23.7 ft-lb	see chapter 7	see note 2

NOTE 1: PEUGEOT CRANKCASES ARE HELD TOGETHER BY SIX BOLTS. FIVE ARE TORQUED TO 0.9 KGM (8.83 NM. 6.5 FT-LB); THE REMAINING BOLT IS TORQUED 1.2 KGM (11.8 NM. 8.7 FT-LB).

NOTE 2: VELOSOLEX ENGINE MOUNT TORQUE LIMITS ARE IN INCH-POUNDS. DIVIDE BY 12 FOR FOOT-POUNDS.

Diagram labels: 1.2 KGM, 0.9 KGM, 0.9 KGM, 0.9 KGM, 0.9 KGM, 0.9 KGM

Exploded view reference numbers: 97, 162, 73, 65, 65, 73, 65

Table 6-2. Torque Limits by Bolt Size

Unit: kgm (lbs-ft)

Part	Torque
6 mm screw	0.7 — 1.0 (5.1 — 7.2)
6 mm hex bolt	0.8 — 1.2 (5.8 — 8.7)
8 mm hex bolt	1.8 — 2.5 (13.0 — 18.1)
10 mm hex bolt	3.0 — 4.0 (21.7 — 28.9)
6 mm flanged hex bolt	1.0 — 1.4 (7.2 — 10.1)
8 mm flanged hex bolt	2.4 — 3.0 (17.4 — 21.7)
10 mm flanged hex bolt	3.8 — 4.8 (27.5 — 34.7)

identical parts; there is always some variation from the blueprint specifications. Moped builders compensate for this by grading and matching parts according to size. Most have three grades of cylinder bores and pistons, so that larger-than-average pistons can service larger-than-average bores. Some have as many as eight grades. The system extends to wrist and crankpins, and even to transmission gears. This concern with precise fit makes inventory problems, but it does much to assure that the engine will live.

Under-stressing the engine and extreme care in assembly has paid off. Mr. Robert E. Drennan is vice-president for customer service at Cimatti, and his comments are typical of what one hears in the industry. Cimatti and several other bikes use the Minarelli engine. Mr. Drennan reports that he has never seen a worn-out Minarelli even though he has inspected scores of them that are used in rental service on East Coast beachfronts.

Reliability—the freedom from sudden, unexpected mechanical catastrophe—appears to be good. While there is no clearinghouse for this kind of information, an informal poll of service technicians has turned up few warranty claims. Nor does the government have many complaints on record. Reliability comes about because of the low power outputs and because of the design stability of these machines. Many of the better known mopeds were designed twenty years ago, and some date back before World War II. Newcomers are usually quite conservative, sometimes going so far as to copy existing designs.

TROUBLESHOOTING

There are three symptoms that should alert you to the need for some serious engine work:

- Power loss (often accompanied by overheating)
- Engine noises
- Temporary or permanent engine seizure

Power Loss

Begin by checking out the running gear, to see if power is being needlessly wasted. Look for:

- Dragging brakes
- Sticking wheel bearings
- Slipping clutch (belt or drive wheel)
- Underinflated tires
- Overtightened or rusty drive chain.

Once you are satisfied that the chassis components are transmitting the power that they receive, turn to the ignition system. Verify that the magneto puts out a healthy spark at cranking speed, change the spark plug, and check the timing. Make a few full-throttle test runs and "read" the spark plug tip as described in Chapter 5.

Next, disassemble the muffler as far as possible; if it is made of steel, soak the muffler for several hours in a bucket of lye and steaming water. Remove the exhaust pipe (sometimes the pipe is integral with the muffler) and, with the help of a flashlight, check out the cylinder condition through the exhaust port. Some carbon is normal, particularily if you are using petroleum-based oil. But thick, slate-like carbon formations on piston and roof of the combustion chamber mean loss of power and overheating. In some cases, performance can be restored by opening the clogged exhaust port. Bring the piston down below the port and scrape the carbon with a dull knife. Remove the spark plug and crank the engine to expel any carbon particles that fell on the piston.

It is useful to examine the rings, or that part of the rings you can see through the port. They should be uniformly bright, without telltale dull stops that show less-than-full contact with the bore. A dull, satiny appearance, as if the rings had been lapped, means abrasive damage from small sand particles that entered through the intake system. Expect to find a torn filter or air leaks between the filter and carburetor. Using something soft like the eraser end of a pencil, push the rings into their grooves. The rings should bottom and spring back. If they do not give, the rings are stuck and should be replaced—in the future use a different brand of oil. If the rings seem lifeless, they have lost tension from overheating. At worst the rings have broken.

A compression check has some utility, but less on a single-cylinder engine than on a multi-cylinder unit. Many factors—ambient air temperature, the percentage of oil mixed with the fuel, the pressure drop across the air filter element, and how vigorously you spin the pedals—influence cylinder pressure. Under average conditions, a moped engine should develop about 90 psi at cranking speeds. If it develops much less than this, you can assume leaks at the:

- compression release
- cylinder head gasket (on engines so fitted).
- piston/cylinder seal.

The seal between piston and bore depends upon contact with the bore by the rings and the piston. In the usual order of things the rings wear first, then the piston, and finally the bore itself. If a few teaspoons of oil squirted into the cylinder improve the gauge readings, the seal is the problem and the engine should at least have new rings. If oil makes no difference, then the problem is above the piston, involving the head gasket or compression release.

Very high compression readings, on the order of 130 psi, mean that carbon deposits have raised the compression ratio. Enough carbon to cause such readings will send the engine into detonation, causing it to overheat and damage the piston. Remove the head and scrape the carbon.

Engine Noise

Engine knocks are associated with the piston connecting rod, and sometimes with the main bearings. The major source—and the one that means a lunched engine unless is it corrected—is the big end of the connecting rod. Because of the uneven loads on the rod, the big end, or crankpin, bearing can be expected to wear about three times faster than the main bearings. The small end, or wrist pin, bearing should give no trouble in a moped engine. Unfortunately, there have been some problems with small end bearings because of manufacturing error.

Individual knocks can sometimes be isolated with the help of a broomstick held against the engine and pressed against

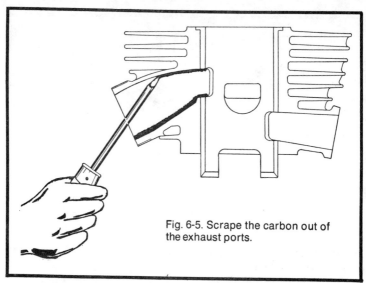

Fig. 6-5. Scrape the carbon out of the exhaust ports.

the bone just behind your ear. The noise is felt rather than heard. But this is usually an academic exercise, since the engine will have to be disassembled anyway and the bearings can than be checked visually.

Whines, shrieks, and wails are usually caused by transmission bearings that have been starved for oil. (Engine bearings would hardly have time to make a peep before they disintegrated.) While no bike should be run with noisy bearings, you can sometimes doctor a transmission bearing with a high film-strength additive such as STP.

Piston Seizure

Piston seizure can be momentary or it can be permanent, in which case the engine must be partially disassembled and the piston forced out of the bore. Seizure is always the result of insufficient lubrication. There may not be enough oil in the premix or the oil may have settled out to the bottom of the tank, causing the engine to run on almost pure gasoline. Oil starvation can also develop on long downgrades if the rider forgets to blip the throttle every few hundred feet.

Other lubrication failures occur because of excessive heat: lugging the engine under load sends temperatures soaring and turns the oil to an abrasive paste. Detonation has the same effect, as does a severely worn piston. When the piston is loose, it makes only partial contact with the bore.

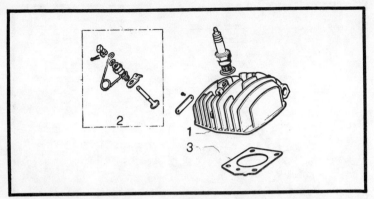

Fig. 6-6. Motobecane cylinder head (1), gasket (3), and compression release (2).

Those areas that touch are subject to the full brunt of piston forces, and overheat.

Upper End

The upper end includes all parts above the crankcase: cylinder head, compression release, head gasket, cylinder barrel, piston and rings, and connecting rod.

CYLINDER HEAD

About half of the mopeds presently imported have detachable cylinder heads (Fig. 6-6); the others have the head and cylinder barrel cast en bloc. Comments here about compression release valves, decarbonizing, and polishing apply to all engines, regardless of their construction. Those with one-piece heads and cylinders must have their barrels removed for access.

Mark the cylinder head and barrel before disassembly, since on many engines the head bolts are spaced evenly, and the head can be installed three ways wrong and one way right. Remove the spark plug and, if present, the compression release control cable. Undo the four cap screws securing the head to the barrel, noting the washer under each screw. Lift the head off.

Compression Release.

The compression release is a small poppet valve, not unlike those used on four-cycle engines. It is opened by a cable-and-lever arrangement and closed by spring tension.

After long service the valve may fail to seat, leaking compression through the port drilled through the head and barrel. Test the valve by covering its face with soap suds and introducing compressed air at the port. Bubbles mean the valve should be disassembled for cleaning.

The pin that holds the valve on the spring collar is as important as any part on the bike. If it should fail, the valve can fall into the cylinder and break the piston. As shown in Fig. 6-6, Motobecane compression releases are fixed by a cotter pin; Peugeot valves are secured by a brass rod, peened over the ends. Other makes use a spring clip. Release the locking mechanism and pull the valve out of the cylinder. Normally, all that is required is to wire brush the valve face and seat.

If the valve appears burnt or warped, it can be resurfaced by lapping, but the job is a little tricky. The valve must be turned against its seat. One way to do this is to glue a small-diameter dowel to the valve head, securing it with one of the potent adhesives such as alpha-cyano-acrylic cement. Dab a little lapping compound on the seat and rotate the valve between the palms of your hands—exactly like a Boy Scout makes a fire. After a few seconds the compound will pulverize and you will no long hear the "swish-swish" sound of it cutting. Raise the valve, wipe off the exhausted compound, and add more. Repeat the operation until the full circumference of the valve and seat are uniformly bright. Take special care to remove all the compound; it must not get into the engine.

In the unlikely event that the whole assembly must be replaced, secure the head in a vise as shown in Fig. 6-7, covering the vise jaws with copper sheet to protect the bolt threads. Unscrew the valve body.

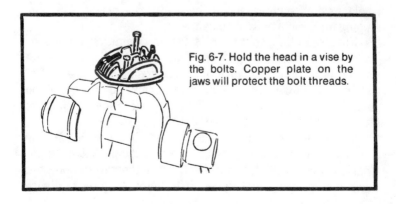

Fig. 6-7. Hold the head in a vise by the bolts. Copper plate on the jaws will protect the bolt threads.

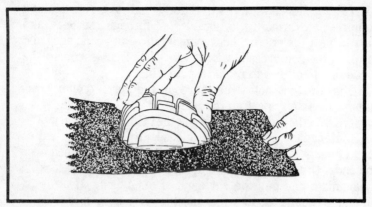

Fig. 6-8. Surfacing a Batavus cylinder head.

Decarbonizing

Even a thin layer of carbon costs power; thick layers send the engine into detonation. Scrape the cylinder head and piston top with a dull knife, trying not to mar the machined surfaces. Nicks and gouges are the sign of amateur work, and make the next decabonizing job more difficult. Move the piston down into the bore and wipe off any loose carbon flakes on the cylinder walls.

Cylinder Head Truing

This step is optional on engines that have not had a history of head-gasket problems. Secure a piece of plate glass—ordinary window glss will not do—to a flat surface and coat it with valve-lapping compound. Place the head, gasket surface down, on the glass and move it in a figure-8 pattern (Fig. 6-8). Your hand should be centered on the head so the whole gasket surface should be uniformly bright. Continue lapping until any low spots disappear.

Note that this operation is not the same as milling or grinding the head. Moped cylinder heads will not tolerate much metal removal before the compression ratio goes out of sight or the squish band, the indentation around the edge of the chamber, is lost. Lapping is a finishing operation which takes off no more than a few thousandths of an inch.

Increased efficiency will result if you polish the combustion chamber and piston top (*not* the gasket surface). Engines have been polished by hand, although the job goes much faster with a high-speed drill motor. Begin with a wire cup brush and progress to finer and finer grades of wet-or-dry sandpaper. Oil speeds the cutting and leaves a smoother surface. After about grade 400, use a buffer and jeweler's rouge. The job is done when you can see your reflection.

Head Gasket

Most engines use a composition gasket that must be replaced each time the head is disturbed: to do otherwise is to ask for leaks. A few mopeds use copper gaskets that can be reused if the gasket is heated with a propane torch and quenched in water. Puch engines employ spacers made of heavy gauge aluminum foil. These spacers are one of the factory tricks to detune the engine for the American market. If you wish, they can be discarded. Seal the head and barrel with a very thin coat of high-temperature silicon cement.

Assembly

Mount the head on the barrel, making sure that the gasket and head are aligned with each other and with the reference marks previously made. Inspect the head bolts for straightness and, particularly, for evidence of thread damage. Lubricate the bolt threads and cap undersides with motor oil or anti-sieze compound.

Run the bolts in until snug. Then, using a torque wrench, tighten the bolts in a diagonal pattern in at least three increments—one-third, two-thirds, and full torque. Torque limit specifications are in Table 6-1. Install the spark plug and compression-release cable.

CYLINDER BARREL

Most machines are constructed so the cylinder barrel can be detached with the engine in place. French belt-drive machines are an exception; the engine must be dropped for cylinder clearance. (Peugeot cylinders can be removed with the engine in the frame if you have access to special tool No. 69260, a belt-pulley spring compressor.)

The barrel, or *jug*, is secured to the crankcase by four capscrews or studs. The studs may double as cylinder-head fasteners. Disconnect the exhaust pipe at the cylinder port and loosen the muffler brackets enough to swing the pipe clear. Disconnect the intake pipe or carburetor, whichever is easier. Undo the capscrews or studnuts in crisscross fashion in order

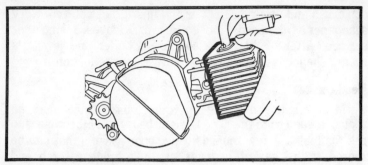

Fig. 6-9. Removing the cylinder barrel on a Jawa engine.

to protect the cylinder bore from distortion. Lift the barrel far enough to see the piston, turn the crankshaft so the piston is at bottom dead center, and pull the barrel off (Fig. 6-9). If the piston were extended, it would drop hard against the crankcase.

It is not unusual for the barrel to be stubborn; unseat it with a rubber mallet, directing the blows against the exhaust port outlet. Do not pound on the fins, which are glass-fragile on some models. Once the barrel is off, scrape the gasket remains from both parting surfaces.

Inspection

Wipe the bore with a clean shop towel and turn it under a strong light. The bore should be uniformly bright and smooth. The various sorts of damage and possible causes are:

- Discoloration—local overheating and distortion.
- Deep grooves running the length of the bore—piston ring or bearing particle damage. Replace or, if possible, remachine the bore.
- Scratches at the exhaust port—carbon damage, a fact of life of two-cycle engines.
- Fine, almost invisible, scratches—sand damage Check the air filter and intake tract joints.
- Peeling or worn-through chrome—manufacturing error or extreme wear. Replace.
- Aluminum splatter—piston damage. Remove the aluminum with muriatic (hydrochloric) acid. Flush with water and immediately oil the bore.

Once you are satisfied that the bore has no obvious defects, have it measured with a bore gauge or inside micrometer. The

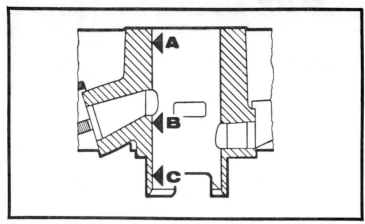

Fig. 6-10. Mike the cylinder barrel at these points, making two measurements parallel with the wrist pin and 180 degrees apart at each point. (Courtesy Steyr-Daimler-Puch of America Corp.)

measuring points are shown in Fig. 6-10; each point is measured twice, parallel with the wrist pin centerline and at 90 degrees to it.

At this juncture things begin to get complicated. Moped engines are put together like a fine watch from parts that are coded for size. Each size code has a wear limit, different with each manufacturer. For example, Puch uses five cylinder bore and piston sizes on the Maxi engine. Permissible out-of-round is 0.00098 in. (0.025 mm) in all cases, but there are five wear limits, varying with the original size of the cylinder. Table 6-3 lists cylinder and piston dimensions for the Maxi engine. Other manufacturers use a different cylinder bore base dimension or

Table 6-3. Puch Cylinder/Piston Tolerances

Cylinder				
Tolerance 1∅ $\frac{inch}{mm}$	Tolerance 2∅ $\frac{inch}{mm}$	Tolerance 3∅ $\frac{inch}{mm}$	Tolerance 4∅ $\frac{inch}{mm}$	Tolerance 5∅ $\frac{inch}{mm}$
1.4950 - 1.4954	1.4954 - 1.4958	1.4958 - 1.4962	1.4962 - 1.4966	1.4966 - 1.4970
37.975 - 37.985	37.985 - 37.995	37.995 - 38.005	38.005 - 38.015	38.015 - 38.025

Permissible ovality of the cylinder 0,00098 in (0,025 mm)

Piston				
Tolerance 1∅ $\frac{inch}{mm}$	Tolerance 2∅ $\frac{inch}{mm}$	Tolerance 3∅ $\frac{inch}{mm}$	Tolerance 4∅ $\frac{inch}{mm}$	Tolerance 5∅ $\frac{inch}{mm}$
1.4938 - 1.4942	1.4942 - 1.4946	1.4946 - 1.4950	1.4950 - 1.4954	1.4954 - 1.4958
37.945 - 37.955	37.955 - 37.965	37.965 - 37.975	37.975 - 37.985	37.985 - 37.995

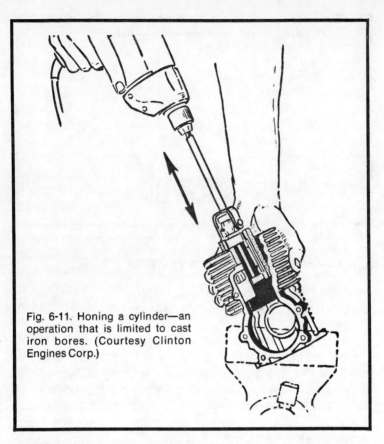

Fig. 6-11. Honing a cylinder—an operation that is limited to cast iron bores. (Courtesy Clinton Engines Corp.)

grade at different size intervals. At any rate, the code will be stamped on the cylinder barrel, usually on the top fin, and the same code number or letter will appear on the piston crown.

Puch and most other moped engines have chromed bores. These bores last longer than plain iron, but complicate matters when they do finally wear out. It is impractical to machine a chrome bore to fit a larger piston. Should the bore be worn past specification, you have two choices: you can purchase a new cylinder and coded piston or you can try to find a piston from one of the larger codes that will restore the fit. If, in the case of the Puch, your machine has a code 5 bore, oversize pistons are not to be had.

Honing

Cast-iron cylinders should be lightly honed before assembly (Fig. 6-11). (This process would be disastrous on chromed liners.) Honing removes small imperfections and leaves a regular pattern of scratches on the bore that help the rings seat (Fig. 6-12). Without honing it is doubtful that chrome-plated rings would ever make a gas-tight seal.

Bona fide engine hones are not available in capacities of less than 2.00 inches. You must therefore use a heavy-duty brake cylinder hone. Hones with three stones, such as the Snap-on B-200, give more consistent results than two-stone models. Mount the hone in a low-speed drill motor, lubricate the cylinder with kerosene or cutting oil, and run the hone up and down in the bore. Adjust the reciprocating speed to give a cross-hatch pattern as shown in the illustration. The exact angle is not important—manufacturers specify anything from 22.5 to 60 deg—what is important is that the pattern have a definite diamond shape. Keep the hone moving, pausing at the end of the stroke only long enough to reverse direction. Stop when the glaze on the cylinder wall is broken. As a practical matter, some patches of glaze may be left, if removing them costs too much metal.

Once the cylinder is honed, scrub the bore with hot water and detergent (Fig. 6-13). Wipe with a paper towel; if the towel discolors, scrub again to float out the remaining abrasive particles. Lightly oil the cylinder to prevent rust.

Reboring

Most cast-iron cylinders can be rebored. Since cylinders retail for between $40 and $50, reboring is certainly worthwhile. The first step is to measure the cylinder accurately to determine how much metal must be taken out. Then purchase a piston in that oversize. The only real complication arises with engines that use tolerance-coded

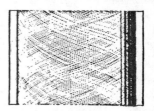

Fig. 6-12. The hone should leave a cross-hatch pattern, with diamond-shaped high spots between the abrasions. (Courtesy Clinton Engines Corp.)

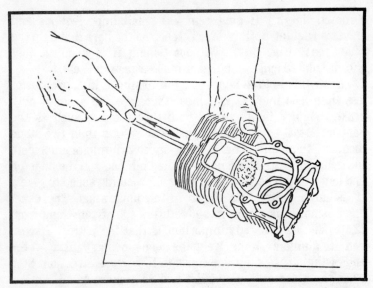

Fig. 6-13. Scrub the bore with hot water and detergent to remove the stone particles. Dry with paper towels and oil immediately. (Courtesy Clinton Engines Corp.)

cylinder/piston assemblies. Jawa is a good example of this practice (see Table 6-4).

Jawa cylinder/piston combinations are supplied in four tolerances. Standard is unmarked; the remaining three are identified by a letter code stamped on the cylinder and piston. Each of these four combinations can be rebored in four quarter-millimeter increments; dealers stock 16 different pistons for this engine. The Yugoslavian Tomos is built on two tolerance codes, A and B. Each can be overbored a half millimeter.

Boring engines and the all-critical matter of piston fitting is best left to the dealer. But there are occasions when this is impractical, and some discussion of the process is in order. There are two ways to bore a cylinder—with a boring bar or with a hone. The former is preferable, since it is faster and more accurate. Cylinders with liners that extend below the fins can be mounted in a standard three-jaw lathe chuck. Those that must be held by the fins require a four-jaw chuck for centering. The cylinder is spun and the boring bar—a heavy bar with a carbide cutter—is fixed to the tailstock. Bore undersize first, then bring the cylinder out to specification with a hone.

The second method of boring a cylinder is to use a coarse hone. The process is similar to glaze breaking, but is, of course, carried further. The drill motor should turn at about 600 rpm and the hone should be reciprocated about 40 strokes a minute. Run the stones clear of both ends of the bore for approximately 0.5 in. You will know when the bore is straight by the steady whine of the drill motor. If the motor bogs down on part of the stroke, that section of the bore is narrow and you should concentrate on it. Keep the stones well lubricated and clean them before abrasive particles scratch the bore. Continually monitor your progress with an inside mike or a cylinder gauge. As you approach the limit, change to a medium stone. Finally, chamber the port edges to prevent ring snag, and scrub the bore with detergent and water.

Assembly

Position a new base gasket on the engine block, aligning it with the transfer port indentations. Some mechanics like to coat both sides of the gasket with a cellophane-thin layer of silicone adhesive. Turn the crankshaft to bring the piston clear of the block and insert a wooden wedge under it (Fig. 6-14). The wedge is a third hand, holding the piston steady while you manipulate the cylinder barrel. Make dead certain that the piston rings are installed with their ends straddling the locating pins: if the closed section of a ring rides over the pin, the ring will snap when the barrel is lowered.

Table 6-4. Jawa Babetta Rebore Limits by Cylinder/Piston Grades

Diameter × H6		A	B	C
Standard	39.00 + 0.016	39.00 + 0.006	39.006 + 0.005	39.011 + 0.005
Rebore I	39.25 + 0.016	39.25 + 0.006	39.256 + 0.005	39.261 + 0.005
Rebore II	39.50 + 0.016	39.50 + 0.006	39.506 + 0.005	39.511 + 0.005
Rebore III	39.75 + 0.016	39.75 + 0.006	39.756 + 0.005	39.761 + 0.005
Rebore IV	40.00 + 0.016	40.00 + 0.006	40.006 + 0.005	40.011 + 0.005

Piston Grading (mm)

Piston Grading		A	B	C
Rebore I	39.116 − 0.006	39.106 − 0.006	39.111 − 0.005	39.116 − 0.005
Rebore II	39.366 − 0.016	39.356 − 0.006	39.361 − 0.005	39.366 − 0.005
Rebore III	39.616 − 0.016	39.606 − 0.006	39.611 − 0.005	39.616 − 0.005
Rebore IV	39.866 − 0.016	39.856 − 0.006	39.861 − 0.005	39.866 − 0.005

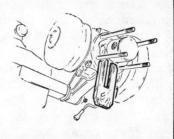

Fig. 6-14. A wedge under of the piston simplifies barrel installation.

Lubricate the piston, rings, and wrist pin. Do the same for the cylinder bore, swabbing oil over every square millimeter of it. Turn the exhaust port down (or, as the case may be, forward) and lower the cylinder barrel. Do not turn it once you contact the piston; angular displacement can send the top compression ring over its locating pin. Gently push the barrel down, (Fig. 6-15) compressing the rings on the chamfer at the base of the bore. (Sachs engines are not chamfered and great care must be exercised not to break a ring.) If the barrel binds, stop and find out why. Once the piston is swallowed, lightly run in the barrel holddown fasteners. Turn the flywheel to detect possible "hard spots."

Torque the cylinder fasteners in several increments, working diagonally across the bore centerline. Mount the exhaust pipe and intake hardware.

PISTON

Examine the piston for heat damage, wear, and distortion. Combustion heat damage starts on the piston crown, or top. Before a hole develops, the metal rises and pits, as if it had been brought to a boil and cooled. Overheating on the cylinder bore sears and blackens the piston skirts, sometimes ripping metal off in splotches. Discard a piston with either kind of heat damage.

No used piston is perfect, but it should be free of deep scratches; wear should be confined to the thrust faces, which are the two areas 90 degrees from the wrist pin centerline. Uneven or skewed wear marks may indicate a bent crankshaft or connecting rod.

Moped piston shapes are more complicated than they appear. The piston must be able to expand under temperature without binding against the bore. When cold, the crown is a few hundredths of a millimeter smaller than the base of the skirt, and the diameter measured along the wrist pin centerline is less than the diameter at the thrust faces. In other words, the piston is an ovoid cone. Once the engine starts, the piston expands to make nearly full contact with the bore.

Where the piston is measured is up to the discretion of the manufacturer—some are silent about this; perhaps half do not even give the piston-bore clearance, never mind how they arrive at it. Those that supply a clearance specification usually want the measurement taken at the base of the piston, across the thrust faces. In other words, the largest dimension is used as the guide. Tomos specifies four measuring points (Fig. 6-16).

Experience and the vailable data suggests that chromed bores tolerate much smaller clearances than plain cast iron. The typical chromed engine is set up at 0.015-0.035 mm (0.0006-0.0013 in.) while cast iron requires 0.060-0.070 mm (0.0024-0.0028 in.). The porous chrome used on these cylinders holds more oil than iron.

Remove the rings from the piston, noting which side is up. The top side should be stamped with an identifying letter near the gap. Handle rings with care, for the edges are razor sharp. Snap one of the rings and, holding it with a file handle or Vise-Grips, use it to clean the grooves. Do not remove metal

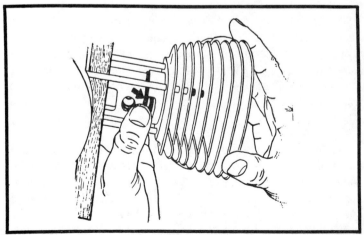

Fig. 6-15. The sleeve cutouts on Batavus and most other engines are a last-chance opportunity to compress the rings before they meet the bore.

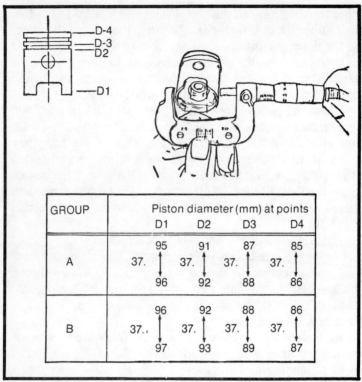

Fig. 6-16. Measurement points and piston diameter specifications for the Tomos engine. Readings range from 37.97 mm (max.) for skirt diameter on a Group "B" piston to 37.85 mm (min.) for crown diameter on a Group "A".

GROUP	Piston diameter (mm) at points			
	D1	D2	D3	D4
A	37. 95↕96	37. 91↕92	37. 87↕88	37. 85↕86
B	37. 96↕97	37. 92↕93	37. 88↕89	37. 86↕87

Insert a new ring into each of the grooves and measure the flank clearance with a feeler gauge It is easier to get an accurate measurement if the ring is backed into the groove as shown in Fig. 6-17. Flank clearance should between 0.03-0.07 mm (0.001-0.003 in.) Much more than this can cause breakage from ring flutter.

Disassembly

Before removing the piston from the connecting rod, mark the leading edge of the crown for guidance in reassembly. Some pistons are already stamped with the letter S or F; most are not. The engine will run with the piston installed backwards, but after a few miles will knock.

The wrist pin is secured in the piston by two spring clips, known in the trade as *circlips*. Place a rag in the block cavity

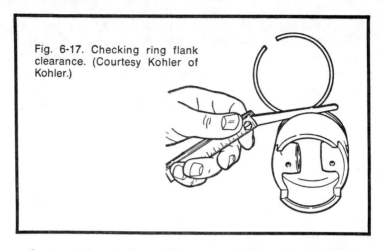

Fig. 6-17. Checking ring flank clearance. (Courtesy Kohler of Kohler.)

and extract the circlips with long-nosed pliers. If you drop one the rag will prevent if from falling into the engine. Discard the circlips: they are too important to be trusted twice.

There are several ways of removing the wrist pin. The easiest way is with a pin extractor such as the one shown in Fig. 6-18. The tool is available from any moped importer and from Kohler engine dealers. Another method is to heat the piston with an electric hot plate or propane torch. If you use a torch, keep the flame moving in circles around the upper diameter of the piston. Stop when the piston smokes. Once heated, the piston will expand enough to release the wrist pin. Do not simply drive the pin out with a punch, for even if you

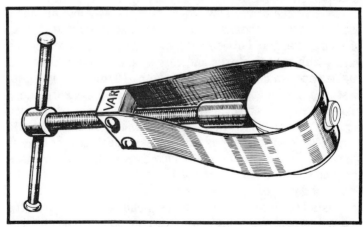

Fig. 6-18. A piston pin extractor from Motobecane.

take pains to support the back side of the connecting rod, some rod distortion is almost inevitable. Some manufacturers insist that the piston be cooled in the cylinder to prevent distortion.

The rod eye, or small-end, bearing takes several forms. It may be a bushing, a caged needle bearing, or merely a collection of needles. If your engine has free needles, be careful not to lose any as the pin is forced past the rod eye. Above all, do *not* allow any needles to drop into the block.

If you wish to replace the piston, you must use one in the same tolerance group. If the cylinder is worn, you may be able to go to a larger diameter. Pistons and wrist pins are best purchased as a matched set. Most moped manufacturers supply wrist pins in two diameters; some supply three. Pins are identified by a color code or by letters stamped on the underside of one pin boss.

Oil the wrist pin and bearings. Position loose needles in the rod eye with grease or, better, beeswax. Warm the piston and slide the pin home. Use new circlips, compressing them just enough to clear the pin bores. Once the circlips are in place, turn them to see that they track in their grooves.

RINGS

Modern rings have a definite top and bottom, indicated by a code letter on the top side. Engines with chrome bores use unplated cast-iron rings; those with iron bores may use chrome rings. Do not interchange the two types. Unless indicated on the parts package, both rings are identical.

Insert each of the new rings about midway into the bore, using the back of the piston as a pilot to keep the ring square. Measure the gap between the ring ends—the specification varies with manufacturer and bore type (Fig. 6-19). Chromed engines are typically set up tight, with 0.30 mm (0.01 in.) gap. Cast iron blocks go as wide as 0.80 mm (0.03 in.) Large gaps allow blowby into the crankcase, but some clearance is needed for ring growth under heat. The minimum dimension is 0.15 mm (0.006 in) If the gap is excessive, suspect that the bore is worn; if it is too small and the ring ends almost touch, check that you have the correct parts. It may be necessary to file the ends, but don't get carried away.

Install the lower or No. 2 ring, slipping it over the top of the piston and past the No. 1 groove. Do not pull the ends farther apart than necessary to clear the piston diameter. Above all,

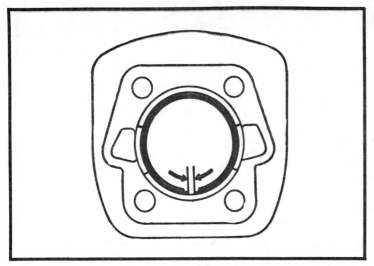

Fig. 6-19. The ring end gap is critical. (Courtesy Batavus Bikeways Inc.)

not twist the ring. Position the ends on each side of the locating pin and repeat the operation for the second ring.

CONNECTING ROD

The piston should pivot by its own weight on the small-end bearing. Steady the rod with one hand and, holding the piston with your thumb and forefinger over the wrist pin ends, move it up and down on the rod. There should be no more than a suggestion of vertical play between the small end bearing and the wrist pin. Holding the piston as before, try to wobble it in a vertical arc parallel to the wrist pin. More than a thirty-secondth of an inch movement means that the small-end bearing is bell-mouthed and should be replaced.

Needle bearings are not difficult to install; bushings are another matter. The new bushing is pressed into place, drilled for oil supply, and reamed for a pin clearance of 0.003 mm (0.0001 inch). Unless you have the tools, it is wise to have a dealer install the bushing.

The connecting rod swings on roller bearings at the crankpin. To get some idea of the condition of these bearings, bring the rod up to top dead center and move it up and down on the crankpin. Some play in the bearing is necessary, but you should not feel the rod release and stop. In other words, if the play is such that you can accelerate the rod with your hand,

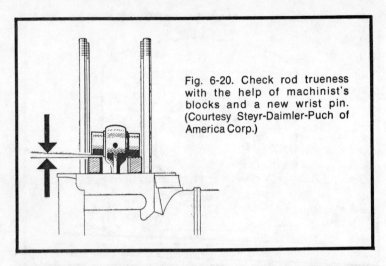

Fig. 6-20. Check rod trueness with the help of machinist's blocks and a new wrist pin. (Courtesy Steyr-Daimler-Puch of America Corp.)

the bearing is shot. Try to move the connecting rod in an arc paralleling the crankpin. If the total arc is more than one-eighth inch, the big-end bearings have tapered and should be renewed.

Check rod straightness with a pair of machinist's blocks and a new wrist pin (Fig. 6-20). Compensate for possible crankcase distortion by switching the blocks from one side of the rod to the other. The rod can be straightened with a homemade bending bar (Fig. 6-21).

II LOWER END

The lower end includes the crankcase, crankshaft, main bearings seals, and the big end of the connecting rod. Lower end repairs are serious matters, not entered into lightly. Some special tools are needed.

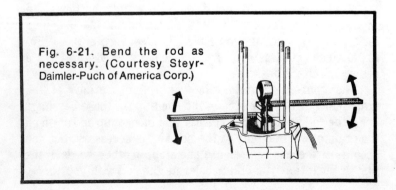

Fig. 6-21. Bend the rod as necessary. (Courtesy Steyr-Daimler-Puch of America Corp.)

PULLING THE ENGINE

Lower end work requires that the engine be taken out of the frame. The engine is secured by bolts and mated to the frame at the fuel, electrical, exhaust, and drive systems. Disconnect these parts:

- Fuel line
- Throttle cable
- Choke cable (if fitted)
- Compression release cable (if fitted)
- Alternator—usually a single, multiprong connection aft of the flywheel.
- Exhaust pipe
- Chain or belt

The belt spring complicates matters on Peugeot bikes. The spring must be compressed by tilting the engine to the rear and then slowly released. Once the fairings, a carburetor, compression release cable, and wiring are dismantled, follow this procedure:

1. Insert special tool No. 69260 into the flywheel hub and one of the sprocket teeth (Fig. 6-22).
2. Push down on the right-hand pedal crank to tip the engine toward the rear of the vehicle.
3. Carefully remove the belt.
4. Raise the pedal and tip the engine toward the front wheel, releasing tension on the spring.
5. Remove the tool.

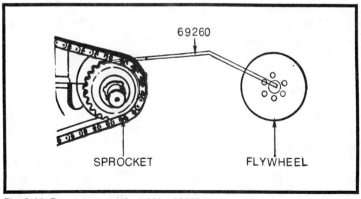

Fig. 6-22. Peugeot special tool No. 69260 is a convenience when removing the engine.

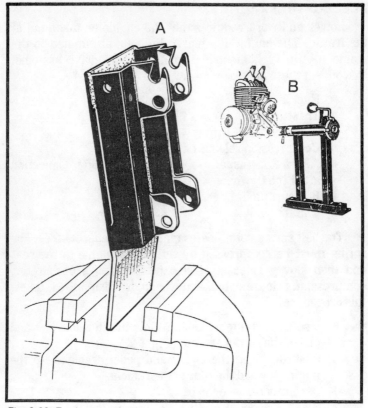

Fig. 6-23. Engine stands range from the spartan Velosolex model (view A) to the elaborate Peugeot stand which allows the engine to be rotated.

6. Carefully undo the support plate fixing bolts, completely disarming the spring.
7. Push out the engine holddown bolt with a 9.5 mm diameter rod, which locks the support arm in place.
8. Now pull the rod back far enough to release the engine. Once the engine is free, insert the rod its full length through the control arm.

Drain the transmission and snug down the drain plug (more than one engine has been lunched by a drain plug that was run in fingertight and forgotten). Clean oil and road grime from the engine castings. These and subsequent operations go faster if the engine is mounted in a holding fixture. Figure 6-23 shows a simple, easy-to-fabricate stand and a top-of-the-line, fully adjustable model.

CRANKCASE

Moped engines are traditionally split vertically through a parting line that divides the crankcases into left- and right-hand pairs. Puch and Sachs engines are built on the more modern horizontal pattern, with the parting line passing through the main bearings. With the exception of Velosolex (discussed in a separate section below) vertically split engines are difficult to open since rotating components—flywheel, sprocket, clutch drum, and the like—must be removed from at least one end of the shafts, and main and transmission bearings are pressed into the crankcase halves.

Vertical pattern

Unless the engine is to be completely stripped, work from the flywheel side. Flywheel removal has been described in the previous chapter. The operations here carry things one step

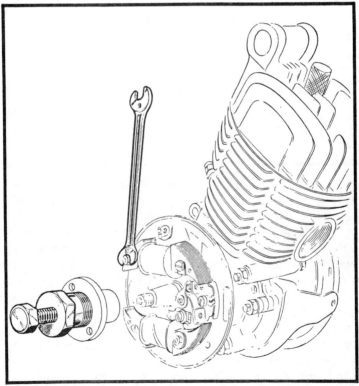

Fig. 6-24. Removing a Motorbecane stator plate. The plate and block should be indexed to ensure correct timing upon reassembly.

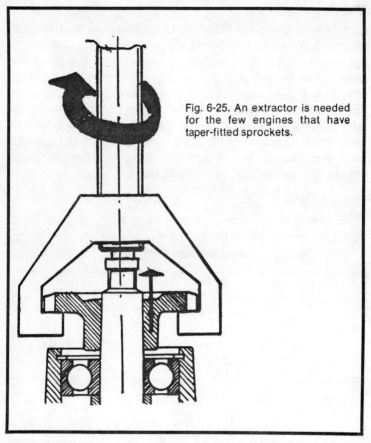

Fig. 6-25. An extractor is needed for the few engines that have taper-fitted sprockets.

further and involve disassembly of the stator plate (Fig. 6-24). Mark the stator and the crankcase so that proper timing will be retained when the engine is reassembled.

Clutch and Pedal Assembly. Remove at least one pedal arm assembly, tapping out the pinch bolt with a brass punch, and file any burrs that may be left on the pedal shaft. Burrs could damage the oil seal. If required, remove the sprocket and the clutch assembly. Most sprockets are held by bolts and splines; a few have the additional security of a taper fit. Figure 6-25 shows a sprocket extractor. Clutches are (almost universally) pressed on tapered shafts; a few are held by splines and snap (Seegar) rings. Pressed clutches are withdrawn with a smaller version of the familiar flywheel extractor. These tools are sometimes available from bicycle dealers as well as moped distributors.

Crankcase Disassembly. The cases are held together by four lines of defense—through-bolts, alignment pins, gasket binds, and the press-fit of the main bearings. Through-bolts are no particular problem: once the nuts are loosened, the bolts can be tapped out with a soft drift. Nor should the pins be of much concern; however, if the pin holes are open on both sides, the pins can be driven out, releasing some tension on the case halves. The gasket will just have to be broken. But the press-fit of the main bearings is a major difficulty which has to be overcome without damage to the shafts or case. There are three ways to do this:

1. The bearing fit on some engines is loose enough that the cases can be jarred apart with a soft mallet. A few glancing blows around the edges of the castings softens things up; the job is finished by driving the crankshaft stub out. Figure 6-26 shows the operation on a Garelli engine.

2. A variation on this technique is to heat the casting adjacent to the bearing with a propane torch (Fig. 6-27). The illustration shows a Motorbecane crankcase half with a single bearing; if you are dealing with a case that supports a transmission bearing as well, it too must be heated. Keep the torch circling around the bearing bosses and stops when the

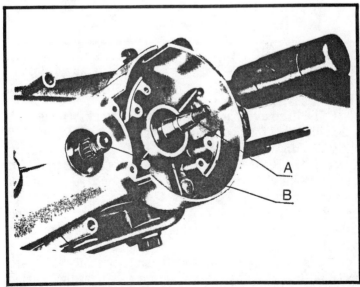

Fig. 6-26. Garelli engines can be opened with a soft-faced mallet applied to the crankshaft (A) and output shaft (B) ends.

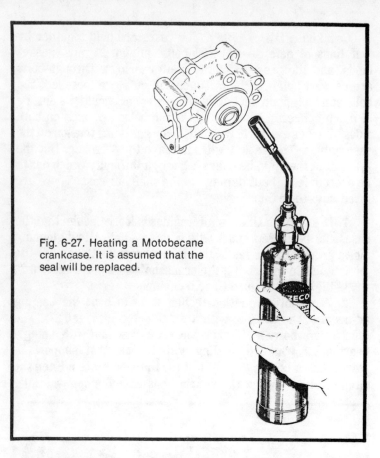

Fig. 6-27. Heating a Motobecane crankcase. It is assumed that the seal will be replaced.

case begins to smoke. Too much heat will fatally distort it. Once the case has expanded, relaxing its grip on the bearings, drive the shafts out with a mallet.

3. The third alternative is to press the crankshaft out with a threaded tool that bolts to the engine casting. Figure 6-28 illustrates three such tools. The first drawing shows an extractor for Peugeot engines; the second, a similar tool sized for the Minarelli V1; the third drawing illustrates a nearly universal model from Bolger Manufacturing. Intended to service Honda 125/250-cc motorcycles, the Bolger tool can be drilled to fit most moped engines. It is available from cycle dealers.

Bearings. The bearings remain on their shafts which are anchored to a case half. Look very carefully at the bearing bosses on the loose case half. Axial scores—scores running the same direction as the centerlines of the shafts—are caused by forcing the bearings out of the case. Unless the aluminum is plowed and raised, axial scores have no significance. If high spots are present, smooth them with a fine half-round file to make assembly easier.

Radial scores—running around the inner diameter of the bosses—mean trouble. The bearing races have broken the

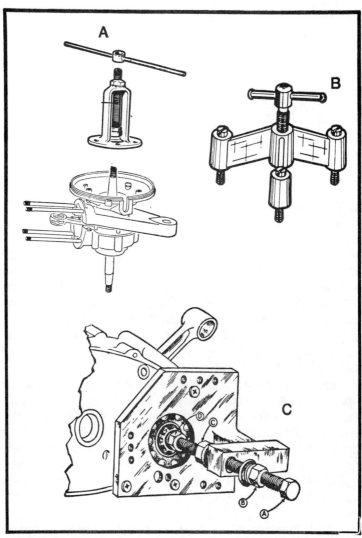

Fig. 6-28. Crankshaft extractor tools from Peugeot (view A), Minarelli (view B), and Bolger Manufacturing (view C).

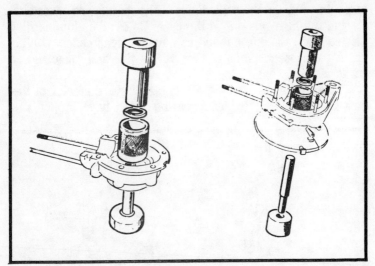

Fig. 6-29. Peugeot tools make seal installation almost foolproof. Each side of the engine is dimensioned differently and requires its own anvils, pilots, and drivers.

interference fit on their bosses, either because the bearings have failed or because the boss diameter and the outer diameter of the races was not controlled properly during manufacture. Disassemble the other side of the engine to check the bosses there. If the bosses are badly spun, look around for another engine. But slight wear, on the order of 0.010 inch, can be corrected by coating the outside diameter of the bearing races with Loctite Stud n' Seal just before assembly. Once the parts are bolted down and air is excluded, Loctite hardens and holds the bearings fast. Do not get any Loctite on the rollers and balls.

Seals. New seals must be installed each time the cases are opened. Pry out the old ones with a screwdriver, being careful not to scratch the seal bosses. Seals are installed with the cupped side outboard, away from crankcase pressure. Factory code numbers are on the side from which the seal is driven. Seal drivers exist and should be used whenever possible. Figure 6-29 shows a collection of Peugeot drivers and pilots for the right- and left-hand cases. A more typical driver is shown in Fig. 6-30.

While factory tools make the work easier and help prevent the embarrassment of leaking seals on a newly overhauled engine, they are not absolutely essential. If the truth were

194

known, probably most rebuilt moped engines have had their seals installed with a wooden dowel.

The seal must go home flat and to the same depth as the original. Some mechanics coat the seal boss with gasket cement. Once the seal is installed, the excess cement must be wiped off and the seal lips lubricated with clean motor oil or transmission fluid. Protect the lips by covering crankshaft keyways, splines, and other sharp irregularities with a layer of masking tape.

Gasket. Mount a new gasket on one crankcase half; the gasket should be soaked in oil first. Heat the bearing bosses on the outboard case, using a large washer to shield the new seal from flame. If one is available, use an extractor tool to pull the crankshaft and inner case into the outer case. Figure 6-31 illustrates the Peugeot setup for this operation. The end of the tool is threaded over the crankshaft and the spacer distributes stress over the circumference of the bearing boss.

Velosolex Vertical Pattern

Velosolex crankcases are split vertically, but other structural features of this engine put it in a class by itself. Once the cylinder barrel, fuel tank, fuel line, muffler, and

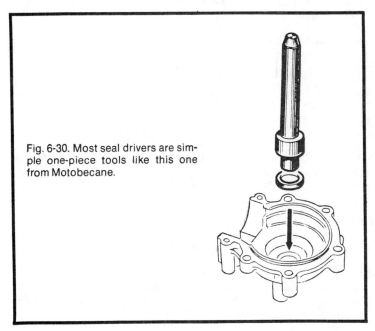

Fig. 6-30. Most seal drivers are simple one-piece tools like this one from Motobecane.

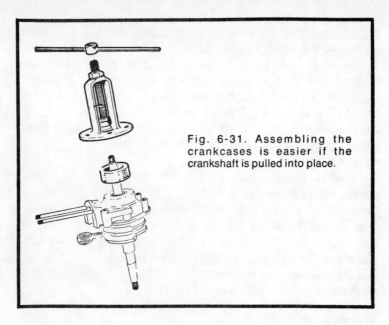

Fig. 6-31. Assembling the crankcases is easier if the crankshaft is pulled into place.

carburetor are dismantled, opening the engine is merely a matter of removing the cover plate over the crankcase (Fig. 6-32). The plate is secured by eight capscrews and gasketed. It does not support the crankshaft, which rides on a single large bearing just inboard of the flywheel. Assemble with a new

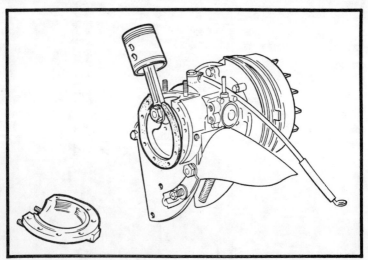

Fig. 6-32. Velosolex engines are unique in many ways, not the least of which is the absence of a second main bearing.

gasket and, working diagonally, torque the capscrews to 0.75 kgm (5.4 ft-lb).

In the event that you need to disassemble the power-takeoff side of the engine, fix the crankshaft with a stroke limiter, available from Velosolex as part No. 01213. Remove the drive roller, clutch, and oil seal. (These operations are described in detail in the next chapter.) Index the stator plate and crankcase to hold the timing dimension. Using Velosolex tool No. 00195, withdraw the stator plate, twisting it as shown in Fig. 6-33. Heat the crankcase at the bearing boss with a propane torch. When the case begins to smoke, it is warm enough and the crankshaft can be driven out with a few mallet blows.

Horizontal Pattern

Puch and Sachs engines have horizontally split crankcases that can be opened as easily as a can of sardines. Drain the transmission lubricant, remove the cylinder barrel and external engine covers, and undo the holddown screws or bolts. The upper crankcase casting lifts off. Crankshaft, bearings, seals, connecting rod, and piston come out as an assembly.

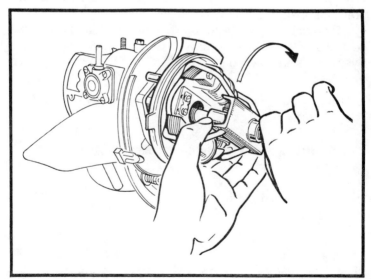

Fig. 6-33. The Velosolex stator plate is removed with special tool No. 01213.

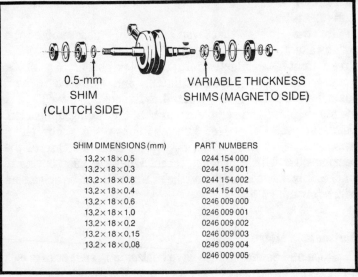

SHIM DIMENSIONS (mm)   PART NUMBERS

SHIM DIMENSIONS (mm)	PART NUMBERS
13.2 × 18 × 0.5	0244 154 000
13.2 × 18 × 0.3	0244 154 001
13.2 × 18 × 0.8	0244 154 002
13.2 × 18 × 0.4	0244 154 004
13.2 × 18 × 0.6	0246 009 000
13.2 × 18 × 1.0	0246 009 001
13.2 × 18 × 0.2	0246 009 002
13.2 × 18 × 0.15	0246 009 003
13.2 × 18 × 0.08	0246 009 004
	0246 009 005

Fig. 6-34. The shim arrangement for the Sachs 501/1 series engine.

Clean the crankcases in solvent and carefully inspect the bearing bosses for evidence that the bearings have spun. Loctite Stud n' Seal will compensate for some bearing wear and, as long as the bearings themselves are serviceable, will prevent reoccurrence of the problem.

The Sachs engine is set up to eliminate end loads on the bearings (Fig. 6-34). Clearance between the bearings and the flywheels is zero, or should be. There are three dimensions involved:

- distance between the outer edges of the bearings   57.75 mm (2.273 in.)

- distance between the outer edges of the flywheels   34.20 mm (1.346 in.)

- combined width of the bearings   22.00 mm (0.866 in.)

Adding the distance between the 'wheels and the width of the bearings determines how thick the shims should be. In the case above, the bearings and flywheels account for 56.20 mm (2.212 in.)—1.55 mm (0.061 in.) shy of the 57.75-mm requirement. The shortfall must be supplied by shims. Place the shims between

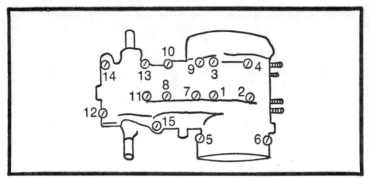

Fig. 6-35. Sachs has developed this torque sequence to prevent crankcase distortion.

the bearings and the flywheels, with the 0.5 mm (0.020 in.) shim on the clutch side and any others needed on the magneto side. Once the crankshaft is shimmed, it can be installed in the lower case. Snug up all the fasteners and, following the sequence in Fig. 6-35, torque to 1.0-1.2 kgm (7.2-8.7 ft-lb).

Puch engines are assembled without reference to thrust washers (other than to be sure that any which are present remain). The only variable is the position of the magneto-side crankshaft seal. It must be approximately a quarter inch outboard of the main bearing; otherwise the bearing will starve for oil (Fig. 6-36).

MAIN BEARINGS

Anti-friction (ball and roller) bearings are manufactured with a clearance of approximately 0.0005 in. between the races

Fig. 6-36. Leave a generous clearance between the main bearing and flywheel-side seal on the Puch engine.

199

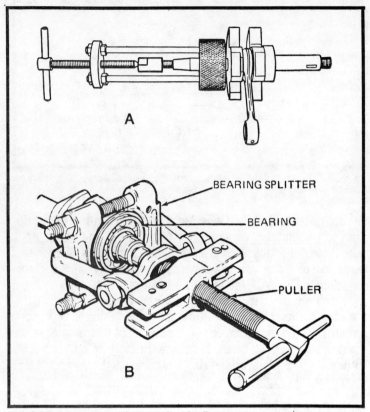

A

BEARING SPLITTER

BEARING

PULLER

B

Fig. 6-37. A bearing puller supplied by Batavus (view A) and the more readily available bearing splitter.

and rolling elements. Unfortunately, changes in clearance cannot be measured directly, and the mechanic must rely on intuition and experience.

The bearings must be clean and dry for assembly. Use a good grade of solvent—trichlorethylene if you have it—and allow the bearings to air-dry: rags or paper towels dirty the bearings with lint and dust. Drying can be speeded with filtered compressed air; the air line should have at least one recently serviced water trap between the nozzle and the compressor. Play the air stream over the bearings, but not against the races. Bearings spinning under a jet of high pressure air generate interesting gyroscopic effects, but almost always are damaged in the process.

Using a wooden dowel, try to pry the outer race off the balls. If the race comes free easily, you can be sure the bearing is worn out of tolerance. Slowly turn the outer races. If the action is rough or catchy, replace the bearing.

Main bearings do not wear at the same rate. The power takeoff bearing takes the worst beating and, unless there is a problem such as a bent crankshaft or off-balance flywheel, should fail first. But it is only reasonable to replace main bearings as a set.

Figure 6-37 shows a Batavus-supplied bearing puller. It is typical of moped tools in that the jaws are very thin to reach behind bearings that are cheek-to-jowl with the flywheels. Tools of this type must be ordered from the importer. The bearing splitter in view B is an auto mechanic's tool that can be adapted to all but the most crowded moped engines. Bearing splitters are available from auto supply houses and from most franchised rental agencies.

In any event, do not give in to impatience and try to wedge the bearings loose. You may get them off this way, but the crankshaft will suffer in the process.

Heat the replacement bearings in a container of oil, keeping the temperature well under the boiling point. The bearings should be supported on a wire mesh, so that they do not come into contact with the sides and bottom of the container. And, for reasons of safety, the operation should be carried on outdoors. Install the warm bearings with the help of a driver (Fig. 6-38). You can use a factory tool or a clean length of pipe whose diameter matches the the inner race. Do not apply force to the balls or outer race. The side of the bearing that has been reinforced to withstand the rigors of installation carries an identification number and the manufacturer's logo. The inboard side is blank and, depending upon the machine, may have a distinctive profile (Fig. 6-39).

CRANKSHAFT

Mopeds use built-up crankshafts with the crankpin pressed into the flywheels. This means that the connecting rod is stronger than it would otherwise be and that there is potential for crankshaft misalignment. It also means that replacing the crankpin (big end) bearings is a formidable operation on machines other than the Velosolex.

Alignment

Serious misalignment can be detected with the crankshaft installed. Mount a dial indicator on the casting as shown in

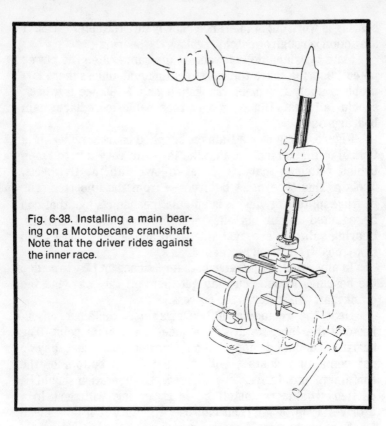

Fig. 6-38. Installing a main bearing on a Motobecane crankshaft. Note that the driver rides against the inner race.

Fig. 6-40 and watch the needle deflection as the crank is turned. A total deflection of more than 0.002 inch should be corrected. Repeat the operation on the other end of the crankshaft.

A more accurate method, and one that *must* be used if the crank is to be straightened, involves two precision V-blocks and a pair of dial indicators. The position of the dial indicators, the distance of the V-blocks from the flywheels, and the distance between the wheels are critical dimensions, although the last one is sacrificed for shaft alignment (Fig. 6-41). In other words, some wheel wobble is tolerated to make the shafts run true.

The wheels are pried away from each other with wooden wedges and the distance between them closed with a C-clamp or with judicious blows from a brass hammer. Figure 6-42 shows the relationship between indicator readings and wheel spacing.

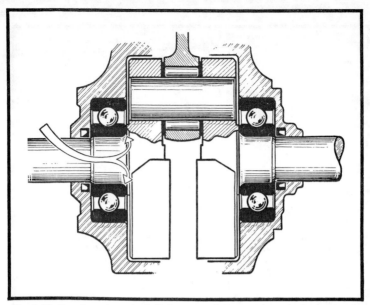

Fig. 6-39. Bearings have a definite up and down side as indicated by the manufacturer's name and bearing identification code. Motobecane is restrictively definite and has arranged matters so the bearings will seize if installed wrong.

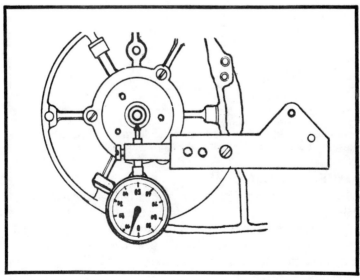

Fig. 6-40. Dial indicator readings with the crankshaft installed give some notion of crankshaft alignment, although the results are compromised by main bearing wear.

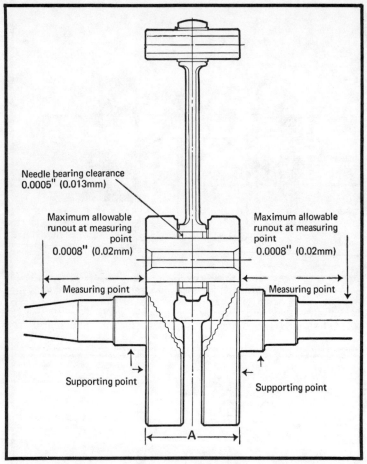

Needle bearing clearance
0.0005" (0.013mm)

Maximum allowable
runout at measuring
point
0.0008" (0.02mm)

Maximum allowable
runout at measuring
point
0.0008" (0.02mm)

Measuring point

Measuring point

Supporting point

Supporting point

A

Fig. 6-41. For best accuracy, the crankshaft should be cradled on precision-ground V-blocks, spaced equidistantly from the flywheels. Dial indicators mounted near the ends of the stub shafts complete the set-up.

CONNECTING ROD BEARING

Play in the big-end bearing can be detected once the cylinder barrel is off. (See "Cylinder Barrels" for details.) As a further check, spin the rod completely around the crankpin. Roughness or rattle means that the bearings and, possibly, the crankpin and connecting rod must be replaced.

Velosolex

Install the stroke limiter (or an equivalent metric bolt) in the side of the crankcase as shown in Fig. 6-43. Mark the

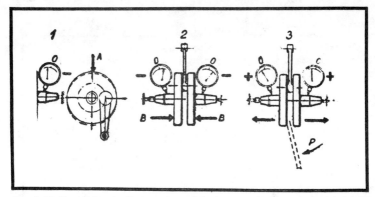

Fig. 6-42. Possible misalignments and their cures: If one stub shaft is high, drive its flywheel down with a brass hammer (view A); If both shafts are low, squeeze the wheels together (view B); if both shafts are high, pry the wheels apart. Note that the crankpin is the fulcrum around which the adjustments are made.

outboard side of the piston as an assembly aid. Remove the 14-mm nut and washer. Lift the piston off the crankpin and extract the bushing. Install a new bushing—flat side toward the crank web—and flood the assembly with oil. Install the

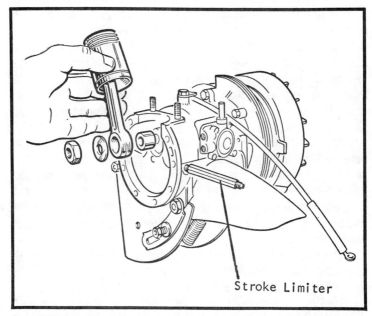

Stroke Limiter

Fig. 6-43. Velosolex connecting rods are secured by a single 14-mm nut and thrust washer.

Table 6-5. Jawa Babetta Connecting Rod, Crankpin Bearing, and
Crankpin Compatibility

Connecting rod	Assembly groups						
I	10 A	9 B	8 C	7 D	6 E	Roller	Pin
II	9 A	8 B	7 C	6 D	5 E	Roller	Pin
III	8 A	7 B	6 C	5 D	4 E	Roller	Pin
IV	7 A	6 B	5 C	4 D	3 E	Roller	Pin
V	6.7 A	5.6 B	4.5 C	3.4 D	2.3 E	Roller	Pin

connecting rod, washer, and nut. In severely worn engines the
washer and connecting rod should also be replaced. Torque the
nut to 1.70 kgm (12.3 ft-lb).

Other Engines

Any moped crankshaft can be disassembled with the help
of a 10-ton arbor press, but most manufacturers do not trust
service personnel with this exacting work. The factory
provides exchange crankshaft assemblies (Batavus) or simply
sells the customer a new crankshaft assembly, already aligned
and ready to be installed. Other manufacturers will provide
crankpins, big end bearing sets, and connecting rods, but
complications arise when parts are installed separately and
not as matched sets.

Table 6-5 illustrates the choices available for the Babetta
engine. Thre are five connecting rods, graded by the diameter
of the big-end bearing surface, five crankpins, and 13,
count 'em, 13 roller bearing diameters. If you have a grade I
con rod, a grade 6 roller set, and a grade D pin, the clearance
will be wrong. With that rod and roller set only a grade E pin
works.

The factories are a long way from American shores and it
is always wise to obtain the parts before the crankshaft is
dismantled. Note the depth of the pin in the face of the
flywheels; on most the pin is flush and never stands proud of
the wheels. Mount the crankshaft in a fixture, supporting the

inside cheek of the uppermost wheel. Mark the wheels with a straight edge and chalk as an assembly guide. Press the pin out of one wheel and then out of the remaining one. Press a new pin in place, mount the bearing and connecting rod. Press work is finished when the remaining wheel is installed. Align the crankshaft as described above and flood the new bearing with oil before installing the crankshaft in the engine.

Chapter 7
Drive Line

Power is transmitted in strange and devious ways in a moped. There are two power sources—human and mechanical. Human power is used to start the engine, help it when it falters, and, if necessary, can become the sole means of propulsion. The engine is the primary power source, connected to the rear wheel by means of an automatic clutch. In addition, some mopeds have automatic torque-multiplying transmissions, so the engine can operate at its most efficient rpm regardless of the forward speed of the vehicle.

CENTRIFUGAL CLUTCHES

The basic clutch mechanism is centrifugal, engaging in response to engine or pedal crank speed. The details vary enormously between makes, but all have these features in common:

- A central hub or yoke that turns at engine speed.
- A drum which is connected to the load.
- Friction shoes or plates that connect the hub with the drum.
- An override mechanism to transfer power from rider to the engine to start it. The override may be at the clutch or at some remote spot on the drive line.

Now we'll take a look at several popular clutches.

Batavus M 48

The M 48 clutch has been very influential in moped technology; one manufacturer has gone so far as to produce an almost identical copy.

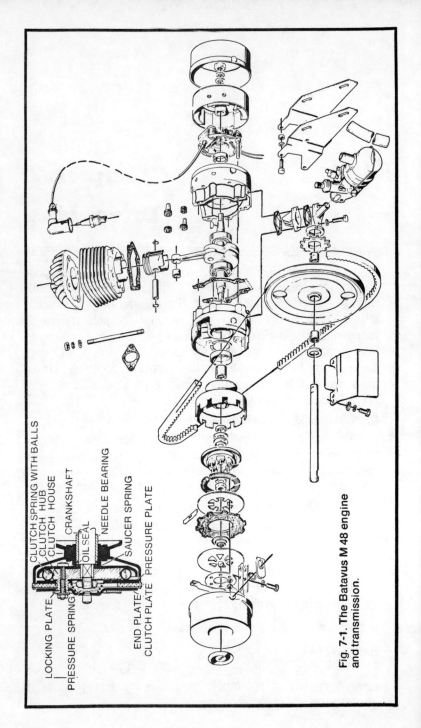

CLUTCH SPRING WITH BALLS
CLUTCH HUB
CLUTCH HOUSE
CRANKSHAFT
OIL SEAL
NEEDLE BEARING
SAUCER SPRING

LOCKING PLATE
PRESSURE SPRING

END PLATE
CLUTCH PLATE / PRESSURE PLATE

Fig. 7-1. The Batavus M 48 engine and transmission.

Operation. The clutch hub, spring, pressure plate, and end plate turn with the crankshaft (Fig. 7-1). The "house," or drum and clutch plate, are connected to the rear wheel by a belt and chain. At low engine speeds the drum floats on the crankshaft, insulated from motion by the needle bearing. As speed increases, ball bearings packed into the clutch spring feel the tug of centrifugal force and move outward, stretching the spring in the process. Ramps on the outer edge of the clutch hub divert this outward motion; the balls push to the left against the pressure plate. While the plate turns at engine speed with the hub, its splines allow some axial movement, and the plate contacts the right-hand friction surface on the clutch plate. The drum begins to receive power. Continued motion of the balls forces the clutch plate to the right where it contacts the end plate. Since the end plate is bolted to the crankshaft, no further axial movement is possible; the clutch plate is sandwiched between the pressure and end plates. Full torque goes to the drum and, hence, to the back wheel.

The starting lever displaces the end, clutch, and pressure plates to the right. Once the pressure plate butts against the spring and ball assembly, no further axial movement is possible: the clutch plate is trapped between the two hub-mounted plates. Power enters at the hub, passes through the clutch plate, and then to the crankshaft.

Service. The only internal adjustment is the clearance between the override lever and the thrust button. Bend the lever to obtain 2.0 mm (0.80 in.) clearance in the disengaged position (Fig. 7-2).

Upon disassembly, clean the parts in solvent—except the clutch disc which should not be wetted. Clutch slippage problems can usually be corrected by replacing the disc. Refusal to disengage completely or harsh, abrupt engagement most often involves the end and side plates. Replace if the plates are warped, scored, or streaked with blue temper marks. Small imperfections can be polished out with crocus cloth. Check the needle bearing for excessive play and, if necessary, replace with a new bearing, driven in from the marked side. Fill the bearing with high temperature grease or heavy transmission oil. Oil the hub, ball and spring assembly, and bronze thrust piece, but do not get any oil on the disc or the pressure sides of the plates.

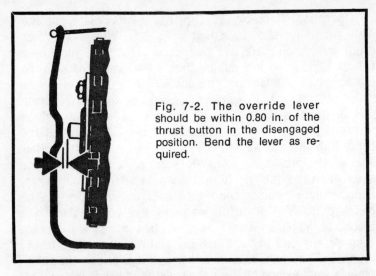

Fig. 7-2. The override lever should be within 0.80 in. of the thrust button in the disengaged position. Bend the lever as required.

Note: Use the seal protector shown in Fig. 7-3 when mounting the hub. Otherwise the seal may be damaged, a condition that leads to bearing failure from loss of lubricant.

Jawa

The Jawa clutch employs shoes rather than a friction disc.

Operation. There are two sets of shoes: the outboard assembly connects the engine with the drive train; the inboard

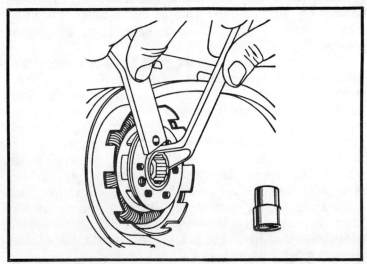

Fig. 7-3. The M 48 clutch wrench and seal protector.

set transfers power from the pedals, via the drive chain. Figure 7-4 shows the arrangement of parts. The flywheel (1), drive clutch shoes (3), segment carrier (4), and sleeve (5) are fixed to the crankshaft and turn with it. The starting shoes (6) and the clutch drum (7) are geared to the drive system and can turn independently of the crankshaft.

During starting, power enters the clutch drum, spinning it and the starting shoes which are pivoted on the drum. At approximately 600 rpm the starting shoes engage the inner lip of the segment carrier, turning it and the flywheel. Once the engine catches, power enters through the segment carrier. The drive clutch shoes pivot out against the garter spring and meet the clutch drum.

Service. Remove the flywheel bolt and the three clutch holddown bolts (Fig. 7-5A). Lift the flywheel off and, using special tool No. 975 1000 1.2, withdraw the segment carrier (Fig. 7-5B). (A substitute for this tool is a steel plate drilled for the segment carrier bolts with a large nut welded over the center.) Remove the sleeve with a small gear puller (Fig. 7-5C); if the shoes are to be separated, assemble them on their springs before installation. Pick out the oil seal and withdraw the drum (Fig. 7-5E).

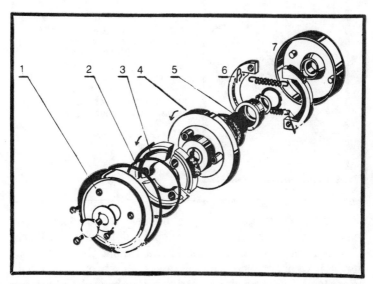

Fig. 7-4. The Jawa clutch is tucked neatly under the flywheel. 1-flywheel; 2-garter (shoe-return) spring; 3-drive clutch shoes; 4-segment carrier; 5-sleeve; 6-starting shoes; 7-clutch drum.

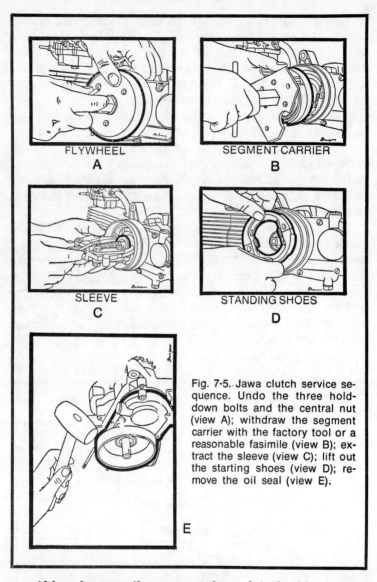

FLYWHEEL
A

SEGMENT CARRIER
B

SLEEVE
C

STANDING SHOES
D

Fig. 7-5. Jawa clutch service sequence. Undo the three hold-down bolts and the central nut (view A); withdraw the segment carrier with the factory tool or a reasonable fasimile (view B); extract the sleeve (view C); lift out the starting shoes (view D); remove the oil seal (view E);

E

Although some oil seeps past the seal, it should not get on the friction surfaces. If the seal should fail, the clutch will drip oil. Engagement will be sudden and harsh, and the drive shoes may smoke under load. The seal and both sets of shoes should be replaced; in a pinch you can replace the seal and dry the linings with repeated applications of Berkebile 2 + 2 Gum Cutter.

Unless there is an oil problem, the starting shoes can be ignored: they get little wear. The drive shoes should be replaced long before the lining has worn down to metal, for once this happens, the drum will be ruined. Early signs of wear are late engagement and clutch slip on hills.

A stretched garter spring allows the drive shoes to engage early, before the engine is up to speed. Replace the spring and examine the shoes and drum for signs of overheating.

Peugeot

The Peugeot clutch is uniquely Peugeot with features that are shared by none other, yet it is a very practical device, having proved itself over millions of miles.

Operation. Figure 7-6 illustrates the mechanism in cutaway and exploded views. It must be remembered that the clutch drum C and ball drum D bolt to the crankshaft and turn

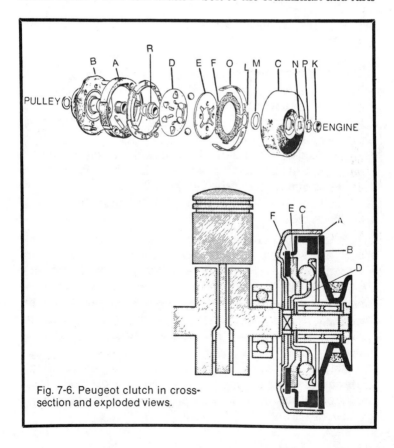

Fig. 7-6. Peugeot clutch in cross-section and exploded views.

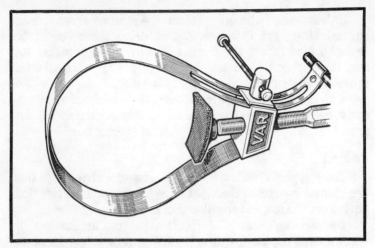

Fig. 7-7. A flywheel holder supplied by Motobecane.

with it. Starting shoes A and clutch disc F turn with the drive pulley B.

During starting, power flows from the pedals to the drive pulley. At about 5 mph the starting shoes A cam out against the drum C, locking the pulley and crankshaft. Once the engine starts, the six ball bearings move out toward the edge of the spinning ball drum D. The bearings are confined to teardrop shaped holes; as they move outward, they cam out of the holes and press against the plate E. The plate moves the clutch disc F against a lip on the inner edge of the drum. Power flows from the drum, to the disc, and through splines on the rim of the disc to the drive pulley. The star spring keeps the plate away from the disc at low rpm.

Service. The clutch mechanism is essentially the same for single- and variable-ratio machines. Hold the clutch drum with a strap wrench (Fig. 7-7) and remove the 17-mm nut (right-hand thread, overhand and left to loosen). Remove the washers and replace the nut with special tool No. 69142. This tool keeps things together when the pulley is removed and takes the guess work out of clutch adjustments. Remove the pulley.

Holding the ball drum D and plate E with one hand, unthread the special tool and pull the clutch drum off. Mark the outboard side of the clutch disc if it is to be reused. Remove parts in this order:

1. disc F
2. spring L
3. adjusting washer M
4. drum C
5. washer N

Place the pulley assembly on a bench, pulley down. Remove the nuts holding the locking ring O and lockwashers, and remove the locking ring. Unhook the springs from the studs in the shoes, noting which of the two studs was used (the first is for direct-drive machines; the second for variable-ratio models).

The shoes are a little tricky. Lightly lubricate the shoe pivot anchors. Assemble the springs on the shoes, with the large hooked ends secured by the slots in the shoes. Mount the shoes on their anchors and hook the small ends of the springs over the appropriate pins. Correctly installed, the open sides of the hooks face toward the center of pulley plate B. Secure the shoes to the plate with two 5-mm nuts and lockwashers. The nuts must be turned so their sides are clear of the clutch disc.

Assemble the rest of the mechanism, reversing the disassembly sequence. Torque the outboard nut 4.0 ts kgm (28.9 ft-lb) and test. If the clutch behaves abnormally—engaging harshly or slipping under load—it will be necessary to check the clearance between pressure plate E and disc F. There are at least three ways to do this.

1. The clutch can be partially assembled with the help of special tools Nos. 69140 and 69141. This is the currently accepted shop practice.
2. The clutch can be assembled in reverse of normal order on the crankshaft. One special tool, formerly available as No. 42018, is needed. This tool can be fabricated from a discarded clutch drum.
3. Assemble the clutch with modeling clay between the pressure plate and the clutch lining. Disassemble and measure the thickness of the clay.

The specification is 0.5-0.7 mm (0.020-0.028 in.). Correct by substituting a different-thickness adjusting washer.

Thickness	Washer Part Number
0.40 mm	45818
0.60 mm	45819
0.80 mm	45820
1.00 mm	45821

If you use method 1, place the assembling shaft 69141 vertically in a vise and assemble these parts on it:

- Washer N
- Adjusting plate No. 69140
- Adjusting washer M
- Spring L
- Disc F
- Pressure plate E
- Balls
- Ball drum D
- Nut

If you choose method 2, turn the engine on its side and assemble the parts in this inverted order:

- Hub ring R
- Ball drum D
- Balls
- Pressure plate E
- Clutch plate F
- Spring L
- Adjusting washer M
- Special tool No. 42018
- Washer N
- Washer P
- Nut K

Method 3 is, as you could expect, the most laborious. The clutch must be disassembled, assembled with modeling clay between disc F and the inboard side of drum C, disassembled again to remove the clay, and assembled one more time.

TRANSMISSIONS

One of the characteristics of mopeds is the high reduction ratio between the engine and the back wheel. The engine may scream at 5000 rpm-plus, but the road speed of the vehicle must be kept under 30 mph. The reduction is accomplished by gears or a pulley-and-belt arrangement. Some machines combine a belt with gears. Most transmissions give a single ratio between the engine and the driving wheel; a few have variable speeds, selected automatically in response to engine rpm.

Belt Drives

The traditional moped (on the French model) uses a V-belt to transmit engine power to the drive sprocket. While this system may look primitive, it has some real advantages. Belt drive is silent, vibration-free, and tends to isolate the crankshaft and main bearings from drive shocks.

Service. The belt must be replaced at intervals. It is a good idea to carry a second belt, wrapped in aluminum foil, on the machine. The aluminum foil will keep the belt dry and free of oil, and will help to protect if from ozone attack.

V-belts transmit power by wedging their angled sides against the edges of the pulley grooves. In time the belt wears and sinks deeper into the grooves, changing the ratio slightly. A machine with a worn belt will have a marginally higher speed than one that has just been fitted with a new belt; conversely, the bike with the new belt should have slightly better acceleration. Wear becomes serious when it is localized; when the flanks of the belt show dips and depressions, or when wear has progressed until the belt rides on the base of the pulley groove. Should this happen, the belt becomes a flat belt, with very little capacity to transmit power.

Belt dressing is one of those shade-tree fixes that help in the short run and cause additional problems down the road. This product, available from auto supply houses in aerosol cans, contains a powerful solvent that makes the belt stickier and better able to transmit power. In the process the belt is softened and wears more rapidly. But it works and will get you home.

Pulley grooves also wear and contribute to the early demise of the belt. The groove flanks should be flat and narrow enough so the belt is supported well above the base of the groove. Wear is more pronounced on the engine pulley, the smaller of the two.

Adjustment. Too much belt tension defeats the wedging action of the belt and loads the crankshaft and pulley bearings; too little tension allows the belt to hump and slip. Some machines do not have provision for belt adjustment, either because of the maker's confidence in steel-cored belts or because adjustment is maintained automatically by means of a spring. Peugeot and Motobecane are examples of the latter method: the engines are pivoted against springs.

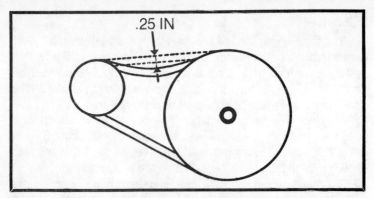

Fig. 7-8. Correct belt tension is important. (Courtesy Batavus Bikeways, Inc.)

In any event, the belt should have approximately one-quarter-inch play under light thumb pressure (Fig. 7-8). The engine is the movable element; the large pulley remains fixed to the frame. Figure 7-9 shows a very elegant tool used to pivot the engine away from the large pulley. The next drawing (Fig. 7-10) illustrates the Batavus procedure. Once the engine holddown bolts are slacked off, a 5-mm rod is inserted into hole A. Lever B rests against this rod and, moved as shown, pivots the engine forward.

Belt-Driven Variable-Speed Transmission

A belt running on fixed pulleys has some built-in ability to multiply torque. Figure 7-11 shows two pulleys with identical

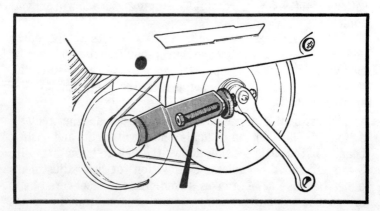

Fig. 7-9. A tool like this is convenient when adjusting belts against spring tension.

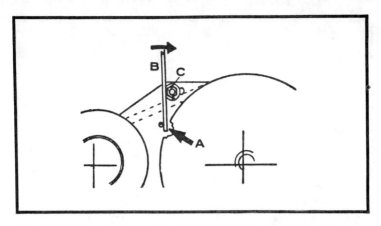

Fig. 7-10. Batavus belts are adjusted with the help of a rod A and lever B.

diameters. Under load, the lower side of the belt tenses and the upper side relaxes. The belt burrows more deeply into the driven pulley and flings outward on the drive pulley. The effective diameters of the pulleys change: the drive pulley becomes larger and the driven pulley shrinks. Torque, or turning force, is multiplied.

While this feature is useful and gives a tractability to belt-driven machines that is absent with gear or friction drives, real torque multiplication requires some mechanical

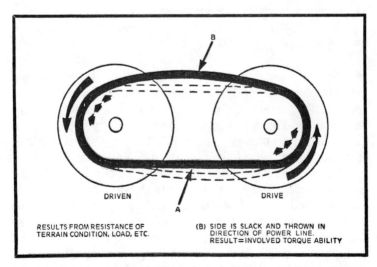

Fig. 7-11. Fixed pulleys benefit from some self-induced torque multiplication. (Courtesy Bombardier Ltd.)

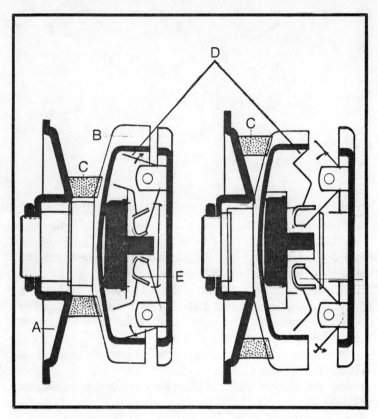

Fig. 7-12. Peugeot speed-sensitive pulley. A-fixed pulley flange; B-movable flange; C-drive belt; D-flyweights

means of changing pulley diameter. Variable-speed transmissions, sometimes called variators, are used on snowmibiles, a few motorcycles, and on at least two light automobiles. These transmissions offer a fairly wide range of ratios and are entirely "stepless." That is, one ratio blends into another without plateaus or steps.

Figure 7-12 illustrates an example from Peugeot. The inboard pulley flange (A) is fixed; the outboard flange (B) moves in and out. At low engine speeds, belt C rides low in the pulley groove, giving a low ratio for starting. As engine rpm increases, centrifugal force pivots the flyweights D out radially, camming the outboard flange inward. The belt is spring-loaded, and thus can respond by climbing higher in the groove. As it does, the ratio is raised for less torque multiplication and more speed. Should the engine bog, rpm falls off, the flyweights relax their pressure on the flange, and the belt burrows deeper into the pulley groove. This device enables the Peugoet 103 LVS-U3 to climb an 18% grade, yet reach 30 mph on level stretches.

Very little maintenance is required of this and similar transmissions. The main concern is the belt, which must be replaced if it shows excessive wear or becomes oil-soaked. The flyweight assembly should be coated with high-pressure grease at the pivots and cam ramps.

Gear Drives

Gear drives may be single-stage or multistage. Single-stage transmissions have one gear pair between the crankshaft and engine sprocket; multistage units have two or more gear pairs in tandem. Figure 7-13 shows power flow through the Jawa Babetta in schematic form. Power leaves the crankshaft by way of a 20-tooth gear meshed with a 34-tooth for a ratio of 1.7 to 1. From there power passes through a second set of gears giving an additional reduction of 3 to 1. The overall reduction is 5.1 to 1. Puch gets a similar ratio from a single stage—a tiny engine gear turns a monstrous wheel on the drive side.

Service. Inspect the gear teeth for wear, giving particular attention to evidence of flaking. Sometimes it appears as if the surface metal has peeled, as indeed it has. One problem with moped (and motorcycle) technology is the unwillingness of

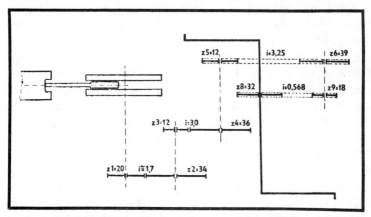

Fig. 7-13. Power flow through the Jawa transmission and rear wheel hub. The numbers represent ratios at each stage.

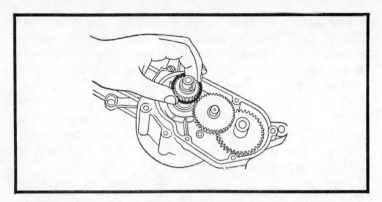

Fig. 7-14. Floating gears can be lifted from their shafts, as is being done here on a Jawa, but watch out for loose needle bearings.

many manufacturers to use the proper alloys. A very soft gear steel is surface-hardened for a few thousandths of an inch. Once this "skin" is broken, the gear rapidly fails. Normally, the damage is limited to the smaller gear of a pair; however, when one meshed gear gives way, the other must be replaced as well, for used gears do not survive long in the company of new ones.

Floating gears—gears that are free to idle—can be removed from their shafts once the bolt or spring clip is undone (Fig. 7-14). However, these gears may float on uncaged needle bearings and some care must be exercised not to lose any of the needles. Installation is easier if the needles are held with heavy grease or beeswax. Gears that turn with their shafts are held by through-bolts and keys. The shaft/gear fit is deliberately tight and a gear extractor will be needed (Fig. 7-15).

Excessive gear wear is often the fault of the shaft bearings. Bushings should be replaced each time the gear set is disturbed. In many cases, the bushings can be reached from outside the castings and driven inwards with a punch. If the bearing boss is blind, that is, if the shaft does not pass through the case, the bushing can be extracted by either of two methods. One way is to split the bushing with a small chisel, being scrupulously careful not to damage the boss in the process. Another technique is to fill the bushing cavity with grease, then drive a rod the same diameter as the shaft into the grease-packed bushing cavity. The grease will displace the bushing, lifting it up onto the rod.

Caged needle or ball bearings should not be disturbed unless the wear pattern on the gears shows they have wobbled. These bearings can be driven out of blind bosses by the same hydraulic technique described above, except that the medium is oil-soaked newspaper confetti. It helps if the casting is heated slightly. When installing needle and ball bearings, the numbered side is out, toward the installation tool. Drive the new bearing home with a hardwood block, seating it to its original depth.

Two-Speed Gear Drives

While three- and four-speed manually shifted mopeds are not unknown in Europe, American laws require that any moped transmission be automatic. The rider cannot be expected to do more than open the throttle. A gear-driven automatic transmission is a fairly complex piece of work, but can give smooth, effortless shifts and is not handicapped by the power losses inherent in belt drive, which can amount to 10% of the input.

Operation. Several mopeds use these transmissions, but all operate on the same theory to give two speeds. At a preset engine speed, one set of drive gears engages and the other simultaneously disengages. The second, or high-speed, set of gears forms a path for power from the pedals to the engine for starting purposes.

These transmissions have the following parts:

- Two sets of centrifugally engaged clutch shoes
- Two sprag clutches
- Two sets of gears that are constantly in mesh

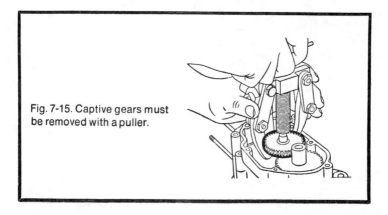

Fig. 7-15. Captive gears must be removed with a puller.

225

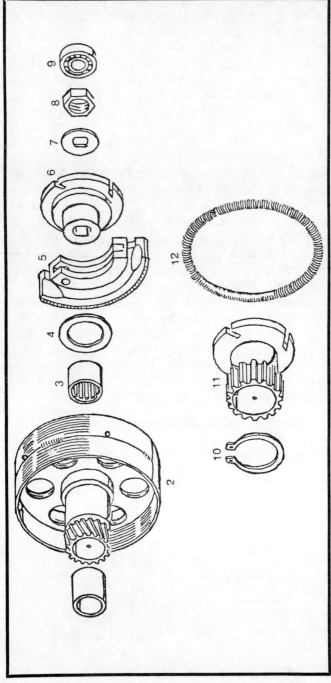

Fig. 7-16. Drive section of the Tomas two-speed, automatically shifted transmission. 1—bushing; 2—clutch drum (double-sided); 3—sprag clutch; 4—spacer; 5—shoe (three on each side of the drum); 6—first-speed hub; 7—lockwasher; 8—nut; 9—bearing; 10—spring clip; 11—second-speed hub and gear; 12—garter spring (one on each shoe set).

Figure 7-16 illustrates the driving parts in a Tomas transmission. The bushing (1) supports the two-sided clutch drum (2) on the engine crankshaft. Note that the clutch drum has an integral gear which turns with it: this is the first speed gear. Both sides of the drum house clutch shoes (5), three shoes on each side for a total of six. Two garter springs (12) restrain the shoes. The first-speed shoes pivot on hub 6, which turns with the crankshaft. The second-speed shoes ride on the hub and gear 11. This second-speed assembly floats inside the drum, on the left-hand side as shown in the drawing.

The drum can be engaged with the crankshaft by either set of shoes or by the sprag clutch (3). Sprag clutches work by means of a wedging action. In the case of clutch 3, the working elements are rectangular in cross-section and held at an angle to the shaft (Fig. 7-7). As this particular example is set up, power can be transmitted from the drum to the crankshaft, but not in the other direction. Once the engine starts, the sprag clutch slips and drum engagement is a function of the shoes.

Figure 7-18 illustrates the driven half of the transmission. The second-speed gear (8) is captive and turns with the countershaft; the first speed gear (6) is mated to the shaft by means of another sprag clutch. While this clutch is somewhat more complex than the one shown in the previous drawing, it operates on the same principle, allowing power to pass in one direction but not in the other. The first-speed wheel can drive the countershat, but the countershaft cannot drive the wheel.

Starting. The engine is started by back-pedaling. Power is transmitted by a small starting chain to the clutch drum and, via the sprag clutch under the drum, to the crankshaft. The chain bypasses one set of transmission gears, and so compensates for the reversed pedal rotation.

Fig. 7-17. Whatever the form, and there are several, a sprag clutch is biased to pass power in one direction and to slip in the other.

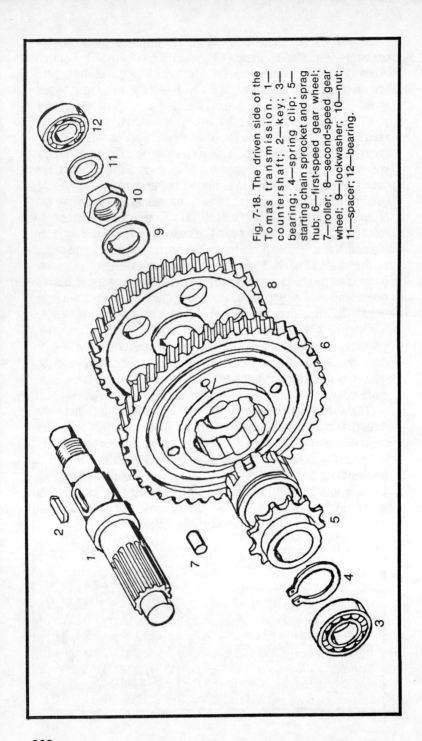

Fig. 7-18. The driven side of the Tomas transmission. 1—countershaft; 2—key; 3—bearing; 4—spring clip; 5—starting chain sprocket and sprag hub; 6—first-speed gear wheel; 7—roller; 8—second-speed gear wheel; 9—lockwasher; 10—nut; 11—spacer; 12—bearing.

Idle. The transmission is in neutral, with no power going to the drum (Fig. 7-19A). The sprag clutch slips, since it is biased to disengage when the crankshaft drives the drum and neither shoe assembly turns rapidly enough to engage by centrifugal force.

First Speed. The first-speed shoes turn with the crankshaft. At approximately 1500 rpm the shoes move out against the drum, mating it with the crankshaft (Fig. 7-19B). Power flows through the low-speed gear set where the flow splits. Almost all power leaves the shaft and goes to the back wheel; a small complement returns to the clutch assembly by way of the second-speed gear set. This power dead-ends at the clutch drum, since second gear is not turning fast enough to engage.

Second Speed. As engine rpm climb, the second-speed shoes reach engagement (Fig. 7-19C). At first glance it would appear that power flows through both gear sets simultaneously, but that interpretation overlooks the sprag clutch under the first-speed countershaft gear. Since the second speed gears drive the countershaft faster than the low speed set, the sprag clutch disengages, releasing the first speed set from the drive train.

Beautiful.

The sprag between the drum and crankshaft engages only during starting, and is rather fragile in comparison with the low-speed sprag clutch. The starting sprag is pressed into the drum and acts directly upon the crankshaft. After a great many starts, the crank may develop waves that interfere with clutch release. Small imperfections can be polished out with emery cloth; deep, fingernail-hanging indentations mean that the crankshaft should be replaced.

The starting sprag should remain undisturbed unless it has failed. In that event, the assembly is driven out of the clutch hub and a new one pressed into place. The numbered end of the sprag assembly is up, toward the arbor.

Test the transmission before final assembly. Hold the second-speed driven gear—the gear pinned to the countershaft—with your left hand and turn the clutch drum with your right. Both sprag clutches should slip when the drum is turned counterclockwise; turning the drum to the right should rotate the crankshaft and the first-speed gear set. If the transmission does not behave in this fashion, check:

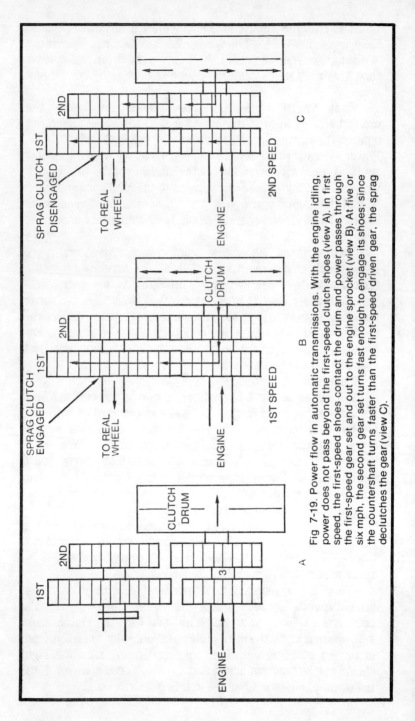

Fig 7-19. Power flow in automatic transmissions. With the engine idling, power does not pass beyond the first-speed clutch shoes (view A). In first speed, the first-speed shoes contact the drum and power passes through the first-speed gear set and out to the engine sprocket (view B). At five or six mph, the second gear set turns fast enough to engage its shoes; since the countershaft turns faster than the first-speed driven gear, the sprag declutches the gear (view C).

- Clutch shoe/drum clearance. The specification for both shoe sets is 0.4 mm (0.08 in.)
- Interference between the crankshaft nut and the drum. With the nut torqued to 2.5 kgm (18.0 ft-lb) there should be 0.1 mm (0.03 in.) axial play between the drum and shaft. Adjusting washers in various thicknesses are available.

Friction Drive

Velosolex bikes drive through the front wheel by means of a roller that bears against the tire. The engine is mounted in a spring-loaded cradle and lowered into the drive position by a lever (Fig. 7-20). While there are objections to friction

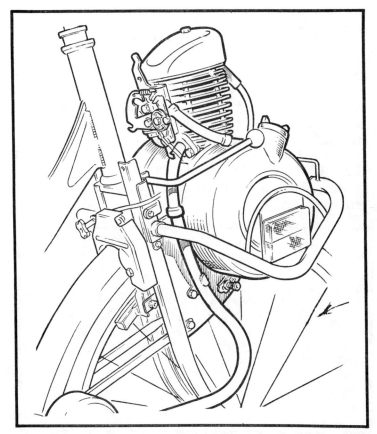

Fig. 7-20. The Velosolex drive mechanism with torque specifications in inch-pounds.

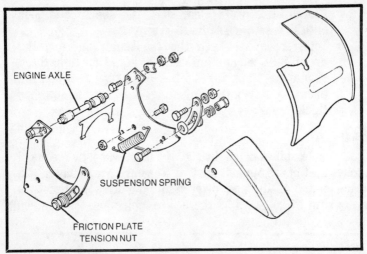

ENGINE AXLE

SUSPENSION SPRING

FRICTION PLATE
TENSION NUT

Fig. 7-21. Engine axle, cradle, and spring assembly. Radical simplicity has always been the Velosolex hallmark.

drive—accelerated tire wear, slip in rain and mud, the pendulum effect of the engine over the front wheel—the concept is elegantly simple. There is no need for elaborate clutch mechanisms or the complexity associated with single chain drives.

Figure 7-21 illustrates the cradle assembly. Spring tension is regulated by the friction plate and tension nut. The next drawing, Fig. 7-22, shows the centrifugal clutch, drive roller, and their torque specifications.

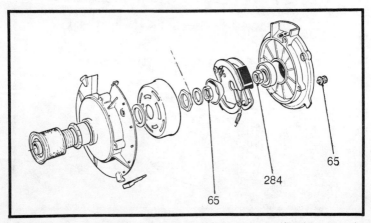

65

284

65

Fig. 7-22. Velosolex drive mechanism with torque specifications in inch-pounds.

To remove the centrifugal clutch, undo the nut securing the shoe assembly to the crankshaft. Squeeze the shoes together and withdraw from the drive roller housing. Inspect the linings for wear and replace if necessary. Assemble with the "X" marks on the shoes toward the drive roller. Run up the nut on the crankshaft and mount the wrench shown in Fig. 7-23 over the nut. The arm extending out of the side of the tool should point toward the front of the engine, where you will find an index hole. Bolt the tool down and torque to 65 inch-pounds (about 5.5 foot-pounds).

To service the drive roller assembly, gently disengage the seal, deforming it with your fingers. Once it has loosened, work the seal over the crankshaft threads (Fig. 7-24). Install the stroke limiter—the threaded rod shown at the left of the drawing—and undo the drive-roller nut and washer. Remove the drive roller.

Lightly grease the roller, confining the grease to the inboard edge where the roller makes rubbing contact with the crankcase flange. Do not get any grease on the friction surface. Align the roller flange with the engine engagement lever bolt hole, and insert a stop bolt. Fit the washer and drive-roller nut and tighten moderately. Replace the oil seal.

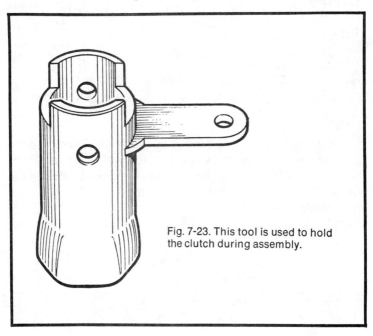

Fig. 7-23. This tool is used to hold the clutch during assembly.

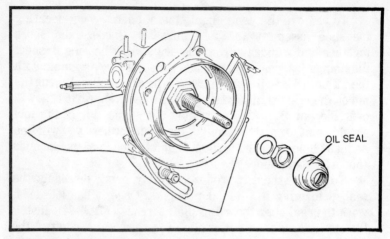

Fig. 7-24. Work the oil seal off with your fingers, being careful not to tear it on the crankshaft threads.

PEDAL CRANKS

The pedal crank is arranged to give three options:

- In *neutral* it is disengaged from the engine and rear wheel.
- In *start* it powers the rear wheel and engine.* Should the engine bog under load, the pedal crank can provide additional energy.
- In *drive* the crank diverts all energy to the rear wheel.

How these options are realized depends upon the type of drive mechanism and, to a lesser extent, upon the manufacturer.

Neutral

In the neutral position, the pedal crank is isolated from the rear wheel and engine. On machines with separate drive chains for pedals and engine, a rachet is placed between the rear-wheel pedal sprocket and the drive hub. The rachet, or freewheel, transmits power in one direction—from the sprocket to the wheel hub—and slips when the wheel hub turns faster than the sprocket.

Machines with a single chain to the rear wheel are fitted with a clutch on the pedal shaft. Figure 7-25 illustrates a

---

*Tomos is an exception; the crank must be reversed to start the engine.

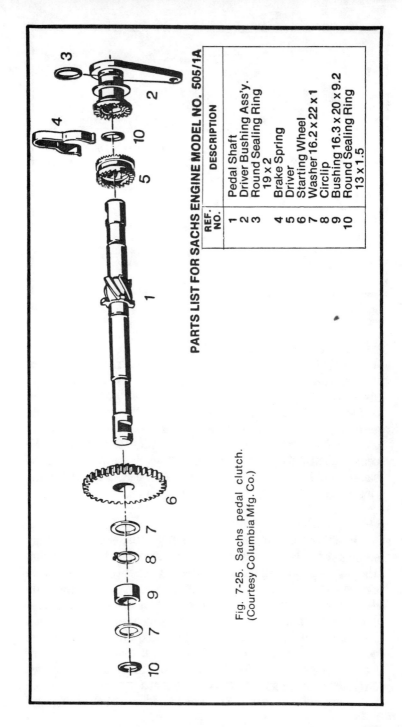

PARTS LIST FOR SACHS ENGINE MODEL NO. 505/1A

REF. NO.	DESCRIPTION
1	Pedal Shaft
2	Driver Bushing Ass'y.
3	Round Sealing Ring 19 x 2
4	Brake Spring
5	Driver
6	Starting Wheel
7	Washer 16.2 x 22 x 1
8	Circlip
9	Bushing 16.3 x 20 x 9.2
10	Round Sealing Ring 13 x 1.5

Fig. 7-25. Sachs pedal clutch. (Courtesy Columbia Mfg. Co.)

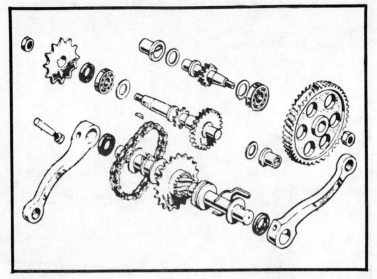

Fig. 7-26. Morini engines employ a short chain between the pedal crank and countershaft.

typical example from Sachs: the driver (5) moves over a thread cast on the pedal shaft in response to friction generated by the brake spring (4). Those of you who are knowledgeable about coaster brakes will be on familiar ground here. In neutral the pedals back off against the driver bushing assembly (2). This example has an external arm whose position can be adjusted to suit the rider, thus locating the pedals positively. (On free wheel designs the pedals can be backed off in a full circle and so offer little support for the rider's feet.)

Start

Pedal torque may be sent directly to the engine or it may enter indirectly, by way of the back wheel and engine chain. The indirect approach is limited to bikes with dual drive chains, and is shown in schematic in Fig. 7-13. Single-chain designs route torque from the pedals directly to the engine clutch. Returning to Fig. 7-25 for a moment, note that driver 5 is toothed on both ends. The right-hand end is for positive neutral stop; the left-hand teeth mate with teeth on the inboard side of the gear wheel (6). Torque from this gear splits in two directions: some goes to the rear wheel and some goes to spin the engine clutch drum. The Sachs engine clutch is engaged manually by the same handlebar control that trips the compression release. Other clutches have starting shoes for automatic, speed-sensitive engagement.

While most manufacturers use gears between the engine clutch and the pedal shaft, a few use a chain. Figure 7-26 illustrates the Morini setup.

Drive

Drive, the condition when forward motion depends solely upon the pedals, means that the engine must be taken out of the circuit. On single-chain machines with manual override on the engine clutch, one merely does not engage the override. With automatic clutches that turn the engine once a preset speed is reached, the uncoupling mechanism is between the clutch and pedal shaft or rear wheel. Figure 7-27 illustrates one form of lockout.

Another lockout one that is typical of belt-drive practice, is shown in Fig. 7-28. The pulley floats on a pair of caged needle bearings (13) on the pedal shaft. It turns with the engine. The pedal crank has its own sprocket, not illustrated here; engine power goes to the back wheel by means of the sprocket assembly 2. The sprocket assembly consists of two toothed wheels; the outboard wheel drives the chain, the inboard wheel can mesh with the lock lever (9 and 15). The lever turns

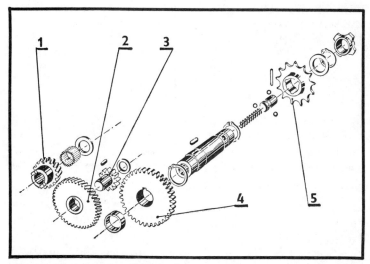

Fig. 7-27. Jawa uses a rather complex collection of parts to lock the engine out of the drive train.

237

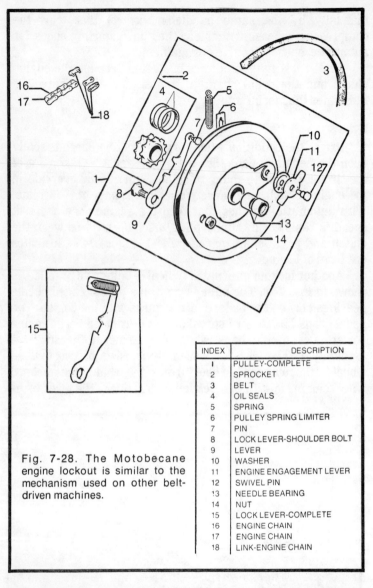

INDEX	DESCRIPTION
1	PULLEY-COMPLETE
2	SPROCKET
3	BELT
4	OIL SEALS
5	SPRING
6	PULLEY SPRING LIMITER
7	PIN
8	LOCK LEVER-SHOULDER BOLT
9	LEVER
10	WASHER
11	ENGINE ENGAGEMENT LEVER
12	SWIVEL PIN
13	NEEDLE BEARING
14	NUT
15	LOCK LEVER-COMPLETE
16	ENGINE CHAIN
17	ENGINE CHAIN
18	LINK-ENGINE CHAIN

Fig. 7-28. The Motobecane engine lockout is similar to the mechanism used on other belt-driven machines.

with the pulley, and is spring-loaded to hold the pulley in engagement with the sprocket. Turning the engagement lever to the right forces the lock lever out of mesh and breaks the connection between pulley and sprocket. Thus the pedals can turn without sending power through the rear wheel and back through the engine sprocket and pulley.

Service

The pedals thread into the crank arms. With reference to the rider's seated position, the inboard ends of the pedal axles are stamped "R" and "L". The right pedal has a standard thread, overhand and counterclockwise to loosen; the left one has a left-hand thread. While the pedals are clearly marked, it is possible to confuse the right and left crank arms if they are detached from the pedal shaft. Mark them.

As shown back in Fig. 7-26, the pedal arms cross-bolt to the shaft. Undo the nuts, remove the lockwashers, and—supporting the shaft with a wooden block—drive the tapered crossbolts out. The shaft must be supported to protect the bushings.

Relax tension on the chain and work it off the more accessible of the two sprockets. On belt-drive machines, disengage the belt and uncouple the pulley from the drive sprocket. Remove the spring clip (reference No. 5 in Fig. 7-29) and lift off the pulley. Removing the second spring clip (8) frees the shaft and sprocket assembly from the frame hanger.

Most other bikes employ integral pedal shafts extending through the crankcase castings. Further disassembly means that the crankcases must be opened, an operation described in Chapter 6. Polish the exposed portion of the shaft with a strip of emery cloth to remove any rust, then gently tap the shaft out of the casting.

Sliding starter engagement clutches, illustrated earlier in this chapter, are subject to brutal loads. The engagement teeth may round off or the thread may split and splinter. Occasionally you will find that the friction spring has lost tension. The clue to this condition is erratic clutching—the engine may engage with a few degrees of pedal crank movement, or it may take several revolutions to move the driver.

Pedal-shaft bushings are normally good for the life of the machine, for no one pedals more than he has to. If there is excessive up-and-down play between the bushings and the shaft, suspect that the shaft or, as the case may be, the frame has bent. Misaligned engine castings are a thought not to be entertained; if this were to happen, the transmission bearings would go first.

Pedal shaft bushings are available for most bikes and, if necessary, can be ordered through a bearing supply house by

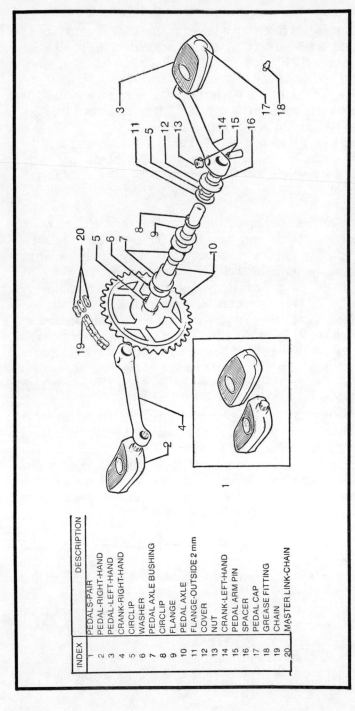

INDEX	DESCRIPTION
1	PEDALS-PAIR
2	PEDAL-RIGHT-HAND
3	PEDAL-LEFT-HAND
4	CRANK-RIGHT-HAND
5	CIRCLIP
6	WASHER
7	PEDAL AXLE BUSHING
8	CIRCLIP
9	FLANGE
10	PEDAL AXLE
11	FLANGE-OUTSIDE 2 mm
12	COVER
13	NUT
14	CRANK-LEFT-HAND
15	PEDAL ARM PIN
16	SPACER
17	PEDAL CAP
18	GREASE FITTING
19	CHAIN
20	MASTER LINK-CHAIN

Fig. 7-29. Motobecane pedal crank assembly. The driven pulley floats between spring clips 5 and 8.

240

dimension (inside and outside diameters and length). Drive the old bushings out with a suitable punch and press the new ones into place. Some distortion is inevitable during installation: correct with an adjustable reamer of the type auto mechanics use. But the importance or relative lack of importance of these bushings is underscored by remarks in one manufacturer's service literature. This manufacturer suggests that new bushings be sized with a rat-tail file.

Axial play is critical for some sliding clutches. The standard specification is 0.1 mm (0.025 inch). Adjust with dealer-supplied or bearing-house shims. Lubricate the internals with light grease and assemble.

The Jawa lockout mechanism deserves special attention. The star-shaped part at the extreme left of Fig. 7-27 is known as the control gear, although it is not a gear in the usual sense of the word. It is secured to the shaft by means of the pin. The pin and control gear ride in a slot on the end of the shaft, milled in the form of the letter L. The plunger is grooved around its circumference and slips inside the shaft where it faces a spring. Engagement occurs between the inside of the sprocket and the three ball bearings. Each bearing is located over a hole in the shaft, one of which is shown.

Turning the control gear counterclockwise allows the plunger to retract so that its groove is under the balls. There is no contact between the balls and sprocket and no power goes to the engine. Moving the control gear in and to the right sends the plunger deeper into the shaft. The groove no longer indexes with the holes and the balls are forced up into engagement with the sprocket. Power can be transfered from the rear wheel to the engine.

To disassemble, drive out the control-gear pin with a small punch (Fig. 7-30A), extract the plunger (Fig. 7-30B), remove the spring clip and spacer (7-30C), lift off the sprocket and, using a copper or aluminum buffer, drive out the countershaft (7-30D). Upon assembly, be certain that the balls index with the holes in the shaft and with the groove on the plunger. Once together, the balls cannot escape and the lockout can be shifted to the "engine on" position.

Engine Chains

Nearly all mopeds use a 1/2 inch by 3/16 inch roller chain for both the engine and the pedals. The first fraction

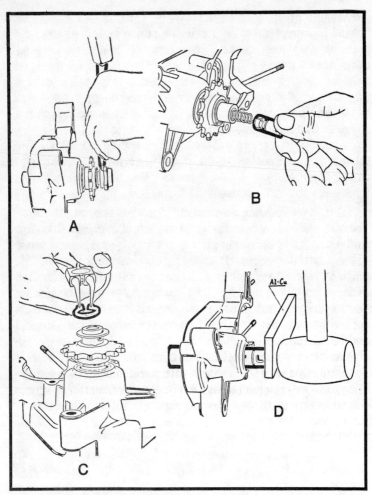

Fig. 7-30. Jawa lockout service. Drive out the control gear pin (view A); extract the plunger (view B); remove the spring clip and sprocket (view C); and tap the countershaft out of the casting (view D). It may be necessary to heat the casting with a propane torch to release the bearing. This technique was described in the previous chapter.

represents the pitch, or the distance between the roller centers; the second represents the width of the inner links. While there is little that can be done about chain pitch, the width of the chain can sometimes be increased for additional durability. The only factor limiting width is the clearance on either side of the sprocket. Wider-than-original chains may foul the spokes or engine case.

Adjustment

Too much chain tension can lead to expensive repairs since the chain, sprockets, and bearings suffer. Too little tension allows the chain to whip and snatch during acceleration and encourages it to jump the sprockets. Adjusted correctly, the chain should have 0.5 inch free upward movement between the sprocket centers. If the bike is equipped with rear spring-shocks, make the measurement with a rider aboard. (The swing arms are never on the same axis as the engine sprocket; weight on the suspension increases chain travel.)

The rear-wheel axle slides in the frame lugs, its position controlled by eye-bolts or cams (Fig. 7-31). Loosen the axle nuts and make the required adjustment. Cams are usually stamped with index marks so that both cams can be adjusted equally. But do not trust these marks to keep the wheel parallel; their value depends upon the trueness of the axle, the precision of the swing-arm bushings, and the integrity of the frame. It is possible to align the cams and have the rear wheel crabbed in the swing arm, a situation that costs power, handling, and tire tread.

A careful owner checks the cam marks against wheel alignment. One way to do this is with parallel boards on either side of the rear wheel (Fig. 7-32). Another, perhaps more accurate, way is to use taut strings. Once the alignment is

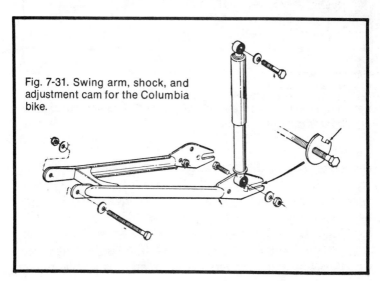

Fig. 7-31. Swing arm, shock, and adjustment cam for the Columbia bike.

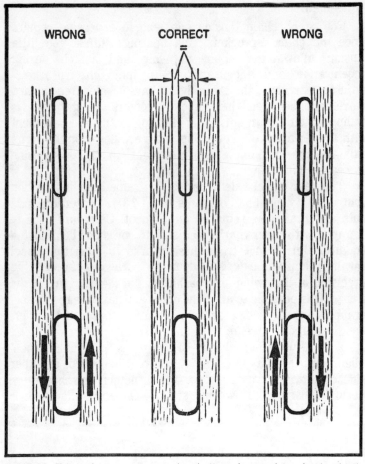

WRONG   CORRECT   WRONG

Fig. 7-32. Triumph suggests wooden battens be used to check wheel alignment.

verified, the cam marks can be corrected and future wheel alignments become almost automatic.

Lubrication

Roller chains are complex, with pins, bushings, and the inside diameter of the rollers masked by other parts (Fig. 7-33). The lubricant must be thin enough to work its way into these parts and, at the same time, tenacious enough to stay on the chain at speed. There are various chain lubes on the market, most of them packaged in aerosol cans and relatively expensive. A more economical alternative is a 50-50 mix of

Varsol and 60-weight motor oil, applied with a small paint brush.

The chain should be removed occasionally and soaked in solvent. Moped chains use three-piece master links easily identified by the spring clip. With a small screwdriver, pry the split ends of the clip apart and push the clip out of engagement with pins. Flex the chain to free the side plate. Once the chain is clean, dip it into a container of lubricant. Allow an hour or so for the excess oil to drain off; then thread the chain over both sprockets. Install the master link from behind, as shown in Fig. 7-34—otherwise the spring clip will not be readily visible. Flex the chain and snap the side plate over the pins. Mount the clip so its closed end is in the direction of travel.

Chain wear is measured by the amount of "stretch," or play between the rollers and bushings. For moderate-duty applications, the allowable stretch is 2%. Since moped chains have an average length of 100 half-inch links, moving the rear wheel back one inch is the absolute limit. If greater movement is required, the chain should be replaced.

SPROCKETS

The engine sprocket is about one-quarter the diameter of the wheel sprocket and therefore wears about four times

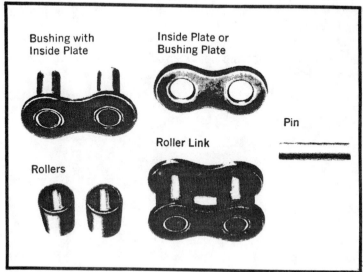

Bushing with Inside Plate

Inside Plate or Bushing Plate

Pin

Roller Link

Rollers

Fig. 7-33. Inner-link components. The outer link consists of two side plates, riveted on the pins. (Courtesy Daido Corp.)

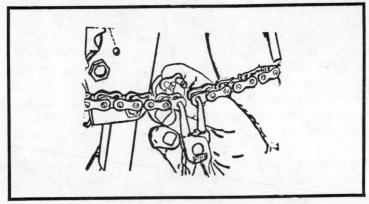

Fig. 7-34. Installing the master link on a Tomos bike.

faster. Moped engine sprockets are quite small, a tooth or so larger than the 9-tooth minimum that most engineers accept. Even discounting the difference in revolutions per mile, a small sprocket wears more than a large one because of the way it exercises the chain.

The best way to detect sprocket wear is to wrap a new chain over it. There should be some clearance between the teeth and the chain rollers, but not enough to be felt when the chain is tugged. As sprocket wear progresses, the symptoms become more obvious: the teeth appear hooked and eventually wear away.

As a rule, the engine sprocket should be changed as often as the chain. Wheel and pedal sprocket should last the life of the machine.

Chapter 8
Frame, Suspension, and Wheels

The frame, suspension, and wheels are, in terms of the rider's safety, the most important components on the bike.

FRAMES

Nearly all mopeds employ pressed steel frames on the pattern of the Motobecane shown in Fig. 8-1. This type of frame is heavier than other types of equal load-bearing ability, but is economical to manufacture and can double as the fuel tank. Batavus follows motorcycle practice and uses mild steel tubing. The HS 50 frame in Fig. 8-2 with its wide-diameter tubing and top tube is probably the strongest in the industry.

Fractures

Frame breakage is rare; when it does occur the fracture is at the steering head—the part that supports the front fork—or the juncture of the seat post with the bottom tube. Have a professional make the repair, using one of the new high-strength brass alloys. Electric arc welding, the process used by the factory, is generally not successful in the field, and tends to weaken the steel adjacent to the weld. Once the damage is corrected, the repair can be disguised with factory paint, available from most importers in aerosol cans.

Engine Mounts

Some manufacturers isolate engine vibration with hard rubber grommets. In time these grommets wear and must be

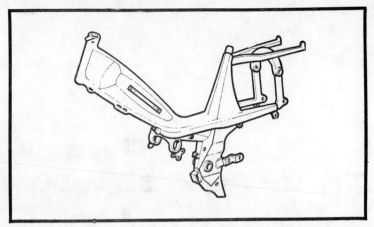

Fig. 8-1. The Motobecane frame is typical in that it's made of steel stampings.

replaced. Figure 8-3 shows an extractor-installer tool which can be purchased from Motobecane dealers or fabricated in the shop. In case parts are not available, grommets can be cut from the rubber blocks used in automobile motor mounts.

SUSPENSION

Suspension components include the swing arms, steering head, front forks, shocks and, to some extent, the wheels.

Swing Arms

Swing-arm distortion is a fairly common aliment which, unless corrected, results in wasted power, excessive tire wear, and rear-wheel steering. The first clue is a misaligned rear wheel, tilted off the vertical or canted to one side. The wheel

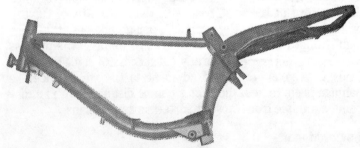

Fig. 8-2. This super-strong Batavus frame, made of steel tubing, is triangulated for additional strength and a motorcycle-like appearance.

can be adjusted in one plane by means of the chain tension cams as describe in the previous chapter. But severe horizontal misalignment or any degree of vertical misalignment means that the swing arm should be dismantled for inspection.

The rear of the arm is secured by the spring/shock units on each side; the front of the arm pivots on the frame. Most bikes use the arrangement shown in Fig. 8-4: the swing arm hinges on a central bolt. Puch arms are flanged to fit against the bearing housing and are secured by four capscrews (Fig. 8-5). Because the pivot flange is flat, it is a fairly simple matter to check the swing arm with a plumb bob: distances AA and BB should be equal. The same check can be made on other swing arms by mounting them vertically in a vise. If either measurement is off,the arm should be replaced or turned over to a first-class frame man for straightening.

Regardless of their construction, swing arms pivot on rubber bushings. Rubber is a mixed blessing. It soaks up minor road irregularities and quiets wheel rumble, but the bushings wear rapidly and tend to collapse with age. The rear wheel develops steering inputs, particularly on hard, fast curves. The bike is slow to enter a curve and remains in it after the rider has shifted weight for the straightaway.

The bushings can be replaced without disassembling the swing arm or removing the rear wheel. Place the bike on its centerstand and undo the pivot nut. Drive the pivot bolt out with a punch, an operation that releases the swing arm and causes its forward end to drop. Drive the bushings out and install new ones to the depth of the originals. Raise the swing arm and wheel and insert the bolt. Coat the bolt threads with Loctite or an equivalent adhesive and torque the nut snugly against the bushings. Snug is enough—do not overtighten and reload the rubber.

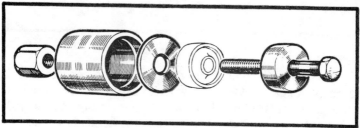

Fig. 8-3. A bushing tool available from Motobecane.

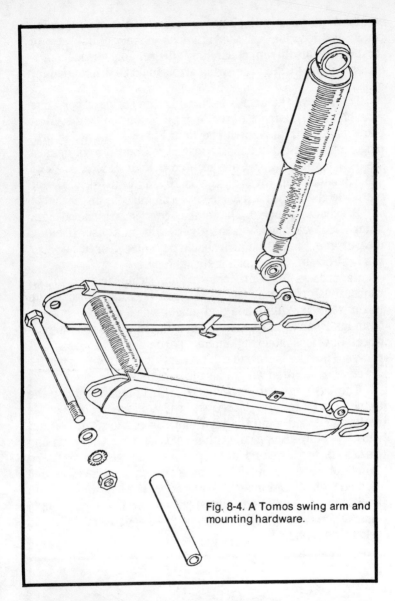

Fig. 8-4. A Tomos swing arm and mounting hardware.

Steering Head

The front fork rides in the steering head on two sets of ball bearings. As the bike rolls forward it tends to wobble from left to right. The rider learns to make corrections, but he is helped by the automatic self-righting tendency generated by the fork and steering head. As the bike falls off to the left, the fork pivots on the steering head bearings to the right, transferring weight away from the direction of fall. A bike with fixed steering is inherently unstable and impossible to ride.

The fork should have little or no up-and-down clearance on the bearings and, at the same time, must not bind at the extremes of pivot. Place the bike on its centerstand and sit on it, raising the front wheel clear of the pavement. Pull up on the forks, as if you were trying to lift them out of the steering head. There should be no free movement. Slowly turn the handlebars from lock to lock to detect binds or rough spots. Excess axial (up and down) clearance can be corrected by loosening the locknut in Fig. 8-6 and tightening the copper cone. Tighten gingerly—too much torque will imprint the balls into their respective cones ruining the steering response. Leave a tiny amount of play and tighten the locknut. Test as before. If the fork binds at the extremes of travel, loosen the adjustment nut a hair. Should the assembly be impossible to adjust—remain loose at the straight-ahead position and tight when the fork is turned—suspect that the fork is bent.

Rough action can mean that the bearings are dry or that they are damaged. The latter is more likely. Fork removal is

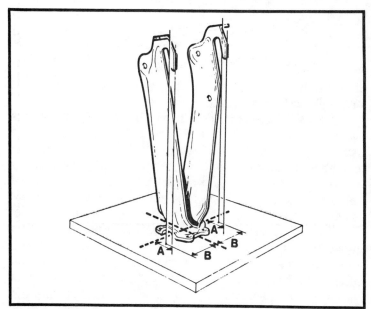

Fig. 8-5. Making an alignment check on a Puch swing arm. The same technique can be used with other makes.

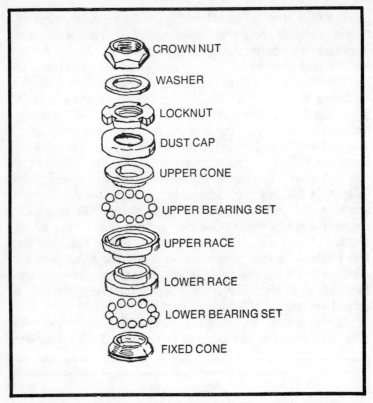

CROWN NUT

WASHER

LOCKNUT

DUST CAP

UPPER CONE

UPPER BEARING SET

UPPER RACE

LOWER RACE

LOWER BEARING SET

FIXED CONE

Fig. 8-6. Some bearing sets vary from this pattern by omitting the locknut.

discussed further on in this chapter; here we will be concerned with replacing the bearings, cones, and races.

Inspect the cones and the races. If the bearing surfaces are pitted or if the bearings have worn deep grooves into the metal, it is best to replace the complete bearing assembly—balls, cones, and races. Sometimes you can get by with a new lower cone or race, but this is not recommended because of the safety aspects involved. At any rate, do not replace a broken or lost bearing with a new one. The whole set must be purchased, since a new bearing would be slightly larger than the others and the assembly might crumple under the strain. The dealer where you purchased the machine is, of course, the best source of parts. But you should know that bearings are a standard item available from houses that cater to this trade. In addition, cones and races can sometimes be purchased at bicycle shops.

The upper cone unthreads to release the fork; the lower cone can be pried off with a knife blade. The races, or bearing cups, are pressed into the fork tube from which they can be driven with a punch. New races are usually driven home with the help of a wood block; professionals use the VAR tool shown in Fig. 8-7.

Front Forks

The solid, springless fork on the Velosolex is a heritage of friction drive; the wheel must not be allowed to move relative to the drive roller (Fig. 8-8). Intramotor's Blanco is one of the few mopeds to employ a leading-link suspension (Fig. 8-9). The links, supported by springs and pivoting on bushings, allow a few degrees of wheel movement. This type of suspension saves money since the forks can be inexpensive stampings, jig-welded together. On the other hand, the forks are susceptible to bending from side forces—the kind of forces that can be generated by skidding into a curb—and the bushings are not up to the job of keeping the wheel parallel. Another disadvantage is that the wheel base, or the distance between the front and rear axles, changes with suspension movement. Handling is always a triffle sloppy.

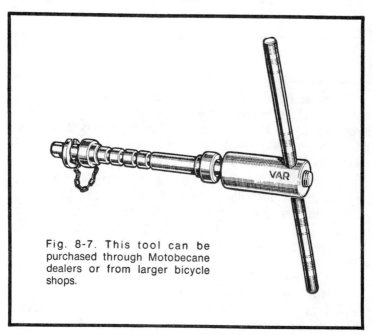

Fig. 8-7. This tool can be purchased through Motobecane dealers or from larger bicycle shops.

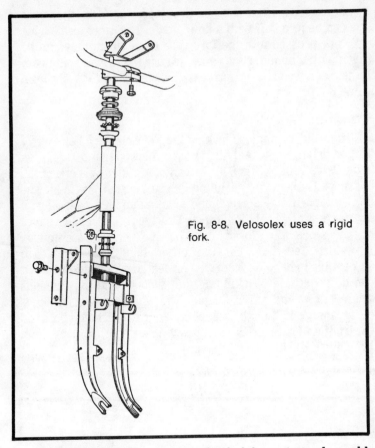

Fig. 8-8. Velosolex uses a rigid fork.

Telescopic forks are the standard of the motorcycle world and are used on the better mopeds. These forks are inherently strong and locate the wheel through large bushings (Fig. 8-10). The more sophisticated designs are oil-dampened on joust and rebound to give a smoother, safer ride.

To remove the forks from the frame, first detach the front wheel and the handlebars. Loosen the handlebar stem bolt, unthreading it so it extends a half-inch above the stem. Rap the bolt head down with a soft mallet to disengage the expansion plug. The handlebars should be free to turn from side to side without moving the wheel. As you turn the bars, pull up, working the assembly out of the fork tube. It may be necessary to use the mallet on the underside of the stem. Lay the handlebars carefully alongside the bike with the wiring and control cables still connected.

Remove the nut securing the forks to the tube and carefully back out the cone. As you do, the fork will drop away from the frame, releasing the lower set of ball bearings. With one or two exceptions, these bearings are uncaged. Given the chance, they will run away and hide, so cup your hand at the fork-steering-head joint and catch them as they fall. Count the bearings. Completely unthread the upper cone and retrieve the upper bearings with a magnet. Count them; the number should be the same as in the lower set. If not, one or more is missing. As mentioned earlier, do not make up the discrepency by adding new bearings to the used sets—replace each set as an entity. Wash the cones, bearings, and races in solvent and grease lightly in preparation for assembly.

The fork is now detached. Normally, a visual examination from several angles will detect distortion, but you can get an accurate picture of the fork condition by mounting it in a vise and taking measurements with a plumb bob.

Further disassembly means removal of the triple crown, the triangular plate at the top of the assembly. The bolts may be exposed as in the Puch design, or they may be hidden under plastic covers. Pry the covers off. Motobecane and a few other bikes secure the tubes with slotted screws that require a specially ground screwdriver.

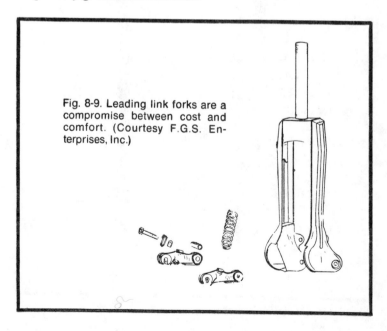

Fig. 8-9. Leading link forks are a compromise between cost and comfort. (Courtesy F.G.S. Enterprises, Inc.)

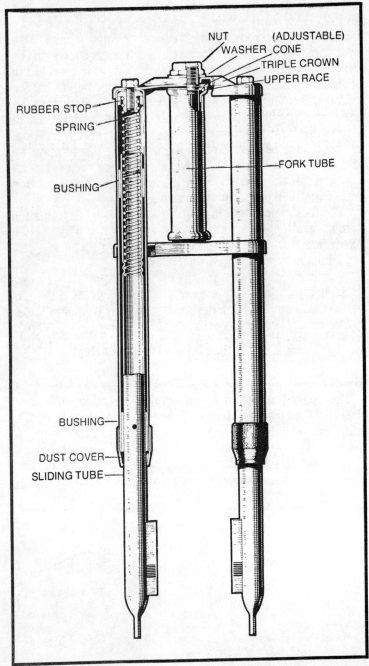

NUT (ADJUSTABLE)
WASHER CONE
TRIPLE CROWN
UPPER RACE

RUBBER STOP

SPRING

FORK TUBE

BUSHING

BUSHING

DUST COVER

SLIDING TUBE

Fig. 8-10. Puch employs a telescopic fork.

Removing the triple-crown bolts releases the springs and allows the lower, or sliding, fork tubes to drop free of the fixed tubes. Jawa is an exception—the sliding tubes are held by the triple-crown bolts and by large knurled nuts (Fig. 8-11).

Clean the parts in solvent and replace the bushings—often made of plastic—and rubber stops. If the unit is oil-dampened, drain the old oil and replace with the correct amount of oil or, more fashionably, automatic transmission fluid. The dealer will be able to tell you how much oil should be used. Lubricate the bushings and assemble in reverse order of disassembly.

Rear Shocks

Rear shocks can be dismantled for cleaning and lubrication, but serious repair is out of the question (Fig. 8-12). Most manufacturers list part numbers for the rubber bushings at the shock mounts; a few can supply internal bushings. Guide rods, springs, and tube assemblies are not obtainable. If the shocks sag or have suffered impact damage, replace them with bona fide, oil-dampened shocks intended for small motorcycles. The best of these are made by aftermarket suppliers such as Koni and Bolger. But even the cheapest Japanese shock is better than original moped quality.

WHEELS

The spoked wheel is a remarkable invention, just now being replaced by cast aluminum wheels. The integrity of the spoked wheel depends upon the strength of steel wire in tension. Only a few spokes are in play at any time: no more than a dozen bear the weight of the rider and the machine, with those near the top of the wheel carrying most of the load (Fig.

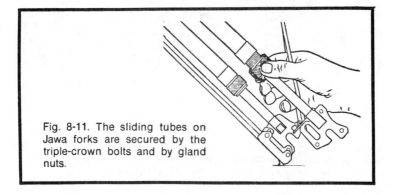

Fig. 8-11. The sliding tubes on Jawa forks are secured by the triple-crown bolts and by gland nuts.

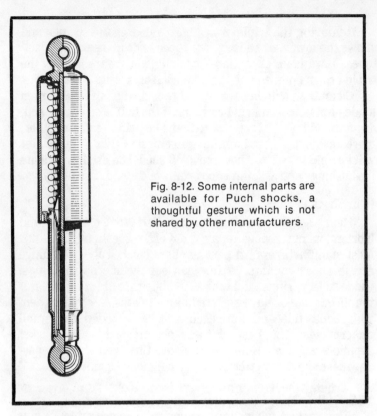

Fig. 8-12. Some internal parts are available for Puch shocks, a thoughtful gesture which is not shared by other manufacturers.

8-13A). Even fewer spokes contain braking and accelerating forces (Fig. 8-13B and C). It is not surprising that spokes "sing" when they break.

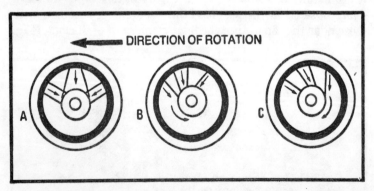

DIRECTION OF ROTATION

Fig. 8-13. Only a few spokes are important at any given moment. The drawings show the normal load distribution (view A), forces generated during acceleration (view B), and during braking (view C).

Tension Adjustments

Restraint is a key work in adjusting spoke tension. Most amateurs overtighten spokes, causing distorted rims, and, occasionally, broken spokes or stripped threads.

An extremely loose spoke will rattle when wobbled with your finger, or you may hear it as you ride. Less severe tension imbalance can be detected by tapping the spokes with a small wrench. The tighter the spoke, the higher and cleaner its resonance; loose spokes will sound flat and sloppy in comparison.

Figure 8-14 shows a VAR spoke-nipple wrench, available from bicycle shops and Motobecane dealers. The nipples are made of brass, but the spokes corrode and penetrating oil is frequently needed. Another stratagem is to loosen the nipple a fraction of a turn before attempting to tighten it. At any rate, work slowly, tightening each loose spoke no more than a quarter-turn at a time; otherwise you may distort the wheel. Under no condition should any spoke be tightened more than two turns without removing the tire to see if the spoke protrudes through the back of the nipple. If it does, the end must be filed off to protect the tube.

Truing

Truing wheels is a minor art form, like orgami or potato carving. The perfect wheel has all spokes torqued to the same tension, retains the original hub offset (or "dish") and is perfectly round, without trace of eccentricity or wobble.

Real success requires a truing stand. Fig. 8-15 illustrates a professional model, equipped with an adjustable pointer. Perfectionists substitute a dial indicator for the pointer at the final stage of the work. But truing stands, with or without the dial indicator, are hardly worth the investment for a moped owner. You can get fair results if you turn the machine over

 Fig. 8-14. VAR spoke wrench.

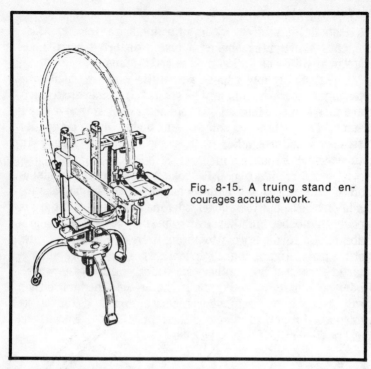

Fig. 8-15. A truing stand encourages accurate work.

and use the front fork as a stand. An Allen wrench secured to the fork leg by an automotive hose clamp serves as a pointer.

Remove the tire, tube and tube protector. Check the rim for local creases or dents that are too defined for the spokes to correct. Unless the rim is folded, these dents can usually be pounded out with a mallet. Mount the wheel in the fork and set the pointer so that it just brushes the rim at the point of greatest runout. Loosen the spokes near the runout and tighten those across from it to pull the rim back into line. Move the pointer to the other fork leg and repeat the operation. You may have to check the other side again, but with patience the wheel will spin with only the shadow of a wobble. Now place the pointer under the flange of the rim, that part that is on the inside and near the bead. This is to determine if the rim is eccentric, or egg-shaped. Loosen the spokes near the bulge and tighten those on the far side of it. These procedures should not shift the hub relative to the center of the rim. The offset will remain as the manufacturer intended.

Once you are satisfied that the rim is true, grind or file off the ends of the spokes flush with the nipples, since protruding spokes will work through the rim protector and gnaw away at the tube.

Spoke Patterns

While respoking wheels is a job for the professional and out of the scope of this book, you should be aware that there are several possible spoke patterns. Most mopeds use the "cross-3" pattern on both wheels (Fig. 8-16): each spoke crosses over three other spokes on the same side of the trim. Cross-3 lacing makes a moderately strong wheel, adequate for most service. Velosolex uses a cross-1 pattern at the front and cross-2 at the rear. In other words, Velosolex wheels are deliberately spindly, a design that makes little sense until you reflect that this bike has no suspension. The only way it can absorb roadshock is to allow the wheels to flex.

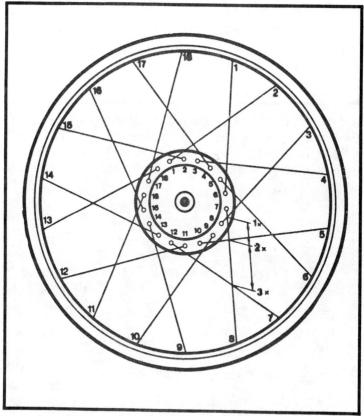

Fig 8-16. The cross-3, 36-hole spoke pattern used on Puch wheels.

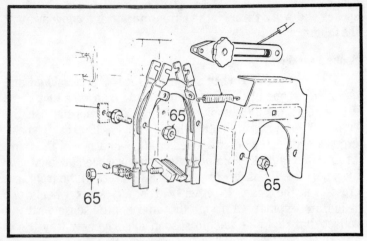

Fig. 8-17. The Velosolex caliper brake with torque limits given in inch-pounds.

Heavy riders can benefit from a stronger rear wheel. Heavy-gauge spokes can be substituted for the originals or the wheel can be relaced in the cross-4 pattern.

Brakes

Mopeds use drum or caliper brakes. The former are lightweight versions of those used on motorcycles; the latter have evolved from the familiar bicycle rim brake.

Caliper Brakes

Figure 8-17 is breakdown of the Velocette front-wheel caliper. When engaged, a pair of rubbing blocks, or shoes, moves into contact with the sides of the rim.

There are two adjustments. Small changes in the shoe position are made at the handlebar end of the control cable. Loosen the locknut and turn the barrel counterclockwise to bring the shoes closer to the rim. There should be approximately one-half inch of play at the end of the handlebar lever.

To make larger adjustments, remove the U-shaped cover over the caliper mechanism. Turn the handlebars to the right for easy access and pull the right brake shoe into contact with the rim. Turn the star wheel to the left (Velocette has a special wrench for this, although you can wrap a shop towel around the wheel and use pliers), which tightens the cable by moving its anchor point. Stop when there is a quarter-inch clearance between the rim and left brake shoe.

To disassemble, attach the brake cable at the caliper and remove the cover plate. The caliper is bolted to the fork and fender. Replace worn brake shoes with factory parts; if you must use bicycle shoes, be certain that the crimped ends of the shoe holders are forward, to lock the shoes against wheel rotation. Position the holders so the shoes contact the rim and not the tire sidewalls. When installing the cover plate, be sure that it engages the brake return spring.

Drum Brakes

Drum brakes are located within the wheel hubs where they are fairly immune to rain and water splash (Fig. 8-18A and B). A cast-iron liner pressed into the aluminum hub is the friction surface; shoes mount on a backing plate that is locked into the fork or swing arm. The actuating lever pivots on the backing plate and terminates in a cam which nestles between the shoes. Moving the lever prys the shoes apart and into contact with the drum. Return springs, sometimes with the addition of a helper spring at the lever, assure that the shoes pull out of engagement when pressure on the lever is relaxed.

Adjustment. The brake cable must be shortened to compensate for lining wear. Depending upon the manufacturer, the cable adjustment may be at the handlebar, the backing plate, or at both locations. In any event, loosen the locknut and thread the adjuster barrel out, toward the center of the machine. Sachs hubs have an additional refinement—the lever and cam are in two parts, geared together. The purpose of this is to restore leverage to worn linings, for as the linings wear, the lever works at a progressively more unfavorable angle (Fig. 8-19). It can be repositioned at right angles to the cable by disassembling the backing plate and meshing the gears for earlier engagement.

Service. The backing plate floats on the axle and drops off once the wheel is out of the frame. Note the position of the shoes for assembly; in most cases the shoes appear identical, but the wear patterns will not be.

Disengage the return springs with the point of a screwdriver, freeing the shoes. Replace the shoes if either lining has worn to half of its original thickness or if either has become grease-soaked. For most bikes, replacement shoes are

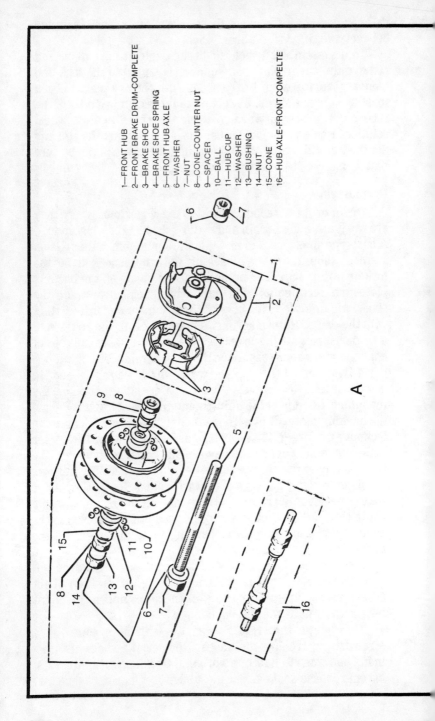

1—FRONT HUB
2—FRONT BRAKE DRUM-COMPLETE
3—BRAKE SHOE
4—BRAKE SHOE SPRING
5—FRONT HUB AXLE
6—WASHER
7—NUT
8—CONE-COUNTER NUT
9—SPACER
10—BALL
11—HUB CUP
12—WASHER
13—BUSHING
14—NUT
15—CONE
16—HUB AXLE-FRONT COMPELTE

A

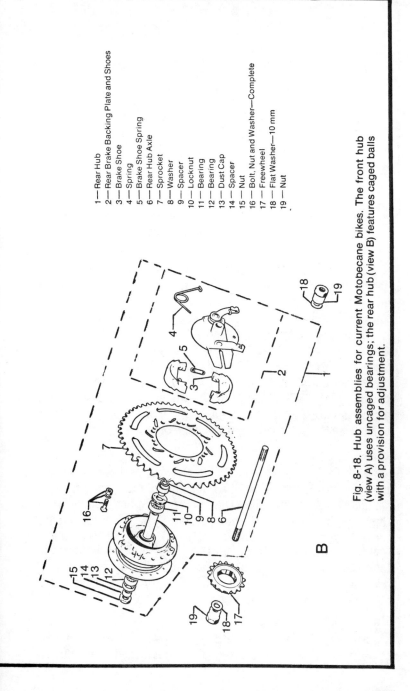

1 — Rear Hub
2 — Rear Brake Backing Plate and Shoes
3 — Brake Shoe
4 — Spring
5 — Brake Shoe Spring
6 — Rear Hub Axle
7 — Sprocket
8 — Washer
9 — Spacer
10 — Locknut
11 — Bearing
12 — Bearing
13 — Dust Cap
14 — Spacer
15 — Nut
16 — Bolt, Nut and Washer—Complete
17 — Freewheel
18 — Flat Washer—10 mm
19 — Nut

Fig. 8-18. Hub assemblies for current Motobecane bikes. The front hub (view A) uses uncaged bearings; the rear hub (view B) features caged balls with a provision for adjustment.

265

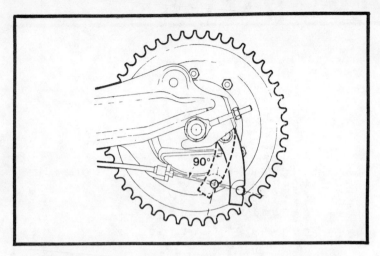

Fig. 8-19. Sachs brake levers can be adjusted for best leverage.

easy to come by; obsolete bikes and orphans, whose distributors have gone on to greener pastures, can be put back into service with the help of the local brake-and-clutch shop. They will cut new linings and glue them to the shoes.

Clean the metal parts in solvent and lubricate the cam and anchor pin with high-temperature grease. Hook the springs over the shoes and place the assembly over the cam, pulling the shoes apart as you install them. Install the spacer and backing plate. When mounting the wheel, be sure that the slot on the backing plate arm engages a pin on the fork or frame. Otherwise the plate will turn when the brakes are applied.

HUBS

Hub maintenance is often overlooked, perhaps because a missed lubrication period has no immediate symptoms. The wheels roll as before. But the factories are not kidding when they insist on frequent maintenance. The specification for most bikes is 6000 miles between hub disassemblies; Motobecane suggests 3600 miles and Velosolex would have you take the hubs down at 3000-mile intervals. Unlike the sealed bearings used in an automobile, moped bearings are vulnerable to dust and water damage.

Front Hubs

Figure 8-18A illustrates a typical front hub as-sembly using adjustable cones (15) and uncaged balls (10). To disassemble, dismount the wheel at the fork and remove the backing plate. Carefully back off the cone with the jam nut ahead of it. In the drawing the cone is on the left side of the wheel. Retrieve the bearings as they become accessible and count them. Slip the axle and cone out the other side of the wheel. Compare the number of bearings on this side with those on the first. If a bearing is lost, replace all bearings on that side; otherwise the new, unworn bearing will be loaded more than the others and may fail. Wash the parts in solvent without disturbing the mounted one. As long as this cone is in its original position, the axle will be centered on reassembly.

Assemble the hub and adjust the bearing clearance, tightening the cone that was unthreaded. Adjust for the tiniest amount of side clearance between the axle and hub. Holding the cone with a thin wrench, tighten the jam nut hard against it. Even though the cone has not moved, the jam nut will take up some of the slack. If you have allowed correctly, the bearings will have zero sideplay, yet be loose enough to allow the wheel to turn from the weight of the valve stem.

Rear Hub

Figure 8-18B shows one hub variety with a sprocket on either side, using caged ball bearings. Other dual- or single-chain hubs may use loose bearings and cones, slightly more hefty versions of the bearings shown in Fig. 8-18A. Caged bearings are normally left in the hub where they are cleaned and packed with grease as well as conditions allow. Wheel wobble or bearing noises—not to be confused with the racheta-racheta of the freewheel—mean that the bearings should be replaced. Drive out the old ones and, using a tube sized to the bearing, drive in the replacements. Where one side of the bearing is closed, that side is outboard. This hub has an endplay adjustment at locknut 10; others are fixed during manufacture.

The freewheel/sprocket assembly can be removed from the hub with a wrench like the one shown in Fig. 8-20. Moped dealers service freewheels as complete assemblies; but springs, pawls, and freewheel wrenches can be purchased at bicycle shops. Lubricate the pawls with light grease.

The Sachs hub, one of the most complex, is shown in Fig. 8-21. In this country, the rear-wheel brake is lever-operated to meet DOT's penchant for standardized controls. In Europe the

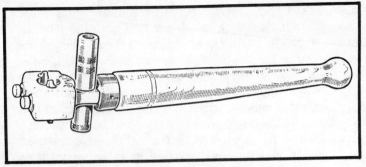

Fig. 8-20. A high-quality freewheel tool

lever is often omitted and the brake is engaged by reversing the pedals. The Sachs hub can be operated both ways.

With power on the pedals, the driver threads the driving cone to the right where it contacts the tapered end of the hub. Although the clutch depends upon metal-to-metal contact, tremendous force is exerted by the driver and there is no slip. In neutral the pedals are stationary and the driving cone is disengaged from the hub: no power passes to the pedals. For braking the pedal direction is reversed, moving the driving cone to the left, toward the end of the driver. The cone engages the coupling which mates with the gear. The gear turns and rotates the brake cam, opening the brake shoes against their spring. In short, the Sachs hub and its imitators amount to a coaster brake with drum and shoes.

The mechanism is disassembled from the brake-drum side. Using a screwdriver, pry off the dust covers for access to the bearings. Wash all metal parts in solvent and lubricate with multipurpose grease, being careful not to touch the brake drum with your somewhat, inevitably, sticky fingers. When assembling, note that the open side of the bearings is inboard, toward the center of the hubs. Replace the dust caps using a wooden block as a driver; once the caps are squarely installed, check that they do not rub against the bearings.

Adjustment is by way of the small cone to the left of the driver. Using finger pressure only, tighten the cone until the axle binds, then back off 1/4-1/2 turn. Check driver action before remounting the shoes: the pedal sprocket should engage the hub during normal rotation, release when sprocket tension is relaxed, and turn the gear when sprocket rotation is reversed.

268

TIRES AND TUBES

The most popular tire sizes are 2.00 or 2.25 by 16. That is, the tread width is two or two and a quarter inches and the inside diameter is 16 inches. In either case the rim is two inches wide. Some owners may wish to fit a larger tire on the rear for marginally better handling. The rim will tolerate a maximum tread with of 2.50 inches, although the frame may not. The outer diameter of the tire increases with the width; a quarter-inch of tread section adds a half-inch to the rolling diameter and the tire may rub against the fender or frame. The overall gear ratio will be "taller," giving fewer engine revolutions per mile and less acceleration.

Changing a tire is not difficult. You will need a valve-stem wrench or one of the almost obsolete slotted valve caps and a pair of motorcycle tire irons. Remove the wheel and follow this procedure:

1. Unthread the valve core to release all pressure in the tube.

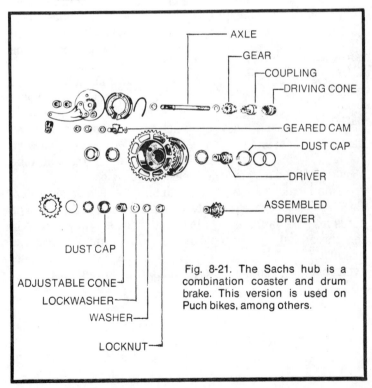

AXLE
GEAR
COUPLING
DRIVING CONE
GEARED CAM
DUST CAP
DRIVER
ASSEMBLED DRIVER
DUST CAP
ADJUSTABLE CONE
LOCKWASHER
WASHER
LOCKNUT

Fig. 8-21. The Sachs hub is a combination coaster and drum brake. This version is used on Puch bikes, among others.

2. Walk around one sidewall to free the bead from the rim. Do the same for the other sidewall.
3. Insert a tire iron at some point near the valve and pry up, levering the sidewall over the rim.
4. Keeping tension on the first iron, insert the second a few inches away from the first. Hold and lever until you can work the rest of the bead off with your hands.
5. Push the valve stem through the hole in the rim and gently pull the tube out.
6. Hold the wheel upright between your knees and work one iron between the mounted bead and the far side of the rim. Pry up, shoe-horning the bead clear off the rim.
7. Keeping the first lever in position, take a bite with the other. The tire should pop off.

To mount the tire, reverse the process. Center the tube protector—the rubber band on the inside of the rim—over the valve stem hole. Mount one side of the tire and install the tube, inflated with just enough pressure to take the wrinkles out of it. Work the valve stem through the hole and tuck the tube well clear of the edge of the rim where it could be pinched by the tire tools. Carefully lever on the bead and inflate the tire.

Moped dealers do not bother with patching tubes. Labor costs mitigate against the practice and European tubes should be replaced by smog-proof American rubber anyhow. But an owner can save money by patching his own tubes if the damage is local and not concentrated at the valve stem. Ozone rot or abrasion from protruding spokes mean that the tube should be replaced, since new leaks will develop.

Small leaks can be found by dipping the tube under water. Once you have located the site, mark it and check the tire. The cords may be damaged or the offending object may still be in the thread where, unremoved, it will promptly give you another flat. The tube can be repaired with either hot (vulcanizing) or cold patches, available at bicycle shops.

Index